TRAINER
ANGLES

TRAINER ANGLES

MAXIMIZING PROFITS USING FORMULATOR AND ADVANCED TRAINER STATS

by

Dean Keppler

DRF Press

NEW YORK

Published by
Daily Racing Form Press
100 Broadway, 7th Floor
New York, NY 10005

ISBN: 1-932910-91-3
ISBN13: 978-1-932910-91-9
Library of Congress Control Number: 2006902944

Cover and jacket designed by Chris Donofry

Text design by Neuwirth and Associates

Printed in the United States of America

All entries, results, charts and related information provided by

821 Corporate Drive • Lexington, KY 40503-2794 Toll Free (800) 333-2211 or
(859) 224-2860; Fax (859) 224-2811 • Internet: www.equibase.com

The Thoroughbred Industry's Official Database for Racing Information

To my dad — the only best bet of the day that always found the winner's circle.

Contents

Acknowledgments

IF SOMEONE HAD TOLD me 10 years ago that I would one day write a book for a popular and successful *Daily Racing Form* handicapping series, I probably would have responded by saying that I had a better chance of dating a supermodel.

I can honestly say that *Daily Racing Form* was the first and only place I ever desired to work. I'm very fortunate to have fulfilled that lifelong dream.

I'm extremely honored to have had the opportunity to put together a handicapping title for *Daily Racing Form*—the greatest handicapping resource ever created—and I have many people to thank for giving me this once-in-a-lifetime opportunity.

Steven Crist is not only one of the best handicappers the game has ever produced, but also always has the racetrack fan and gambler in mind. Steven and his wife, Robin Foster, who copyedited this book, are two of the most talented individuals I've ever had the pleasure of working with. Their editing expertise, unique insight, and love for the sport have made this manuscript that much better.

A special thanks to Charlie Hayward and Mandy Minger for recognizing my enthusiasm and dedication to this fabulous game, and giving me the opportunity to work at *Daily Racing Form*. Thanks also to Brent Diamond for allowing me to write the book, and to Duane

Burke for assisting in gathering many of the useful stats for the manuscript. A great deal of gratitude to two fabulous designers: Chris Donofry and Meg Wren. Thanks to my other *Daily Racing Form* friends, colleagues, and handicappers for their contributions and support, both past and present: Jim Amoroso, Marc Attenberg, Ed Bain, Mike Beer, Hirma Carter, Maria Cavalari, Bob Cinnerela, Mark Cramer, Gary Dworet, John Eastwood, Geoff Faustman, Sarah Feldman, Brad Free, Lonnie Goldfeder, Steve Grabowski, Dan Illman, Tom Ingate, Jim Kachulis, Lila Kearns, Chuck Kuehhas, Jennifer Lusk, Paul Malecki, Steve Marcinak, Jim Mazur, Harry McAlpin, Kenny Peck, Robert Perocier, Brian Pochman, Eddie Schiffer, Barbara Seidenberg, John Short, Tom Spellman, and James Quinn.

This book could not have been written without the unwavering support of priceless friends and family: to James Carboy, my lifelong friend and partner in crime; my brother, Gregg; my mother, Mary Ann; Ray Hunziker; and Bruce Stallworth. And, finally, a universe of thanks to my lovely wife, Lou-Ann, for her unconditional love and support. Thanks for always having that spare $40 for the late double secretly hidden within the side pocket of your purse. It has bailed us out on many occasions.

INTRODUCTION

MOST 7-YEAR-OLD New York City kids spend their spring-time Saturday afternoons peering cautiously into a lion's den at the Bronx Zoo or chasing butterflies in left field at the local Little League matchup. I had my own unique childhood regimen. I usually traded 7:00 a.m. Saturday-morning cartoons for a *Daily Racing Form* and my mother's red and green real-estate markers. These weren't for shading in any Hardy Boys or Nancy Drew coloring books. Instead, I used them for circling hot jockey and trainer combinations and superior times. This fascination all started about 28 years ago, somewhere in between the Kabanger craze, metal roller skates, Rubik's Cube, and the original GI Joe era.

Nowadays, most thirtysomething adults from the Tri-State area can reminisce about those weekend trips to Cape Cod, the Jersey Shore, or Lake George while traveling via the old man's station wagon. We had several old, beat-up station wagons. The truth is, we had about 17 in a span of eight years. My father had a horrible habit of crashing one a week. However, when the wagon was in driving condition and not overheating from lack of fluids, the old junker was usually barreling down the Cross Island Parkway or the Van Wyck Expressway at about 83 miles an hour. My dad drank like a fish and habitually tossed each empty can of Rheingold out the open window of the passenger seat. If it was winter, he slipped in a slug of blackberry brandy.

The scenery was fantastic as we passed by the usual landmarks—an abandoned burnt car, a rubber tire, and some Italian folks picking dandelions on the side of the road for their Sunday salads. I usually sat calmly handicapping the daily double, using those same green and red markers. I'd occasionally blurt out a fact or two about a first-time starter in the fifth, or a recent Oscar Barrera claim that was coming off three days' rest and moving from a $10,000 claimer to a nonwinners-of-two allowance race. This was all part of Thursday-afternoon payday, which conveniently occurred twice each month. The poor nuns at Mt. Carmel St. Anthony grade school must have thought I was a very sick child when I was escorted from social studies class at 11:00 a.m. I was my dad's partner in crime. I was an innocent child enjoying every minute of his truly degenerate journey. Horse racing became my passion.

Any horseplayer alive can remember how and where he was first introduced to this fascinating game. For many, that introduction may have come from a parent, uncle, aunt, a high-school or college buddy, or the next-door neighbor. Some days, when you lose that tight photo and miss that pick four or pick six by an annoying snout, you may wish you had never begun this humbling adventure. Most days, though, despite a winning or losing afternoon, it's a game we all embrace with open arms. It's a love like no other. I've had it every day of my life and I honestly couldn't be more thankful.

I'd like to welcome you to the journey of studying trainer statistics and the introduction to Formulator 4.1. I hope you find the following pages and chapters entertaining and helpful in all your handicapping endeavors. If you're looking for a rags-to-riches handicapping guide, you've come to the wrong place. What I can promise you, however, is that you'll become aware of profitable trainer angles and maneuvers that you may not have easily uncovered before reading this book. Furthermore, you'll learn to recognize what trainer angles are worth researching and what angles are basically worthless. Hopefully, you'll spend less time handicapping unimportant trainer data and more time constructing profitable wagering techniques. Enjoy the ride.

TRAINER
ANGLES

1

TRAINER FORM

*T*RAINER FORM WAS FIRST introduced into the *Daily Racing Form* in October 2000. Before *Daily Racing Form* started incorporating its own unique trainer statistics into the past performances, it was up to the individual handicapper to keep his or her own trainer-stat records. The practice was tiresome and time consuming, but extremely rewarding for those with the patience and diligence to scan through thousands of result charts. At the impressionable age of 16, I had both the time and the patience.

Many years ago, in the 1980's, I was playing the New Jersey circuit fairly exclusively. This included the Meadowlands in the fall, Garden State Park during the winter months, and the Monmouth Park/Atlantic City racetrack afternoon/evening doubleheader during the late spring and summer. At the time I was armed with my own five to six years of trainer stats, which I had accumulated by cutting out daily DRF result charts and placing them in a plastic binder. My artillery included a cheap pair of scissors, some loose-leaf paper, and a small bottle of Elmer's glue. With these limited supplies I had single-handedly started my own business.

During this adolescent gambling journey, I stumbled across some intriguing trainer angles—many of which weren't highly publicized and available to the rest of the horseplaying community. My teenage gambling run was a good one. In fact, there was a point when I traded in catching feeder goldfish and cleaning ferret cages one summer at Nature's Children Pet Shop for a full-time escapade at the Monmouth Park third-floor grandstand. It wasn't long before I realized that Monmouth Park's Joseph H. Pierce Jr. (first off the claim) combined with Chris Antley on board paid far better than the $4.75 an hour that store owner "Dr. Dan the Pet Shop Man" was willing to part with.

There were a few memorable trainer-angle scores. One unforgettable hit included a 60–1 bomb from veteran trainer Timothy Hills in a small New Jersey-bred stakes race. The sly New England horseman moved his older colt up in class, from dirt to turf, and retained the jockey services of Abigail Fuller. According to my yellowed racing charts and Timothy Hills stats, it was a winning angle. Needless to say, I was hooked on trainer stats for life. A similar angle in today's highly technological era, however, would likely produce a much smaller payoff, with the data now available in print and online for thousands of handicappers to read, utilize, and wager on.

Don't despair. Despite the fact that today's player is slightly more sophisticated, and armed with various tools to uncover these types of overlays, there are still some valuable angles that produce overlays day in and day out. The key is having the patience and ability to sift through the extensive trainer-stat "data dump." There are still some golden nuggets left lying for recovery. The Trainer Form created and printed by *Daily Racing Form* is a wonderful inclusion to past-performance data, and is an excellent starting point for the trainer-angle enthusiast.

Over the last six years, the DRF editorial staff has slowly added Trainer Form categories they felt were relevant to producing winning angles. Although all the categories can be considered a supportive feature, it becomes relatively obvious that some of them are far more helpful and relevant than others. At the present time DRF is tracking almost 40 trainer statistics, which cover every trainer's record over this year and last year in a variety of situations. There are as many as six individual categories listed under the past performances for each horse, depending on the number of applicable statistics. Each trainer stat will list:

- The number of starts for the trainer in each category
- The win percentage for the trainer in that category
- The $2 Return on Investment for the trainer in that category

2 Brother Derek — Own: Cecil N. Peacock — 3–5 Teal, multi-colored peacock, — Solis A (235 51 42 31 .21) 2006:(220 49 .22)

B. c. 3 (Mar) BARMAR05 $275,000
Sire: Benchmark (Alydar) $10,000
Dam: Miss Soft Sell (Siyah Kalem)
Br: Mary H. Caldwell(Cal)
Tr: Hendricks Dan L (39 7 3 4 .17) 2006:(37 6 .16)

L 122

Life	7	5	0	1	$712,080	108	D.Fst	7	5	0	1	$712,080 108
2006	2	2	0	0	$210,000	108	Wet (366)	0	0	0	0	$0 -
2005	5	3	0	1	$502,080	102	Turf (289)	0	0	0	0	$0 -
SA	3	3	0	0	$330,000	108	Dist (400)	0	0	0	0	$0 -

Entered 6Apr06 - 3 EQ
4Mar06-5SA fst 1 1/16 :231 :461 1:101 1:414 StCtlina-G2 102 6 3½ 3nk 2hd 11 11¾ Solis A LB122 *.50 91-06 BrthrDr12211¾ ScrdLht1152¾ LttHt1183¾ Vied 3wd,led into lane 8
14Jan06-6SA fst 1 :232 :464 1:102 1:36 SnRafael-G2 108 2 11 11 11½ 11½ 11½ Solis A LB122 1.30 88-22 *BrthrDr* 12211½ StWndrb12231¼ WRr11691½ Inside,held on gamely 4
17Dec05-8Hol fst 1 1/16 :233 :47 1:102 1:42 HolFut-G1 102 5 2½ 2hd 12 11½ 11 Solis A LB121 3.60 91-12 *BrthrDr* 1211 YrTntOrMn1214 *BbdJh* 1211¼ Broke in,bump,game 8
29Oct05-4Bel fst 1 1/16 :23 :453 1:103 1:413 BCJuvnle-G1 89 13 42 41½ 21 45½ 48½ Solis A L122 56.75 83-11 StWndrb12211¼ HnnHhs1222 FrstSmr12255¼ 3 wide move, tired 14
2Oct05-6OSAfst 1 1/16 :224 :461 1:104 1:441 Norfolk-G2 82 1 1½ 1½ 11 12 1¾ Solis A LB122 3.50 84-15 BrothrDrk122¾ *A.P.Wrrr* 12231½ JlsPrft122½ Inside,held gamely 8
5Sep05-1Dmrfst 6f :212 :433 :553 1:083 [S]ImSmokiN100k 81 1 5 47½ 46½ 47 38½ Solis A LB118 3.00 87-10 BroLo11871½ MoonlitRomnc1161 *BrothrDrk* 1181 Broke in,slowly 5
14May05-3Hol fst 4½f :212 :453 :514 Md Sp Wt 57k 77 2 2 66¾ 63¾ 1½ Solis A LB120 *1.80 95-10 BrthrDrk120½ SwssSnt1201 *Bshrt* 120¾ Rallied btwn foes,game 7
WORKS: Apr2 SA 5f fst 1:001 B *9/50* ●Mar26 SA 6f fst 1:11 B *1/5* Mar20 SA 4f fst :492 B *30/59* ●Feb23 SA 6f fst 1:121 H *1/23* ●Feb12 SA 5f fst :592 B *1/37* Feb5 SA 4f fst :492 B *8/30*
TRAINER: 2Off45-180 (22 .23 $2.41) 31-60Days (45 .27 $2.85) Dirt (146 .21 $2.20) Routes (91 .18 $1.86) GrdStk (12 .42 $5.25) J/T 2005-06 SA (38 .24 $1.67) J/T 2005-06 (58 .29 $2.61)

The complete list of comprehensive trainer stats includes the following, and the abbreviations indicated in parentheses are what appear under the past performances of each horse.

1. First North American Start (1stNA)
2. First race after claim (1stClaim)
3. First race with trainer (1stW/Trn)
4. More than 180 days since last race (+180Days)
5. 61–180 days since last race (61–180Days)
6. Second off a layoff of 45–180 Days (2Off45–180)
7. Second off a layoff of more than 180 Days (2OffOver180)
8. 1–7 days since last race (1–7Days)
9. First-time starter (1stStart)
10. Second starts with maidens (2ndStart)
11. Maiden special weight to maiden claimer (MSWtoMCL)
12. First-time turf (1stTurf)
13. First-time blinkers (1stBlink)
14. First-time Lasix (1stLasix)
15. 2-year-olds (2YO)
16. Dirt to turf (Dirt/Turf)
17. Turf to dirt (Turf/Dirt)
18. Blinkers on (BlinkOn)
19. Blinkers off (BlinkOff)
20. Sprint to Route (Sprint/Route)
21. Route to Sprint (Route/Sprint)
22. Two sprints to a route (2Sprints/Route)
23. 31–60 days since last race (31–60 Days)
24. Won last start (WonLastStart)

25. Dirt (Dirt)
26. Turf (Turf)
27. Sprint (Sprint)
28. Routes (Routes)
29. Maiden claiming (MdnClm)
30. Maiden special weight (MdnSpWt)
31. Claiming (Claim)
32. Allowance (Alw)
33. Stakes (Stakes)
34. Graded stakes (GrdStk)
35. Debut in maiden claimer (DebutMCL)
36. Debut at a distance greater than or equal to one mile (Debut>=1Mile)

Of the 36 Trainer Form variables listed, I have found nearly half of them (or roughly 16) to be immediately supportive to one's daily handicapping regimen. They include those that fall under the following trainer patterns: (1) recent claims; (2) layoff runners; (3) debut starters; (4) new barn acquisitions; and (5) any horse undergoing a makeover or modification (such as adding or removing blinkers or Lasix, stretching out or cutting back in distance, or moving from one surface to another).

What separates these categories from the others is that these Trainer Form stats are specific, and often indicate a favorable trainer maneuver that is likely to improve a runner's performance. It's this immediate improvement in performance we're interested in capitalizing on. In the upcoming chapters, I'll discuss how these Trainer Form stats can sometimes be misleading. As you become familiar with the DRF Formulator software and learn how to utilize it, you'll discover that many of the Trainer Form categories listed in the daily paper contain completely different win percentages and ROI's when separated according to a horse's age, sex, or a trainer's performance at an individual racing circuit. It's this hidden trainer data that requires some work and digging on the part of the handicapper. This is the data we'll be concentrating on.

HOW TO USE TRAINER FORM

I COULD EASILY FILL 400 pages with examples of how using Trainer Form data exclusively from the daily paper produced box-car payoffs. That's not my intention. However, I will list a few examples of how the data produced from my Top 16 can be utilized almost immediately without any further "filtering" (a term you'll become very familiar with when using the Formulator software).

Let's take a look at one average, chilly March Wednesday afternoon from 2006 and see which Trainer Form statistics could have steered you toward some potential runners. More importantly, the following examples will show you how this unique handicapping feature could be used in addition to other standard handicapping tools, such as speed figures, trip and form-cycle analysis, pace examination, etc.

---

3 Saalb
Blue   Own: Gladwell Martha
   Red, White Chevrons, Red Cap   **$50,000**
HILL C (303 24 31 33 .08) 2005: (1157 135 .12)

B. c. 4 (Apr) KEESEP03 $300,000
Sire: Unbridled (Fappiano) $200,000
Dam: Majestic Legend (His Majesty)
Br: ClassicStar LLC (Ky)
Tr: Asmussen Steven M (58 9 11 6 .16) 2005: (2227 473 .21)

① 123

	Life	1 M 0 1	$2,500	–	D.Fst	1 0 0 1	$2,500	–
	2005	1 M 0 1	$2,500	–	Wet(405)	0 0 0 0	$0	–
	2004	0 M 0 0	$0	–	Turf(298)	0 0 0 0	$0	–
	Aqu ⊡	0 0 0 0	$0	–	Dst(317)	0 0 0 0	$0	–

Previously trained by Saeed bin Suroor

24Feb05 Nad Al Sheba (UAE) ft *7f LH 1:24³   San Isidro Maiden   35½   McEvoy K   121   –   Parole Board1214½ British Isles121¾ Saalb1211½   15
Timeform rating: 82   Maiden 25000   Led to 2f out, faded. Dubai Wings 6th
WORKS: Mar5 Bel tr.t 4f fst :48² B 6/56 Feb18 Bel tr.t 4f fst :48³ B 7/48 Feb8 Bel tr.t 5f fst 1:03 Bg 21/28 Feb1 Bel tr.t 5f fst 1:03³ B 8/12 Jan25 Bel tr.t 4f fst :52 B 43/46 Jan18 Bel tr.t 4f my :52² B 10/10
TRAINER: 1stNA(6 .50 $4.60) 1stW/Tm(156 .24 $1.87) +180Days(69 .14 $1.27) 1stLasix(42 .26 $2.16) Dirt(2224 .21 $1.45) Sprint(1727 .21 $1.41)   J/T 2005-06 AQU(47 .17 $1.60) J/T 2005-06(55 .16 $1.63)

SECOND RACE
Aqueduct
MARCH 8, 2006

6 FURLONGS. (1.074) MAIDEN CLAIMING . Purse $25,000 INNER DIRT (UP TO $4,750 NYSBFOA) FOR MAIDENS, THREE YEAR OLDS AND UPWARD. Three Year Olds, 118 lbs.; Older, 123 lbs. Claiming Price $50,000, For Each $5,000 To $40,000 1 lb.

Value of Race: $25,000 Winner $15,000; second $5,000; third $2,500; fourth $1,250; fifth $750; sixth $500. Mutuel Pool $227,248.00 Exacta Pool $204,397.00 Quinella Pool $20,962.00 Trifecta Pool $135,547.00

Last Raced	Horse	M/Eqt.	A.	Wt	PP	St	¼	½	Str	Fin	Jockey	Cl'g Pr	Odds $1
24Feb05 NAS³	Saalb	L	4	123	3	6	1hd	1hd	12½	12	Hill C	50000	2.35
17Dec05 7Aqu⁵	Chicago Nate	L b	3	118	2	3	22½	25	23½	2½	Espinoza J L	50000	4.70
1Jan06 2Crc⁸	Honored Nation	L b	3	118	5	2	6	53½	4hd	3nk	Dominguez R A	50000	4.40
15Feb06 2Aqu²	Better Get Busy	L	4	123	4	1	3hd	33	32	44½	Coa E M	50000	1.40
4Mar06 4Aqu⁷	Keep n' Line	L	3	115	1	4	41½	41½	58	58¾	Kaenel K⁵	50000	20.30
15Feb06 2Aqu⁶	Funny Jello	L bf	4	121	6	5	51½	6	6	6	Santagata N	40000	20.90

OFF AT 1:30 Start Good. Won driving. Track fast.
TIME :22⁴, :45³, :57⁴, 1:11¹ (:22.86, :45.68, :57.86, 1:11.37)

Despite getting off a step slowly at the start and being forced to gun to the early pace, then racing erratically in the stretch, this 4-year-old colt by Unbridled, trained by Steve Asmussen, kicked away from a group of $50,000 maiden claimers for a comfortable two-length victory. Reading from left to right, you can see Asmussen's past success with these types of runners, and a scholarly Trainer

Form handicapper could have assumed that this colt could be ready for a nice performance despite the nearly 13-month layoff.

Asmussen was winning at a rate of 50 percent with a profitable $4.60 return on investment for North American starters (1stNA: 6 .50 $4.60); he had a 24 percent win percentage and slight ROI loss for new acquisitions (1stW/Trn: 156 .24 $1.87); and he had a 26 percent win percentage with a small 16-cent-profit return for starters adding Lasix for the first time (1stLasix: 42 .26 $2.16). Some fairly decent numbers for a trainer winning 16 percent (58 9 11 6 .16) at the current Aqueduct meet.

I would like to add that there is no magic win-percentage number that one should be looking for or focusing on when evaluating Trainer Form stats. As a general rule, however, I like to see win percentages that are considerably higher than the trainer's general stats at the meet with all starters; have a minimum of seven starts within a specific trainer category; and, finally, if you're the kind of person that insists on being married to a number, a minimum of an 18 percent win percentage or higher for the specific Trainer Form angle. I believe this is a reasonable beginner-bettor's guideline, and one that will help you familiarize yourself with the Trainer Form handicapping feature while eliminating those stats that are cumbersome.

Our next example's group of $40,000 3-year-old claimers was filled with about a half dozen entrants who were not only stretching out to the $1\frac{1}{16}$-mile route for the first time, but also making their initial attempt on the turf. A great betting race and a Trainer Form fan's gala for finding potential overlay trainer patterns and angles. The number 4 horse, Full In, had a lot of interesting angles for Southern California-based trainer Mike Mitchell, who was having a rousing Gulfstream Park meet, clicking with 35 percent of all his starters (20 7 3 1 .35).

Mitchell had already had tremendous success in 2005, and continued his winning ways when setting up a small army of original claiming stock along with those he recently acquired 3,000 miles away from his home base. Despite having some Trainer Form numbers that were slightly below his overall win percentage, there were a lot of positive trainer maneuvers (makeovers) that should have tipped you off to his winning intentions.

In addition, for those of us using the Formulator software (please see the next chapter), there was one general layoff angle that screamed "Play me!" like a pink neon sign blinking in a completely lightless room. It was the 31–60 days since last running date category (87 .30 $2.26). Although the Trainer Form stat indicated a 30 percent win percentage for the year (which was accurate), a careful filtering process focusing just on Mitchell's Gulfstream Park entrants produced an astounding 80 percent win percentage. If that angle wasn't enough, the collection of other positive modifications, such as 1stClaim (111 .29 $2.02), 1stBlink (13 .31 $2.65), Dirt/Turf (32 .22 $2.58), and BlinkOn (19 .32 $3.17) may have swayed you to seriously consider this mediocre 2–1 betting favorite. If you dug even farther and noticed the talented New York jockey John Velazquez taking over the mount for J. C. Leyva—a 33 percent winning combination thus far (J/T 2005–06 GP: 12 .33 $2.57)—it was surely a winning scenario no matter how you decided to spin it. Well, maybe not.

Part of the running line in the following result chart for Full In reads: "FULL IN reserved off the pace, rallied inside FAMOUS FROLIC to reach near even terms for command inside the eighth pole, then dueled with that rival and was just edged to the wire."

It just goes to show you that despite the most favorable Trainer Form numbers and stats available, you still need the trip and some racing luck. That favorable trip and luck went to number 10,

Famous Frolic, who won the photo over the rallying Full In to produce a $127.60 exacta based on a $2 bet. Trainer gurus who selectively establish their own records, and perhaps even devise their computerized database for the meets they play regularly, may have been aware that trainer Milton Wolfson had had only two turf winners on the Florida circuit in the past 12 months, making it a little bit of a stretch to bet assertively on Famous Frolic. There were, however, a few Trainer Form stats that might have stirred your interest in this 14–1 Charismatic colt making his third start off a layoff. The first important angle was the 25 percent win percentage Wolfson had accomplished with horses making their first grass attempt (1stTurf: 4 .25 $3.20). The second was the basic surface switch from dirt to turf (7 .14 $1.83). You could have made a reasonable case that Milton was in a position to end his 0–9 skid at the Gulfstream meet, based on some positive trainer stats in a couple of categories where he had enjoyed previous success.

SIXTH RACE
Gulfstream
MARCH 8, 2006

1¹⁄₁₆ MILES. (Turf) (1.38) CLAIMING . Purse $23,000 FOR THREE YEAR OLDS. Weight, 122 lbs. Non-winners of a race at a mile or over since February 6 Allowed 2 lbs. Claiming Price $40,000, For Each $2,500 To $35,000 1 lb. (Maiden and Claiming races for $32,000 or less not considered) (Condition Eligibility)(Registered Florida Breds Preferred). (If deemed inadvisable to run this race over the Turf course, it will be run on the main track at One Mile) (Rail at 60 feet).

Value of Race: $23,000 Winner $13,800; second $4,830; third $2,300; fourth $1,150; fifth $230; sixth $230; seventh $230; eighth $230. Mutuel Pool $272,073.00 Exacta Pool $214,700.00 Trifecta Pool $173,131.00 Superfecta Pool $64,391.00

Last Raced	Horse	M/Eqt.	A.	Wt	PP	St	¼	½	¾	Str	Fin	Jockey	Cl'g Pr	Odds $1
22Feb06 9GP10	Famous Frolic	L	3	120	8	8	4¹	4¹	4¹½	3½	1hd	Trujillo E	40000	14.30
5Feb06 10GP4	Full In	L b	3	120	3	3	5½	6²	6³	4²	2⁴½	Velazquez J R	40000	2.50
5Feb06 10GP5	The Business Man	L	3	120	7	4	7³	7³½	7²	7½	3hd	King E L Jr	40000	21.10
10Feb06 10GP10	Little Response	L b	3	120	4	7	6hd	5½	5¹	5²	4½	Bejarano R	40000	4.90
2Feb06 7GP1	Jet Propulsion	L bf	3	118	5	6	1³	12½	11½	11½	5hd	Cruz M R	35000	2.90
24Feb06 7Tam3	Smoke Em Again	L	3	120	2	2	3³	3⁴	2¹½	2hd	6²½	Castellano J J	40000	3.10
2Mar06 2GP6	Takemywife Please	L	3	118	6	5	8	8	8	8	7³½	Leyva J C	35000	72.20
5Feb06 10GP3	Newfy	L bf	3	120	1	1	2hd	2hd	3hd	6hd	8	Prado E S	40000	8.10

OFF AT 3:15 Start Good. Won driving. Course firm.

A final illustration of how the *Daily Racing Form* Trainer Form works, and how it can be used in addition to your daily handicapping routine, takes us to race 4 at Oaklawn Park on March 8, 2006. This $15,000 maiden-claiming route for 3-year-olds and up featured some of the cheapest and most unreliable horses at that track. From a handicapping standpoint, total chaos was expected, and that's exactly what happened when 31–1 shot Requiem of Dreams crossed the wire three widening lengths in front.

5 Requiem of Dreams Own: Benny Campo
Green Lime, Black Bc On Back $12,500
QUINONEZ L S (164 23 15 14 .14) 2005: (1233 171 .14)

Dk. b or br c. 4 (May)
Sire: Cat's Career (Mr. Prospector) $2,000
Dam: Maddux (Shadeed)
Br: Merie Log Farm (Ky)
Tr: Cannon Charles(10 1 0 0 .10) 2005:(101 10 .10)

L 120

Life	4	M	0	0	$360	56	D.Fst	2	0	0	0	$0	40
2006	3	M	0	0	$360	56	Wet(299)	2	0	0	0	$360	56
2005	1	M	0	0	$0	21	Turf(256)	0	0	0	0	$0	-
OP	2	0	0	0	$360	56	Dst(310)	1	0	0	0	$0	15

Previously trained by Bindner Walter M Jr 2005: (125 21 22 21 0.17)
26Feb06-3OP fst 5½f :222 :47 :5931:06 Md 15000 **40** 5 6 64 64½ 78½ 710½ Graham J L124 6.50 77-15 Blues Talkin'1181¼ Cypress Star1243¼ **C J's Jet**124½ Never dangerous 12
10Feb06-6OP sly 6f :222 :472 1:0011:13 Md 15000 **56** 3 11 66½ 43 23½ 57¼ Graham J L123 20.50 71-21 Haajes1175½ *Awesome Richard*1171 **C J's Jet**123nk Pinballed start 12
13Jan06-3LaD fst 1$\frac{1}{16}$:231 :474 1:1521:492 Md 12500(12.5-10) **15** 10 21½ 2hd 2hd 1010 1025¼ Burch L L122 13.40 44-23 Key Race1225 Arcd'angeli1192¾ Uncle Tater122¾ Pressed, vied, stopped 12
15Dec05-4LaD gd 6½f :231 :472 1:1241:20 Md 25000(25-20) **21** 5 9 64½ 65¾ 913 822¼ Graham J L122 f 12.10 57-24 Bamboozled118½ TropicRocket1221¾ *SlemSchoolRod*1222¾ Tired after half 9
WORKS: Feb5 LaD 3f fst :39 B *15/18* Jan29 LaD 4f gd :472 B *3/47* Dec28 LaD 5f fst 1:031 B *14/23*
TRAINER: 1stW/Trn(19 .21 $1.88) Sprint/Route(19 .05 $0.32) Dirt(106 .10 $1.17) Routes(60 .08 $0.63) MdnClm(39 .13 $1.16) J/T 2005-06 OP(2 .00 $0.00) J/T 2005-06(2 .00 $0.00)

1 Mountain Jett Own: Don Eberts
Red Orange, White Chevron, White Diamonds On $12,500
MARQUEZ C H JR (79 11 12 5 .14) 2005: (632 80 .13)

Ch. c. 3 (May)
Sire: Groovy Jett (Groovy) $1,000
Dam: Ajax Mountain (It's Freezing)
Br: Donald Eberts (Tex)
Tr: Nicks Morris G(39 5 8 6 .13) 2005:(238 57 .24)

L 114

Life	1	M	0	0	$0	50	D.Fst	1	0	0	0	$0	50
2006	1	M	0	0	$0	50	Wet(323)	0	0	0	0	$0	-
2005	0	M	0	0	$0	-	Turf(293)	0	0	0	0	$0	-
OP	1	0	0	0	$0	50	Dst(355)	0	0	0	0	$0	-

24Feb06-1OP fst 1⅛ :5021:161 1:4311:571 Md 15000 **50** 7 89 99¾ 89½ 79 67½ Marquez C H Jr L118 8.40 44-30 Timber Hunt1181½ ColoradoJazz1242 BlackCard124½ Wide, erratic stretch 9
WORKS: Feb13 OP 5f fst 1:024 B *8/12* Feb7 OP 5f fst 1:041 B *13/20* Feb1 OP 5f fst 1:032 Hg *24/44* Jan25 OP 5f fst 1:041 Bg *35/56* Jan12 OP 4f fst :51 Bg *13/33*
TRAINER: 2ndStart(24 .25 $2.36) Dirt(231 .23 $1.74) Routes(136 .20 $1.23) MdnClm(80 .28 $2.41) J/T 2005-06 OP(4 .25 $1.10) J/T 2005-06(6 .17 $0.73)

9 Critical Acclaim Own: Wind Hill Farm
Turqse Purple, White Emblem $15,000
ELLIOTT S (89 15 10 10 .17) 2005: (860 143 .17)

Ch. g. 3 (May)
Sire: Acceptable (Capote) $2,500
Dam: Privileged Speech (General Assembly)
Br: Wind Hill Farm (Ky)
Tr: Fires William H(30 1 2 6 .03) 2005:(160 26 .16)

L 118

Life	5	M	0	0	$851	57	D.Fst	4	0	0	0	$271	35
2006	2	M	0	0	$696	57	Wet(304)	1	0	0	0	$580	57
2005	3	M	0	0	$155	35	Turf(203)	0	0	0	0	$0	-
OP	1	0	0	0	$580	57	Dst(329)	1	0	0	0	$100	22

25Feb06-6OP gd 6f :221 :472 1:0021:133 Md 30000 **57** 7 11 1213 129½ 97¼ 55 Carmouche K L121 b 75.80 70-19 GoodOffer1211 SlyDimondJim1211¼ DixilndGnrl121¾ Stride late midtrack 12
Previously trained by Stidham Susan 2005: (27 2 1 0 0.07)
4Jan06-2TP fst 6½f ◈ :232 :481 1:1531:224 Md 30000(30-20) **30** 1 6 98 99½ 812 811¾ Medina L 122 44.70 59-25 Whack1221½ Brian J1222¼ Folding Money122¾ Outrun 9
22Dec05-7TP fst 1$\frac{1}{16}$ ◈ :243 :501 1:1641:521 Md Sp Wt 23k **22** 5 128¼116¼ 911 917 830¼ Woods C R Jr 122 67.10 - - I'm Waiting for U1221¾ *Bahri and Grill*1224 Han Solo1221¾ 7 wide 3/8 pole 12
10Dec05-12TP fst 1 ◈ :24 :481 1:1431:42 Md Sp Wt 23k **35** 7 910 812 1117 1121 1225 Woods C R Jr 122 177.10 - - *TemporrySint*1222 StrspngldGtor1222¼ Extortion1224 Never in contention 12
19Nov05-7CD fst 7½f :231 :46 1:1111:312 Md Sp Wt 41k **32** 9 11 1012 1013 1017 1019¾ Charkoudian J5 115 83.70 63-15 AdmirlsArch1201 RighteousRuler1201 HllowedFlg1204¼ Never prominent 12
WORKS: Feb15 OP 5f fst 1:031 B *25/45* Jan28 OP 4f fst :511 B *27/41* ●Dec30 CDT 3f gd :362 B *1/9*
TRAINER: 2Off45-180(22 .14 $1.09) Sprint/Route(20 .20 $2.72) Dirt(180 .14 $1.67) Routes(97 .15 $2.11) MdnClm(33 .15 $1.94) J/T 2005-06 OP(3 .00 $0.00) J/T 2005-06(3 .00 $0.00)

3 General Genius Own: Ernie Witt
Blue Turquoise & Purple Quarters $12,500
HERNANDEZ B J JR (65 7 4 7 .11) 2005: (989 100 .10)

B. g. 4 (Mar)
Sire: American General (Danzig) $1,000
Dam: Bold Genius (Beau Genius)
Br: Ernie Witt (Ark)
Tr: Hewitt Michael(9 1 3 0 .11))(—)

L 115

Life	13	M	1	2	$3,461	51	D.Fst	11	0	1	2	$3,311	51
2006	2	M	0	0	$0	25	Wet(317)	1	0	0	0	$0	-
2005	7	M	1	1	$2,390	51	Turf(351*)	1	0	0	0	$150	15
OP	4	0	0	0	$0	25	Dst(325)	2	0	1	0	$1,470	51

23Feb06-3OP gd 6f :223 :471 1:0031:141 [S]Md Sp Wt 32k – 11 7 65½ 1017 - - Theriot H J II L124 b 31.80 - 21 GrdyO1181½ AirBorneEtbur1181¾ CountryDiggr1243¼ Gave way 4-w, eased 11
Previously trained by Goodman Randy J 2005: (133 13 19 16 0.10)
5Feb06-3OP fst 1 :232 :474 1:14 1:42 [S]Md 20000 **25** 6 42 32 43½ 711 618¾ Berry M C L123 b 12.70 55-19 Junior Adams1231¾ Etbauer's Kitty1172¾ Pine Bar1238¼ Forward, empty 12
24Jly05-4Cby fst 6f :221 :452 :5811:122 Md 10000 **25** 4 6 56 46 510 511 Ziegler M G LB117 b 2.70 71-15 Loud Enough1171½ Dun122nk Jimbo's King1175 Btwn foes, gave way 11
9Jly05-8Cby fst 170 :224 :464 1:1131:424 Md 10000 **51** 1 13 12½ 1½ 2hd 2nk Toro M LB116 b 9.90 87-13 AmrcnMud116nk GnrlGnus11612½ *Shouldboghtm*119½ Resisted grudgingly 9
17Jun05-3Cby fm *1$\frac{1}{16}$ Ⓣ 1:464 Md Sp Wt 15k **15** 2 3nk 2hd 22½ 79 817¼ Black J A LB116 b 23.90 56-23 Turnthhtup122no Tuplo1161¼ ClirsConnction116¾ Dueled inside,gave way 12
29May05-3Cby fst 170 :222 :454 1:1111:434 Md 10000 **39** 5 41½ 31½ 21½ 22 56 Black J A LB116 b 5.90 76-15 Deltatron1231¼ Mister Bel1161 Ranger Ryan122nk 5wd 1st turn, emptied 11
20May05-3Cby fst 1 :234 :48 1:1411:431 Md 10000 **27** 6 2hd 1hd 1hd 2½ 31¾ Black J A LB116 b 13.80 58-25 RigningGold122no MrktKing1161¾ GnrlGnius116¾ Veered brk, bumped foe 10
25Feb05-3OP fst 6f :222 :47 1:0021:134 [S]Md 15000 **–0** 10 5 74¼ 77¾ 1224 1230½ Oro E L117 b 62.70 43-16 Polly's Pistol1242 *Stormin Bleu*1172¾ *Easy Luck*1171¾ Backed up 12
16Feb05-7OP fst 6f :224 :474 1:0041:133 Md 15000 **–0** 4 9 62¼ 104¼ 1222 1224½ Scantling V L117 b 123.90 50-18 Lanslide Lerblance1221 Uncle Toodie122½ *CorpusSand*1222¼ Finished early 12
Previously trained by Cox John M 2004(as of 11/6): (95 8 5 11 0.08)
6Nov04-4RP fst 6f :221 :46 :5821:12 Md 15000 **–0** 10 7 54½ 55 828 930 Scantling V LB120 fb 8.00 54-11 Okie Dream1153¾ Our Runnin Buddy1202¼ Spec Tater1201¾ Gave way 10
WORKS: Mar2 OP 6f fst 1:152 Hg *2/3* Feb14 OP 3f fst :354 H *2/15* Jan30 OP 3f fst :354 H *2/10* Jan23 OP 5f my 1:052 H *33/42* Jan8 OP 5f fst 1:034 B *13/16* Dec31 OP 4f fst :492 B *14/55*
TRAINER: Sprint/Route(2 .50 $3.00) Dirt(10 .20 $1.34) Routes(2 .50 $3.00) MdnClm(5 .20 $1.20)

The optimistic and creative horseplayers who had backed the winner were rewarded handsomely, and deservedly so. This struggling 4-year-old colt had been beaten a combined 65 lengths in four lifetime starts for trainer Walter Bindner Jr. After what was described as a "pinballed start" in his February 10 outing on a sloppy track, when he rushed into contention with a quarter-mile to go after getting off slowly, he was fairly well-backed at 6–1 when he returned a little over two weeks later at the same $15,000 class level. The result was a disappointing seventh-place finish. What happened next, however, might have provided the clue to the sudden wake-up call on March 8.

Requiem of Dreams changed barns and landed under the care of Charles Cannon and owner Benny Campo. The colt's first Trainer Form line read 1stW/Trn (19 .21 $1.88). Not exactly the type of trainer stat that jumps off the page and makes you do an Irish jig on the kitchen floor while holding your *Form* above your head, but worth noting nonetheless. It's important to stress that it is always advisable to take a second look when a horse changes barns, despite its dismal previous form. Whether it is the influence of better general care, different feed, new medications, implementation of some ground-breaking equipment or remedy, or something as simple as a little TLC and change of scenery, it can make a world of difference in a horse's performance.

The second-place finisher, number 1, Mountain Jett, was a more realistic play, and offered the following pair of notable Trainer Form stats: 2nd Start (24 .25 $2.36), MdnClm (80 .28 $2.41). Morris G. Nicks showed a profitable ROI in two important stat categories, and there was reason to believe there was a little talent hidden within this colt after a wide trip and green "erratic" stretch run in his debut. Furthermore, the trainer was winning at a decent rate with general route runners (Routes: 136 .20 $1.23) and Mountain Jett had attracted some betting action at 8–1 in his initial start.

Rounding out the trifecta and mammoth superfecta were number 9, Critical Acclaim, and number 3, General Genius. The trainer of Critical Acclaim was only 1 for 30 at the current meet, and his assets weren't immediately visible to the untrained eye, but those who took the time to do a little more research could have used him on their exotic tickets. His 15 percent win percentage in general maiden-claiming events was worth noting (MdnClm: 33 .15 $1.94), especially if you took it a step farther and filtered out only his Oaklawn Park starters. You would have quickly discovered that his mediocre win percentage was easily overshadowed by his juicy prices in the Oaklawn wagering pools. This was a key stat that could have only been uncovered by utilizing the Formulator software, which leads us to the subject and the introduction of the program in Chapter 2.

FOURTH RACE

Oaklawn

MARCH 8, 2006

1$\frac{1}{16}$ MILES. (1.40[1]) MAIDEN CLAIMING . Purse $9,700 (includes $2,400 Other Sources) FOR MAIDENS, THREE, FOUR, AND FIVE YEAR OLDS. Three Year Olds, 118 lbs.; Older, 124 lbs. Claiming Price $15,000, if for $12,500, allowed 4 lbs.

Value of Race: $9,700 Winner $5,820; second $1,940; third $970; fourth $582; fifth $388. Mutuel Pool $90,919.00 Exacta Pool $65,880.00 Trifecta Pool $52,697.00 Superfecta Pool $27,437.00

Last Raced	Horse	M/Eqt.	A.	Wt	PP	St	¼	½	¾	Str	Fin	Jockey	Cl'g Pr	Odds $1
26Feb06 3OP7	Requiem of Dreams	L	4	120	5	9	85½	87½	2hd	11½	13	Quinonez L S	12500	31.10
24Feb06 1OP6	Mountain Jett	L	3	116	1	5	4hd	5½	3½	3½	2no	Marquez C H Jr	12500	4.10
25Feb06 6OP5	Critical Acclaim	L b	3	120	9	7	73	6hd	5hd	45	32¾	Martinez S B	15000	2.50
23Feb06 3OP10	General Genius	L b	4	115	3	4	2hd	11	13½	22½	43½	Hernandez B J Jr	12500	64.40
16Feb06 8OP3	Aliyev's Joy	L b	5	119	7	10	10	9hd	82	53	51¾	Burress B5	15000	8.30
29Dec05 3LaD7	Beau Trieste	L	4	124	4	6	6½	72½	9hd	64	68½	Graham J	15000	8.50
26Feb06 3OP3	C J's Jet	L bf	4	124	10	3	54½	44	6½	71	7nk	McKee J	15000	4.90
24Feb06 1OP4	C'Mon Moon	L f	4	120	6	8	9½	10	10	8hd	87	Johnson J M	12500	11.60
16Feb06 8OP4	Strike It North	L b	3	118	8	2	32	22½	41½	93½	9¾	Pettinger D R	15000	4.60
10Feb06 6OP9	Grand Fappy	L f	3	118	2	1	1hd	3hd	71½	10	10	Carmouche K	15000	20.50

OFF AT 2:53 Start Good. Won driving. Track fast.

TIME :23³, :47³, 1:13⁴, 1:41¹, 1:48¹ (:23.74, :47.70, 1:13.81, 1:41.29, 1:48.24)

$2 Mutuel Prices:				
5 – REQUIEM OF DREAMS	64.20	20.80	10.80
1 – MOUNTAIN JETT		6.00	3.80
9 – CRITICAL ACCLAIM			3.60

$2 EXACTA 5–1 PAID $478.80 $1 TRIFECTA 5–1–9 PAID $1,352.50
$1 SUPERFECTA 5–1–9–3 PAID $72,125.00

Dk. b or br. c, (May), by Cat's Career – Maddux , by Shadeed . Trainer Cannon Charles. Bred by Merie Log Farm (Ky).

REQUIEM OF DREAMS off slow, raced back, strong move four wide into contention in the second turn, bid, drove clear. MOUNTAIN JETT unhurried early, came on the outside when advancing into the stretch, proved determined for the place while no threat to the winner. CRITICAL ACCLAIM settled off the pace, staged a mild rally, outfinished for the place. GENERAL GENIUS vied early, got well clear the middle half, faltered when confronted by the winner turning for home. ALIYEV'S JOY off the pace, came six wide into the stretch, had little left for the stretch run. BEAU TRIESTE lacked a late bid. C J'S JET within striking distance three wide in the second turn, gave way. C'MON MOON was never involved. STRIKE IT NORTH forwardly placed for a half, faded. GRAND FAPPY with the early pace, stopped.

Owners– 1, Campo Benny; 2, Eberts Don; 3, Wind Hill Farm; 4, Witt Ernie; 5, Warchol Ronald M; 6, Robinson J Mack; 7, Danaher James E; 8, Reddog Racing; 9, Singer Craig B; 10, Champion Racing Stable Inc

Trainers– 1, Cannon Charles; 2, Nicks Morris G; 3, Fires William H; 4, Hewitt Michael; 5, Cox John E; 6, Trosclair Jeff; 7, Danaher James E; 8, Hartlage Gary G; 9, Von Hemel Donnie K; 10, Tomlinson Michael A

2

FORMULATOR

PROGRAM DEVELOPMENT

THE DEVELOPMENT OF THE Formulator concept first began in the early 1990's. Before it became a mainstream consumer product in April 2000 as Formulator 1.0, the exclusive handicapping software was first distributed as a test run to expert handicappers and horse-racing pioneers Andrew Beyer, Steven Crist, Mark Hopkins, and national *Daily Racing Form* handicapper Mike Watchmaker. David Ward, a longtime horse-racing enthusiast and the founder and president of EquiSoft Inc. of Marblehead, Massachusetts, was the team leader in the product's development.

Formulator's main function is to give on-line horseplayers the ability to customize and manipulate DRF's past performances while creating race lines to their specifications. The software allows each user the luxury of creating his or her own personalized, customized *Daily Racing Form*. In addition, it gives users the ability to call up each horse's lifetime past performances—an invaluable asset for in-depth handicapping analysis.

Ward, assisted by a fine group of software developmental engineers and a stable of marketing and business consultants, continues to serve the horse-racing community while also offering his software infrastructure to various other organizations outside the racing industry. Since 1996, EquiSoft has been providing consulting services that include staff augmentation, systems analysis, programming, and total project development. Today, in just the horse community alone, EquiSoft has expertly assisted Beyer Associates, *Daily Racing Form*, Magna Entertainment Corporation, the Maryland Jockey Club, various Thoroughbred and Standardbred trainers, breeding farms, and even equine veterinarians.

THE BIRTH OF FORMULATOR

FROM 2000 TO 2006, Ward and his team of developers greatly improved upon the original Formulator 1.0 software. There have been numerous upgrades that have not only improved the basic product, but have also offered consumers handicapping enhancements far superior to any available on-line handicapping software data. The current 4.1 version of Formulator has improved by leaps and bounds since the software's inception. The original format gave users the ability to choose or combine such factors as distance, surface, track conditions, early pace, last racing date (recency), and medication. It also allowed users to compare Beyer Speed Figures through colorful graphic charts, merge workouts chronologically into a horse's running line, and incorporate scratches and betting information directly into their customized past performances.

Formulator 2.0 debuted in October 2000 and offered additional functionality, filtering, and elements from the daily paper print edition that were missing from the first version. Formulator 3.0 offered users what many consider to be the program's greatest advantage: the ability to access the lifetime past performances for every horse on the racecard. Formulator 3.1 followed soon thereafter, and introduced the popular feature FormNotes, which allowed customers to write and insert their own comments into the past performances.

The April 2004 version of Formulator 4.0 enabled users to look beyond the basic trainer statistics and perform in-depth analyses of a trainer's patterns, add personalized trip and track-bias notes, customize pace figures, pull up and analyze race result charts, and assemble and explore an almost infinite amount of specific trainer data. Another feature of Formulator 4.0 was ChartNotes, which allowed users to enter notes for a specific horse, race, or entire card from the Chart View that would appear in all future Formulator past performances that were accessed.

FORMULATOR 4.1

BEFORE I GET INTO some of the specifics of the software we'll be dissecting, I would strongly recommend that those of you who are new to or unfamiliar with the program visit the DRF website, www.drf.com, and work through the on-line Formulator 4.1 tutorial. Once you familiarize yourself with the program and its general handicapping features, you'll be better prepared to understand and utilize it. The trainer-tool feature is the one function we'll be focusing on the most throughout this book, and I believe that it stands alone as the most useful resource of the entire Formulator program. What makes the program truly fascinating is the almost endless supply of statistics and the capacity for past-performance manipulation available at your fingertips. Whether you're handicapping a $3,500 maiden-claiming event on a winter Wednesday afternoon at Beulah Park or a Grade 1 stakes race from Saratoga on a summer Saturday afternoon, you'll be able to manipulate your past-performance and Trainer Form data to feature the statistics you're interested in viewing.

The newest Formulator version, 4.1, was released to the public in April 2006. As with the previous versions, it allows horseplayers the flexibility to massage past performances to their personal preferences, but now the trainer tool has been enhanced even further. The current version offers the user the ability to save Trainer Profile (TP) Filter Settings as queries, thus allowing users the ability to apply them during their analyses. Some of the 4.1 filtering options include:

1. The ability to search the same track as the entry you're looking at (Track Filter)
2. The ability to search the same jockey as the entry you're looking at (Jockey Filter)
3. Main Dirt Track (Surface Option)
4. Second-Time Lasix (Medication/Lasix Option)
5. 3-year-olds vs. Elders (Age Option)

6. Maiden Winner Next Start (Winner Option)
7. Claiming to Allowance (Class Option)
8. Allowance to Claiming (Class Option)
9. Optional Claiming (Class Option)

More importantly, Formulator 4.1 added a Trainer Pattern Summary line. This feature automatically provides the number of horses in the analysis sample and the median payoff. The median payoff can be compared to the ROI to help determine if the ROI is magnified by one or more large payoffs. This is a huge advantage to Formulator users, as opposed to relying on straight Trainer Form stats printed in the daily paper.

GETTING STARTED

ASSUMING YOU HAVE A DRF account set up, you can download a racecard directly from the Formulator program. If you don't have a DRF account, I'd suggest you read no farther, and get a personal account up and running before attempting to comprehend the Formulator program. Once you've gotten through the setting-up and downloading process, you're ready to get to work. For example purposes, let's take a look at the Aqueduct card for St. Patrick's Day, March 17, 2006. Once you've opened the Formulator program, you'll notice a "Race Information" heading, which lists the name of today's track, the date, and the card you've selected. Below the track and date will be the race conditions and race listing for all nine races on today's Aqueduct afternoon program. For the purpose of getting you familiar with the software, we'll go through race number 1.

Race	Post	Race Conditions
1st	1:00	5 1/2 Furlongs(Inner Dirt) **MAIDEN SPECIAL WEIGHT. Purse $41,000 INNER DIRT FOR MAIDENS, FILLIES AND MARES THREE YEARS OLD AND UPWARD FOALED IN NEW YORK STATE AND APPROVED BY THE NEW YORK STATE-BRED REGISTRY** Three Year Olds, 116 lbs.; Older, 123 lbs.

Next, click on "1st" under the race heading. You'll immediately be forwarded to the past performances of Aqueduct's first race, which is a maiden-special-weight 5½-furlong sprint event.

1 Aqueduct

ⒻⓈMd Sp Wt 41k

5½ Furlongs. (Inner Dirt) (1:034) MAIDEN SPECIAL WEIGHT. Purse $41,000 INNER DIRT FOR MAIDENS, FILLIES AND MARES THREE YEARS OLD AND UPWARD FOALED IN NEW YORK STATE AND APPROVED BY THE NEW YORK STATE-BRED REGISTRY. Three Year Olds, 116 lbs.; Older, 123 lbs.

Coupled – Don't Drop In and Esopus Jet
Exacta, Trifecta, Daily Double

2 Missing Shirley
Own: Kilstein, Matthew
12–1 Green and Black Halves, Black and Green
Pezua J M (40 1 1 3 .02) 2005:(196 24 .12)

Ch. f. 4 (Apr)
Sire: Carry My Colors (Roanoke) $5,000
Dam: Susita Bonita (Lejoli)
Br: Matthew Kilstein(NY)
Tr: Kilstein Matthew (8 0 0 0 .00) 2005:(8 0 .00)

L 123

Life	1	M	0	0	$137	13	D.Fst	0	0	0	0	$0	-
2005	1	M	0	0	$137	13	Wet (298*)	1	0	0	0	$137	13
2004	0	M	0	0	$0	-	Turf (198*)	0	0	0	0	$0	-
Aqu⊡	0	0	0	0	$0	-	Dist (283*)	0	0	0	0	$0	-

22May05-1Bel gd 6½f :23 :47 1:12 1:182 3↑ⒻⓈMd Sp Wt 41k 1311 7 72¼ 98¼1024 1028 Velasquez C L118b 6.40 52-20 ChmpgnEndng11810 *HsBty* 118nk Hrshs1187½ 5 wide trip, tired 11

WORKS: Mar11 Bel tr.t 4f fst :502 B *52/70* Feb26 Bel tr.t 4f fst :50 B *17/24* Feb11 Bel tr.t 3f fst :39 B *32/36* Feb4 Bel tr.t 3f fst :374 B *9/14*

TRAINER: 2ndStart (2 .00 $0.00) Dirt (11 .00 $0.00) Sprint (6 .00 $0.00) MdnSpWt (9 .00 $0.00) J/T 2005-06 AQU (7 .00 $0.00) J/T 2005-06 (7 .00 $0.00)

---

3 Magee and Maggie
Own: McGettigan, Sr., Edward, T.
20–1 Neon Pink, Black Hoop, Pink Sleeves,
Smith C (9 0 1 0 .00) 2005:(277 6 .02)

Dk. b or br f. 4 (Feb)
Sire: Mighty Magee (Cormorant) $2,000
Dam: Irish Miricle (Go and Go*Ire)
Br: E. T. McGettigan Sr.(NY)
Tr: Jerkens Steven T (13 0 2 1 .00) 2005:(51 2 .04)

116 7

Life	2	M	0	0	$342	31	D.Fst	2	0	0	0	$342	31
2005	2	M	0	0	$342	31	Wet (294)	0	0	0	0	$0	-
2004	0	M	0	0	$0	-	Turf (261*)	0	0	0	0	$0	-
Aqu⊡	0	0	0	0	$0	-	Dist (279)	1	0	0	0	$205	31

28Oct05-9Bel fst 6½f :224 :464 1:122 1:192 3↑ⒻⓈMd Sp Wt 41k –0 9 6 3nk 96¾ 1018 1022¾ Maragh R 120 50.75 52-18 LDvl1151¾ WyrdLz1224¼ ThrtyEghthSt.113½ Brief speed, tired 11
5Oct05-4Bel fst 5½f :232 :463 :584 1:051 3↑ⒻⓈMd Sp Wt 41k 31 8 7 77¼ 78¾ 714 712 Amy J 120 25.75 73-15 Tiamo Mia1225 Vesuvius120½ **Sudden Burst**1221 Had no rally 9

WORKS: Mar5 Bel tr.t 4f fst :523 B *58/60* Feb16 Bel tr.t 4f fst :522 B *69/70* Feb7 Bel tr.t 3f fst :38 B *13/15*

TRAINER: 61-180Days (5 .00 $0.00) Dirt (61 .03 $0.28) Sprint (33 .06 $0.52) MdnSpWt (14 .00 $0.00) J/T 2005-06 AQU (1 .00 $0.00) J/T 2005-06 (1 .00 $0.00)

---

4 Majestic Risk
Own: Team Manhattan Stable
2–1 Red, Black Diamond, Two Black Hoops on
Fragoso P (236 24 32 30 .10) 2005:(988 92 .09)

Dk. b or br f. 3 (Feb)
Sire: More Than Ready (Southern Halo) $30,000
Dam: Hidden Valentine (Lost Code)
Br: Blue Lake Farm(NY)
Tr: Hennig Mark (58 5 8 10 .08) 2005:(413 75 .18)

L 116

Life	2	M	0	1	$6,150	39	D.Fst	2	0	0	1	$6,150	39
2006	1	M	0	1	$4,100	31	Wet (352)	0	0	0	0	$0	-
2005	1	M	0	0	$2,050	39	Turf (391)	0	0	0	0	$0	-
Aqu⊡	1	0	0	1	$4,100	31	Dist (387)	2	0	0	1	$6,150	39

17Feb06-4Aqu fst 5½f ⊡:221 :474 1:011 1:08 ⒻⓈMd Sp Wt 41k 31 7 2 2hd 1½ 21 38 Fragoso P L120 3.05 71-26 WcdSrcrss1205½ HlKrptt1202½ MjstcRs120¾ Vied outside, tired 9
30Jun05-4Bel fst 5f :22 :451 :573 ⒻⓈMd Sp Wt 41k 39 4 6 1hd 2hd 33½ 410½ Velasquez C L118 3.05 85-07 Chf'sDghtr1182¼ *Wmpm* 1187½ Dr.Cpt118¾ Between rivals, tired 7

WORKS: Mar12 Bel tr.t 4f fst :51 B *46/64* Mar2 Bel tr.t 4f fst :514 B *20/25* Feb9 Bel tr.t 5f fst 1:022 Bg *9/17* Feb2 Bel tr.t 5f fst 1:04 B *30/39* Jan25 Bel tr.t 4f fst :48 B *8/46* Jan17 Bel tr.t 4f fst :501 B *56/99*

TRAINER: 2OffOver180 (13 .31 $2.50) Dirt (359 .18 $1.84) Sprint (147 .14 $1.35) MdnSpWt (170 .12 $1.16) J/T 2005-06 AQU (60 .08 $0.70) J/T 2005-06 (103 .11 $1.08)

---

5 Sudden Burst
Own: Kaufman, Robert, Iselin, James, H.
8–5 Red and Purple Diagonal Quarters, Red
Kaenel K (437 58 60 67 .13) 2005:(669 112 .17)

Ch. m. 5 (Apr)
Sire: Goldminers Gold (Crafty Prospector) $2,500
Dam: Sudden Affair (To the Quick)
Br: Marvin Little Jr. & James H. Iselin(NY)
Tr: Stoklosa Richard (39 4 14 5 .10) 2005:(98 8 .08)

L 118 5

Life	16	M	5	4	$60,089	57	D.Fst	10	0	4	3	$48,429	57
2006	3	M	1	1	$12,440	57	Wet (310)	5	0	1	1	$11,450	54
2005	13	M	4	3	$47,649	57	Turf (219*)	1	0	0	0	$210	-
Aqu⊡	7	0	2	2	$25,520	57	Dist (313)	6	0	4	1	$37,840	57

16Feb06-6Aqu fst 5½f ⊡:23 :473 1:00 1:063 4↑ⒻⓈMd Sp Wt 41k 57 6 2 1hd 12 1½ 11¼ Kaenel K5 L117fb 4.90 86-16 ⒹSddnBrst1171¼ FgGrnd122nk Sklpr1222½ Weaving in stretch 9
Disqualified and placed second
29Jan06-9Aqu fst 6f ⊡:224 :47 :592 1:124 4↑ⒻⓈMd Sp Wt 41k 47 2 4 12½ 3½ 2hd 32¼ Kaenel K5 L116fb 7.10 73-17 QutRndton1142¼ Skylopr121no SddnBrst1162¼ Set pace, tired 10
19Jan06-4Aqu gd 5½f ⊡:222 :47 :593 1:06 4↑ⒻⓈMd Sp Wt 41k 50 3 4 1½ 11 1hd 61¾ Kaenel K5 L116fb 3.45 87-13 MssCplyHll121½ PtchsfDx121no **CtDmnd**121½ Bumped stretch 11
16Dec05-6Aqu my 5½f ⊡:23 :481 1:003 1:07 3↑ⒻⓈMd Sp Wt 41k 54 8 1 11 1hd 21 21 Kaenel K5 L117fb 3.30 — — ThrtEhthSt1211 SddBrst1174¾ DstctL1221½ Set pace, gamely 11
10Dec05-9Aqu gd 6f ⊡:224 :462 :591 1:122 3↑ⒻⓈMd Sp Wt 41k 49 6 4 32½ 33½ 21 54¼ Kaenel K5 L117fb 7.50 73-16 DxJm1212¾ StgDncr121nk *ConqstBond* 121½ Bumped after start 10
30Nov05-2Aqu gd 6f ⊡:223 :463 :591 1:123 3↑ⒻⓈMd 25000 42 6 1 22½ 25½ 28 38½ Coa E M L122fb *1.40 67-18 CrkdWmn1155 Chzl1133½ SddnBrst1223 Chased inside, tired 8
12Nov05-2Aqu fst 6f :224 :463 :59 1:12 3↑ⒻⓈMd Sp Wt 41k 49 3 2 31½ 33 36½ 37¼ Sutherland C L122fb 5.90 71-19 Stphnt1215½ CstBd1211¾ SddBrst122hd Chased inside, no bid 11
5Oct05-4Bel fst 5½f :232 :463 :584 1:051 3↑ⒻⓈMd Sp Wt 41k 49 3 2 21½ 31 25½ 35½ Sutherland C L122fb *1.55 79-15 TmoM1225 Vsuvus120½ SuddnBurst1221 Chased inside, tired 9
21Sep05-2Bel fst 6f :233 :481 1:003 1:134 3↑ⒻⓈMd Sp Wt 41k 44 3 1 1hd 2hd 2hd 21 Sutherland C L122fb 3.80 69-23 LStt1191 SddBrst122½ ThrtEhthSt1195¾ Vied inside, stubborn 8
11Aug05-9Sar fst 5½f :223 :463 :592 1:06 3↑ⒻⓈMd Sp Wt 45k 57 3 1 1½ 13½ 1hd 22 Sutherland C L122fb 14.50 87-11 *ChppnWd* 1182 SddnBrst122¾ DstnctJl1182¼ Pace, clear, gamely 12

WORKS: Jan11 Aqu ⊡ 4f fst :501 B (d) *11/14*

TRAINER: Dirt (117 .09 $1.68) Sprint (76 .08 $1.87) MdnSpWt (64 .05 $0.70) J/T 2005-06 AQU (13 .15 $4.60) J/T 2005-06 (13 .15 $4.60)

---

6 Cut Diamond
Own: Oleanik, Jacqueline, E.
5–1 Black, Fluorescent Orange Collar,
Hill C (330 26 33 38 .07) 2005:(1157 135 .12)

Ch. f. 4 (Mar)
Sire: Diamond (Mr. Prospector) $2,500
Dam: A Merry Prankster (Three Or Less)
Br: Judith Gurren(NY)
Tr: Oleanik Jacqueline E (4 0 0 2 .00) 2005:(11 0 .00)

L 123

Life	8	M	0	3	$10,636	54	D.Fst	4	0	0	2	$6,069	48
2006	3	M	0	2	$5,864	54	Wet (391)	2	0	0	1	$4,237	54
2005	5	M	0	1	$4,772	48	Turf (174)	2	0	0	0	$330	37
Aqu⊡	4	0	0	2	$6,001	54	Dist (299)	2	0	0	1	$4,237	54

1Mar06-1Aqu fst 6f ⊡:232 :481 1:011 1:141 4↑ⒻⓈMd 25000 33 10 2 2½ 2½ 2hd 31¾ Hill C L122fb *1.40 66-18 Borngoddss1171¾ JudyLnrS.122hd CtDmond1225 Outfinished 10
29Jan06-9Aqu fst 6f ⊡:224 :47 :592 1:124 4↑ⒻⓈMd Sp Wt 41k 34 3 7 75¼ 77¼ 77¾ 97¾ Arroyo N Jr L121fb 9.40 67-17 QtRndton1142¼ Skylopr121no **SddnBrst**1162¼ Inside trip, tired 10
19Jan06-4Aqu gd 5½f ⊡:222 :47 :593 1:06 4↑ⒻⓈMd Sp Wt 41k 54 5 9 67 66¾ 52¾ 3½ Hill C L121fb 24.00 88-13 MssCplHll121½ PtchsfD121no CtDnd121½ Game finish outside 11
16Dec05-6Aqu my 5½f ⊡:23 :481 1:003 1:07 3↑ⒻⓈMd Sp Wt 41k 20 10 3 31 31 66½ 713¾ Gomez O L121fb 11.50 — — TrtEtSt1211 **SddBrst**1174¾ DstctL1221½ Chased 3 wide, tired 11
Previously trained by O'Brien Leo 2005(as of 11/16): (72 5 7 19 0.07)
16Nov05-2Aqu fst 6f :223 :464 1:001 1:141 3↑ⒻⓈMd Sp Wt 41k 48 4 4 42½ 53 53¼ 35¾ Kaenel K5 L116 30.75 61-27 BrrsWst1215¾ Drscctr121hd CtDd116no Outfinished for place 9
10Nov05-9Aqu gd 1$\frac{1}{16}$Ⓣ:231 :484 1:144 1:463 3↑ⒻⓈMd Sp Wt 42k 37 3 115¾ 119½ 127½ 1213 915¼ Kaenel K5 L115 65.25 58-22 *Aly'sClrs* 1201½ StgDncr1151 AStrfrShnnn1205¼ Outrun inside 12
19Oct05-6Bel fst 6f :222 :461 :583 1:113 3↑ⓈMd Sp Wt 41k 38 5 4 67 79¾ 716 613¾ Kaenel K5 L114 18.60 67-15 SvnBllsforbb1203½ OurLd120hd PrlfcAppl1201¾ No response 9
21Sep05-6Bel fm 1⅛Ⓣ:4741:13 1:38 1:50 3↑ⒻⓈMd Sp Wt 42k –0 8 21½ 22½ 66½ 730 930¾ Smith M E 118 *1.00e 46-15 KnLssi118¾ IncIsClling1183¼ Crzyluck1151 Tired after a half 9

WORKS: Mar10 Bel tr.t 4f fst :491 B *14/28* Feb10 Bel tr.t 4f fst :493 B *16/30* Jan10 Bel tr.t 4f fst :49 B *11/23*

TRAINER: Dirt (13 .00 $0.00) Sprint (4 .00 $0.00) MdnSpWt (3 .00 $0.00) J/T 2005-06 AQU (3 .00 $0.00) J/T 2005-06 (3 .00 $0.00)

---

1 Don't Drop In
Own: Candlin, John
30–1 Yellow, Black Diamond Hoop, Black
Millwood C (2 0 0 0 .00) 2005:(27 0 .00)

B. f. 4 (May) EASSEP03 $2,700
Sire: General Meeting (Seattle Slew) $10,000
Dam: Remember When (Dixie Brass)
Br: Donald & R. Mary Zuckerman, as Tenants by the Er
Tr: Candlin John (56 1 1 2 .01) 2005:(210 5 .02)

L 113 10

Life	2	M	0	0	$411	15	D.Fst	2	0	0	0	$411	15
2006	1	M	0	0	$137	15	Wet (371)	0	0	0	0	$0	-
2005	1	M	0	0	$274	-	Turf (301)	0	0	0	0	$0	-
Aqu⊡	1	0	0	0	$137	15	Dist (369)	0	0	0	0	$0	-

11Mar06-6Aqu fst 6f ⊡:23 :464 :59 1:112 3↑ⒻⓈMd Sp Wt 41k 15 11 4 84½ 916 921 1023 Smith C7 L116fb 82.75 59-13 StinEnd1167½ HerRoylNibs1231 Skyloper1234 Wide trip, tired 11
21Sep05-2Bel fst 6f :233 :481 1:003 1:134 3↑ⒻⓈMd Sp Wt 41k –0 5 8 813 815 820 724 Gomez O 119 65.00 46-23 LnSttn1191 **SddBrst**122½ ThrtEhthSt1195¾ Bumped after start 8

WORKS: Mar2 Bel tr.t 4f fst :503 B *15/25* Feb24 Bel tr.t 4f fst :50 B *46/62* Feb11 Bel tr.t 4f fst :501 B *64/114* Feb4 Bel tr.t 3f fst :384 Bg *13/14* Jan28 Bel tr.t 3f fst :372 B *8/22* Jan22 Bel tr.t 4f fst :52 B *48/49*

TRAINER: 2Off45-180 (16 .06 $4.69) 1-7Days (27 .00 $0.00) Dirt (206 .02 $0.65) Sprint (120 .03 $0.37) MdnSpWt (111 .04 $1.74)

Friday, March 17, 2006

7 Take a Gem
20–1 Own: Unadilla Stable
Emerald Green, White Yoke, Gold
Samyn J L (79 3 8 13 .03) 2005:(437 29 .07)

Dk. b or br f. 3 (Apr)
Sire: Take Me Out (Cure the Blues) $5,000
Dam: Britesparkle (Private Terms)
Br: Milfer Farm Inc.(NY)
Tr: Sedlacek Michael C (30 0 0 2 .00) 2005:(94 4 .04)

116

Life	1	M	0	0	$205	11	D.Fst	1	0	0	0	$205	11
2006	1	M	0	0	$205	11	Wet (339)	0	0	0	0	$0	-
2005	0	M	0	0	$0	-	Turf (245)	0	0	0	0	$0	-
Aqu [•]	1	0	0	0	$205	11	Dist (344)	1	0	0	0	$205	11

17Feb06-4Aqufst 5½f [•]:221 :474 1:011 1:08 (F)(S)Md Sp Wt 41k 11 3 6 816 816 814 715½ Samyn J L 120f 29.50 63-26 WckdSrcrss1205½ HlKrptnt1202½ MjstcRsk120¾ Bumped start 9

WORKS: Mar11 Bel tr.t 4f fst :491 B 29/70 Mar1 Bel tr.t 4f fst :51 B 47/55 Feb10 Bel tr.t 4f fst :493 B 13/30 Feb4 Bel tr.t 5f fst 1:014 B 17/25 Jan30 Bel tr.t 5f fst 1:053 B 4/4 Jan25 Bel tr.t 4f fst :49 Bg 19/46

TRAINER: 2ndStart (7 .00 $0.00) Dirt (105 .04 $0.67) Sprint (57 .05 $1.14) MdnSpWt (40 .05 $0.86) J/T 2005-06 AQU (43 .02 $0.46) J/T 2005-06 (74 .04 $0.56)

8 Melinda's Star
5–1 Own: Winter Park Partners
Royal Blue, White Diamonds on Sleeves,
Dominguez R A (324 86 58 49 .26) 2005:(1221 312 .26)

Ch. f. 3 (Apr) SARAUG04 $30,000
Sire: Precise End (End Sweep) $10,175
Dam: Arizona Star (Afleet)
Br: Thomas/Lakin(NY)
Tr: Contessa Gary C (251 53 40 31 .21) 2005:(610 92 .15)

(L) 116

Life	0	M	0	0	$0	-	D.Fst	0	0	0	0	$0	-
2006	0	M	0	0	$0	-	Wet (417)	0	0	0	0	$0	-
2005	0	M	0	0	$0	-	Turf (230)	0	0	0	0	$0	-
Aqu [•]	0	0	0	0	$0	-	Dist (414)	0	0	0	0	$0	-

Entered 16Mar06 - 4 AQU

WORKS: Mar10 Aqu [•] 4f fst :484 Hg (d) 3/6 Mar3 Aqu [•] 6f fst 1:182 B (d) 1/2 Feb26 Aqu [•] 6f fst 1:183 H (d) 3/3 Feb18 Aqu [•] 5f fst 1:042 H (d) 2/4 Feb11 Aqu [•] 5f fst 1:04 B (d) 8/9

TRAINER: 1stStart (69 .13 $1.60) 1stLasix (41 .15 $0.92) Dirt (702 .18 $1.82) Sprint (446 .17 $1.86) MdnSpWt (231 .15 $1.36) J/T 2005-06 AQU (71 .34 $2.28) J/T 2005-06 (84 .29 $1.93)

1A Esopus Jet
30–1 Own: Loughlin, Eugene, Pascaretti, Nicholas,
Green and White Diamonds, Orange
Gomez O (20 0 0 1 .00) 2005:(249 10 .04)

Dk. b or br f. 4 (Apr)
Sire: A. P Jet (Fappiano) $5,000
Dam: La Femme M (Cure the Blues)
Br: Tranquility Farm(NY)
Tr: Candlin John (56 1 1 2 .01) 2005:(210 5 .02)

L 123

Life	15	M	0	0	$4,488	35	D.Fst	12	0	0	0	$2,290	28
2006	5	M	0	0	$445	25	Wet (344)	2	0	0	0	$2,030	35
2005	10	M	0	0	$4,043	35	Turf (229)	1	0	0	0	$168	31
Aqu [•]	8	0	0	0	$2,680	35	Dist (363)	1	0	0	0	$1,230	34

1Mar06-1Aqufst 6f [•]:232 :481 1:011 1:141 4↑(F)(S)Md 25000 10 4 10 87¼ 58 68¼ 611 Gomez O L122b 20.80e 57-18 Borngoddss1171¾ JudyLnrS.122hd CutDmond1225 Had no rally 10
23Feb06-9Aqufst 1 [•]:241 :482 1:141 1:401 3↑(F)Md 25000 19 2 79½ 710 716 724 724 Rivera J L Jr L123b 74.50 58-26 ActsIf1168¼ FrstbyFv1161½ Nothn'ButSss111no Outrun inside 8
8Feb06-5Aqufst 6f [•]:231 :464 :592 1:122 4↑(F)(S)Md 25000 25 3 5 85½ 612 712 614¼ Gomez O L122b 115.00 63-17 BrookHly1178 Chzl1221¼ DstnctvLvn1151 Inside trip, no rally 11
22Jan06-4Aqufst 6f [•]:232 :48 1:004 1:14 4↑(F)(S)Md 25000 8 9 6 1013 918 822 820½ Pimentel J L122b 56.25e 49-21 J. D.'s Girl1226¼ Chazal1223¾ *Brooke Haley* 115½ No response 12
13Jan06-9Aqufst 170 [•]:242 :493 1:15 1:463 4↑(F)(S)Md Sp Wt 42k 24 5 815½ Lopez D M7 L114b 60.25 52-21 WnErly121nk *PcflDwngn* 1143 BtyOnDck1211½ 3 wide, tired, fog 10
16Dec05-6Aqumy 5½f [•]:23 :481 1:003 1:07 3↑(F)(S)Md Sp Wt 41k 34 7 9 85½ 74¼ 45 58¼ Toups R7 L114fb 40.50e — — TrtEtSt1211 SddBrst1174¾ DstctL1221½ Inside, flattened out 11
30Nov05-2Aqugd 6f [•]:223 :463 :591 1:123 3↑(F)(S)Md 25000 35 1 8 810 611 416 411½ Gomez O L120fb 58.00 64-18 CrkdWmn1155 Chzl1133½ SddnBrst1223 Came wide, no rally 8
3Nov05-1Medfst 6f :222 :454 :582 1:114 3↑(F)Md 10000 24 3 4 43½ 57 510 512¾ Kaenel K5 L117fb 10.20 68-14 YouGo1222¾ WildctPrincess1223¼ TerrCynthus1185 No factor 6
23Jun05-1Bel fst 6f :224 :461 :583 1:112 3↑(F)(S)Md Sp Wt 41k 24 7 8 74¼ 77 711 713¾ Rojas R I L118b 71.50 68-11 JumpJudy1185 SkLov118½ BrookHly1184½ 3 wide trip, tired 8
2Jun05-1Bel fst 6f :23 :471 :592 1:114 3↑(F)(S)Md Sp Wt 41k 28 6 6 74 67 513 719 Rodriguez R R L118b 61.50 61-20 CSccss1188¾ ClsscEprss1185½ Vss1181¾ Between rivals, tired 10

WORKS: Mar14 Bel tr.t 3f gd :372 B 5/9 Feb17 Bel tr.t 4f fst :511 B 41/54 Feb2 Bel tr.t 4f fst :501 B 37/60 Jan7 Bel tr.t 3f fst :40 B 37/37 Dec24 Bel tr.t 4f fst :503 B 135/165

TRAINER: Dirt (206 .02 $0.65) Sprint (120 .03 $0.37) MdnSpWt (111 .04 $1.74) J/T 2005-06 AQU (36 .06 $2.71) J/T 2005-06 (59 .03 $1.65)

You'll now have the option of clicking on each of the entrants' jockeys, trainers, and each horse's last racing date, which will allow you to begin the Formulator 4.1 filtering process. By clicking on trainer name Matthew Kilstein of number 2, Missing Shirley, you'll immediately be sent to Kilstein's trainer stats for the 4-year-old filly he has entered and the relevant information that goes with it. It would look something like this.

Trainer:	Kilstein Matthew/Current Horse: Missing Shirley
Currently Applied TP Query:	Default Query
Track: Aqueduct/Date:	March 17, 2006/First Race
Race Conditions:	5 1/2 F (Inner Dirt) 3-Year-Olds and Up Fillies and Mares

Horses	Starts	Wins	ITM	Win%	ITM%	$2ROI	Median Payoff
4	4	1	1	25	25	$1.00	$7.20

Below the currently applied query you'll have the ability to review the past performances of the current entry, return to the racecard, reset TP filters, modify TP filters, save the TP query, and go to a help function. In addition, you'll be able to see the four other maiden-special-weight starters trainer Matthew Kilstein previously entered. In this case it would include the horses Dynamite Rose, Marree Magee (who appears twice), and Ruby of Royalty. It would also include the racetrack, date, class level, distance, track surface, Beyer Speed Figure, post position, finishing position, margin of defeat or victory, odds, the assigned jockey, and the number of starters. With one simple click of the computer mouse, you have a mountain of information to evaluate and sift through.

Modify TP Filters is the main component of the program, and it's the one we'll be spending 90 percent of our time utilizing in order to find interesting and valuable trainer statistics we can wager on with confidence. By clicking on the Modify TP Filter option, you're sent to three main filtering options: Basic Filters, Filters with Ranges, and Track/Jockey Filters. The Basic Filters include the assortment of options listed below. The TP Query is set at General because we haven't modified anything yet. The General function below the TP Query gives you a specific time frame from which to choose your trainer analysis. When you use the Modify TP Filters dialogue box to customize the settings you want Formulator to use, you can then save these settings and use them again in subsequent sessions. At first, the Trainer Pattern tool will display some stats that are relevant to the race under review. By simply clicking on Modify TP Filters, you can decide exactly what stats you're interested in reviewing. The options are endless.

BASIC FILTERS

GENERAL
Time Frame: (Past Five Years), (Past Four Years), (Past Three Years), (Past Two Years), (Past Year), (Past 6 Months), (Past 90 Days), (Past 30 Days).

AS A GENERAL RULE, the greater the time frame allowed, the larger and more accurate a sample you're likely to generate. I prefer to keep this setting at five years unless there's a reason to believe a trainer may be on a sizzling win streak, and perhaps hitting with a strong win ratio in the last three or six months within a certain category. The explanations for his or her sudden success can vary for a number of reasons or circumstances. Perhaps a new owner has provided the trainer with a dozen well-bred, track-ready, talented 2-year-olds filled with win-early pedigrees such as In Excess, Not For Love, or Tale of the Cat. In this scenario, there would be good reason to believe that the trainer's first-time-starter/2-year-old win percentage could increase sharply in a limited time frame. If that was the situation, it could be relevant to set your time-frame filter for the last six months or 90 days as opposed to two or more years.

The next basic filter is Surface, and it's one of the strongest Trainer Form variables. As you'll see in upcoming chapters, different trainers excel on different surfaces, and the surface change often indicates positive trainer intent. This is a Trainer Form filter that we'll want to be aware of at all times and definitely include in our calculations.

Surface: (Include All Starters), (Dirt), (Turf), (Inner Dirt), (First-Time Turf), (Off the Turf), (Dirt to Turf), (Turf to Dirt), (Wet), (Main Dirt).

The Winners, etc. option will show the trainer's percentage for winners, horses that finished in the money, etc., when each specific category is selected (see list, below). For our purposes, I'm most interested in seeing the Winners column, although one other category that could be of some interest is Maiden Winner Last Out. This grouping allows us to see how our trainer does with horses that have recently broken their maiden. Some trainers may make nine or ten attempts with the horse before winning another race, while others have the ability to keep their stock sharp and in form for greater lengths of time. Therefore, these types of conditioners may be more likely to have their horses win their next race following a maiden victory.

Winners, Etc.: (Winners), (In the Money), (Place & Show), (Winner Last Out), (ITM Last Out), (Maiden Winner Last Out).

The Beyer Speed Figures category allows you to see how the trainer does with horses that have recently achieved their top Beyer (see list below). In many situations, depending upon the trainer, the age and class of the horse, and the racing surface and distance, some trainers' horses who have achieved a lifetime best effort based on speed figures in their most recent start are more inclined to "bounce," or not repeat this giant effort, in their next race. With so many different variables going into the cycling of peak and nonpeak performances in an individual horse's running cycle, I find it most favorable to include all starts, not just the Top Beyer Last Out.

Beyer Speed Figures: (Include All Starts), (Top Beyer Last Out), (Last Three Ascending Beyers).

HORSE RELATED

The Horse Related Formulator filters are some of the strongest and most constructive statistics. We will concentrate primarily on them, and they provide the basis for most value-oriented wagers a bettor can make. There's no question that some trainers excel with horses of different ages and sexes. Some have the ability to get young horses ready to run off a series of workouts, while others use an actual race or even several races as "hands-on" training sessions. At the very least, it's imperative that you become aware of what, if any, age or sex specialties the trainers possess at the racing circuit you're following and betting. As you'll see in greater detail in some of the later chapters, a single positive trainer angle in a specific category is not always as favorable as it may first appear once you've applied the Age and Sex filters. A trainer may have an incredible win percentage with 3-year-old first-time-starter colts, but a horrendous percentage with 2-year-old first-time-starter fillies. Using the first-time-starter Trainer Form angle as a stand-alone for horses making their debut can be a beginner's costly mistake.

Age: (Include All Starters), (2 YOs Only), (3 YOs Only), (3 YOs & Older), (4 YOs & Older), (3 YOs vs. Older).
Sex: (Include All Starters), (Males), (Females).

There was a time when the addition of the diuretic Lasix (generic name: furosemide) was a noteworthy medication change. Used as an anti-bleeding medication, it often significantly improved a horse's performance when administered for the first and second time. Today, Lasix and the anti-inflammatory medication Butazolidin (phenylbutazone) are so widely administered that their addition does not produce the sudden improvement it once did, but I've found the Lasix angle still important with young horses that have had minimal starts, and with those arriving for their first start on American soil. An improved performance is almost always likely in these two scenarios when Lasix is given.

> **Lasix:** (Include All Starters), (First Time Lasix), (With Lasix), (Without Lasix), (Switch to Lasix), (Switch Off Lasix), (Second Time Lasix).

The addition or removal of blinkers is an important change of equipment that's used regularly by trainers of all types. It's a useful indication of trainer intent and one that can improve a horse's running line by several lengths and several Beyer points. It's especially important in young, green horses that are easily distracted and/or have difficulty concentrating on the racing task at hand. A young and immature horse that has flashed halfway decent speed in one or two prior outings usually improves significantly with the addition of blinkers. On the flip side, the removal of blinkers can sometimes make a horse run more aggressively and be more keenly aware of the horses around him as the race unfolds. The Blinkers On and Blinkers Off categories are two significant Trainer Form equipment filters that are sure to lead you to several winning tickets at generous odds. Do your homework and familiarize yourself with the local conditioners that have successfully used this equipment change.

> **Blinkers:** (Include All Starters), (First Time Blinkers), (First Time Blinkers Off), (Blinkers On), (Blinkers Off), (Switch to On), (Switch to Off).

TRAINER

View Trainer-Pattern Past Performances

THE FORMULATOR PROGRAM GIVES you unprecedented access to the past performances that make up trainer-pattern statistics. The tool is unique in that it helps the user get an inside look into a trainer's numbers. It provides the option of comparing the past performances of an entrant running today with similar past performances from that trainer's previous starters.

Once a stat is pulled, by simply clicking on the View TP PPs option, you can easily see the relevant past performances for the horses that make up the statistic. The default setting here puts only the relevant running lines from each horse's past performances in black, while the less relevant running lines are in gray. The View TP PPs option is a great way to compare today's runner with a trainer's runners from the past in similar circumstances. The hope is that a profitable pattern will emerge.

Trainer Workout Patterns

THE FORMULATOR PROGRAM ALSO allows you to compare the workouts of horses that are running today with the workouts of relevant horses in other Trainer Pattern past performances. After you've set your Trainer Pattern options, click on View TP PPs to see the PPs of the relevant horses. Keep in mind that the black running lines are the ones that are relevant to the statistics, and the gray lines are not. Next, go to the TP Options drop-down menu at the top of the page and select the last option, TP Workouts. Now you will see the last six workouts prior to the relevant black PP lines within View TP PPs. Next, click on the Return to Racecard button at the top of the page. You can view the workouts for today's horse within the racecard's PPs. By using the red "back" arrow within the racecard's PPs, you can then return to the TP PP view to compare these to the workouts from the relevant horses from the past.

Trainer Changes: (Include All Starters), (First After Claimed By), (Second After Claimed By), (First After Claimed From), (First After Trainer Switch).

Some of the finest horsemen make a good living at the claiming box and are true craftsmen at getting the best bang for their buck. They have the ability to spot improving, sound horses and to take over another conditioner's stock and drastically improve those horses' performance. These men and women are the individuals we're interested in studying, tracking, and pursuing. Some trainers have immediate success (First After Claimed By) while others may need a race or two (Second After Claimed By) to figure out what conditions best suit their newly acquired purchase. A recent claim combined with a surface or distance change, jockey switch, class drop or increase, or equipment change offers some of the best and most profitable trainer angles and intent available.

A class move in either direction can be a positive or a negative sign, depending on the trainer we're evaluating. Some trainers are able to move a horse up the claiming and allowance ranks, grabbing purse after purse under various distances and circumstances, while others have a difficult time finding the winner's circle unless they drop a runner significantly in class. Cashing tickets depends on familiarizing yourself with the patterns of the conditioners on hand and the class maneuvers they've had the most success with.

For example, it's no handicapping secret that one of the biggest class drops in racing is the move from maiden special weight to maiden claiming. The drop is even more significant when the horse has shown some natural front-running ability, or the capability to be within early stalking or striking position in either one or a few of its prior attempts against better stock. In many cases, while making this initial drop in class, these types of horses can shake clear of maiden-claiming runners with relative ease. When the real running begins at the top of the stretch, they are frequently long gone with gate-to-wire scores. However, there are many trainers that have had paltry success with such maiden class-drop maneuvers. For these types of trainers, the class drop is often a negative and desperate attempt to unload a sore or disappointing runner or perhaps a last-resort effort to grab a purse. Without the Formulator class-filtering process, it's almost impossible for the handicapper to know when the drop is a positive or negative trainer tactic.

Class Moves: (Include All Starters), (50% Claiming Tag Jump), (50% Claiming Tag Drop), (First Time For Tag), (MdnSpWt to MdnClm), (Allowance to Claiming), (Claiming to Allowance).

The final basic filter that the Formulator user is able to modify is the Shipper option. Occasionally, a conditioner will march into another circuit or arrive with a foreign invader and pop at a big price. Bettors are not as perplexed as they once were when evaluating the form and class of a horse from unfamiliar surroundings. The availability of Beyer Speed Figures, and precise class and track pars, make evaluating the ability of these out-of-towners far easier than it once was. With this data at your fingertips, you can make an educated guess as to how a $15,000 Philadelphia Park older claimer matches up against $20,000 Delaware Park claiming stock. Despite what's available by calculating raw class and speed-figure data, there are still a handful of trainers out there that specialize in shipping horses in and out of racing circuits from this country and abroad. The form on these types of horses from these types of conditioners is occasionally dark and uninviting. Do you know which ones have had success at your circuit?

Shippers: (Include All Starters), (All Shippers), (Domestic Shippers), (Foreign Shippers).

Filter with Ranges

THE FILTER WITH RANGES option begins with giving the user the ability to see how a specific trainer does with horses making their first or second start, or those coming off a brief, middle-of-the-road, or extensive layoff. In addition, the Days Between Starts option allows a careful examination of how some trainers perform when putting a horse on the track for the first, second, and third time after a layoff. This is a valuable Formulator tool and one that will quickly guide you to favorable trainer patterns and generous payoffs.

The simple fact is that some trainers have the skills to have their horses perform well with limited time off between starts, and others achieve maximum success with horses that have been well rested. It's interesting, however, to evaluate how the Days Between Starts handicapping factor has changed based on updated Thoroughbred care, medications, and 21st-century training methods. For example, about 10 years ago, it was very encouraging to see a horse run back within a limited time frame, such as three or four days' rest. It was often a sign of physical soundness, and positive trainer confidence and intent. During this same era, a horse coming off any type of layoff often needed a race or two to get his running legs back underneath him. A layoff runner wouldn't be expected to perform at his optimum level returning to the track off an extended vacation.

Today, for the most part, just the opposite holds true. Many successful trainers have become masters of patience. They have shown the ability to have a horse ready through only workouts and private training sessions, and readily score with a runner after several months or even years of rest. It's imperative that you know the Days Between Starts specialty of the trainers at the circuit you're betting and following.

Days Between Starts: (Include All Starters), (First Time Starters), (Second Career Start), (1st After Layoff +45), (2nd After Layoff), (3rd After Layoff), (1 to 7 Days), (8 to 30 Days), (31 to 60 Days), (61 to 180 Days), (>180 Days), (User Min and Max Days).

Some trainers and stables like to bet just as much as you or I. In fact, there are some outfits that bet quite heavily when it appears they have a live entrant on the track. The Formulator Closing Odds filter option, however, is one that I rarely utilize. I'm usually inclined to keep the setting at the Include All Starters option when working with the Formulator program. I'm a firm believer in early tote action within individual races on major racing circuits, and so I don't pay much attention to the Closing Odds selection. The "early-money" angle is especially deadly when a reliable morning line is in place and the first couple of tote-board flashes indicate a solid, informed wager. A morning-line 8–1 shot at Aqueduct or Santa Anita that opens up at 2–1 or 9–5 indicates meaningful tote-board action that deserves a bettor's respect and attention. Therefore, attempting to utilize the Closing Odds range field, as a measurement of trainer intent, is irrelevant.

Closing Odds: (Include All Starters), (Favorites), (Beaten Favorite), (Odds On), (2/1 and Less), (>2/1 & < = 5/1), (>5/1 & < = 10/1), (>5/1 & < 10/1), (> 10/1), (User Min and Max Odds).

A distance change when combined with some other positive handicapping factor usually indicates a positive trainer maneuver. There are some trainers that are speed-oriented and others that are stamina-oriented. Some trainers are equally effective in both sprint and route events. A cut-back or stretch-out in distance is usually a training tactic indicating at least an attempt to improve a horse's performance. It could also be a training exercise or experiment to see if a horse will improve with a change of distance. This is a Formulator filter that is extremely useful and one that can be combined with several others to sift out some solid, winning angles.

Distance: (Include All Starters), (Sprints <1 Mile), (Routes > = 1 Mile), (First Route), (Second Route), (Sprints to Routes), (Routes to Sprints), (User Min and Max Distances).

The purse of a specific race has little value in regard to attempting to uncover profitable trainer angles. I prefer to keep the setting at the Include All Starters option. If you do decide to filter to the exact purse of today's event and the trainer's success at that level, there's no harm in doing so. Throughout the Formulator trainer modifications, the more specific you can get, the better results you'll achieve. However, the negative side to being too specific is that there are usually fewer races and circumstances to evaluate, and the amount of race samples to sort through will be too small for an accurate conclusion. For example, if trainer Dale Romans is 2 for 3 in allowance route races on the turf at Churchill Downs with a purse range of >$40,000 & <=$60,000, is that convincing enough data to run to the windows with a fistful of hundreds? The answer is probably no when dealing with such a small sample.

Purse: (Include All Starters), (<=$10,000), (>$10,000 & <= $20,000), (>$20,000 & <= $40,000), (>$40,000 & <= $60,000), (>$60,000), (User Min. and Max. Purses).

The class-filter Formulator options are some of the longest but the most important for filtering out the strengths and weaknesses of each trainer. Whether we're evaluating a low-profile Suffolk Downs trainer who specializes in bottom-level claimers or a high-profile conditioner at Santa Anita who has racked up a dozen Grade 1 victories over the past few seasons, it makes no difference. It won't be long after familiarizing yourself with the software program that you will come to realize that trainers have a tendency to excel at their own comfortable class level and they rarely venture outside their specialty.

Of all the class options available, I've found the Maiden, Claiming, and State Bred & Restricted Races Only options to be the most profitable and useful. You'll often stumble across some solid longshots in the State Bred & Restricted Races Only category, offering incredibly high win percentages and an excellent ROI. The downside to evaluating some of the other better-quality events (Allowance, Graded, and Non-Graded Stakes) is that there's usually one or only a handful of exceptionally talented horses within a stable. One consistently classy runner that frequently wins or picks up a check against the best horses on the grounds often carries an average or below-average training outfit and therefore recurrently produces tainted results.

For example, let's take John Servis, the Philadelphia-based trainer of 2004 Kentucky Derby and Preakness winner Smarty Jones. If you were a beginning handicapper, or happened to be living in an underground chamber the past few racing seasons, you could easily be misled by evaluating Servis's Graded Stakes stats upon the conclusion of the 2004 Triple Crown season. Servis, although a talented midlevel trainer and very successful with his graded-stakes superstar, "Smarty," was a Philadelphia Park claiming prodigy with Charles Town roots. To use the success of Smarty Jones's graded-stakes victories in evaluating Servis's ability to perform in some of the classiest races in the country would be erroneous and counterproductive.

Class: (Include All Starters), (All Maidens), (Maiden Claiming), (Maiden Special Weight), (Maiden Winner Last Out), (All Claiming), (Low Clm. <$10,000), (Mid Clm. $10,000-$40,000), (High Clm. >$40,000), (Optional Claiming), (Conditional Claiming), (Allowance), (Handicap), (Non-Graded Stakes), (Graded Stakes), (Grade One Stakes), (Grade Two Stakes), (Grade Three Stakes), (User Min. and Max. Claiming), (State Bred & Restricted Races Only).

Track/Jockey Filters

ONE THING YOU'LL APPRECIATE by using the Formulator track-filter option is that there are various racetracks and specific circuits that are the highlight of a trainer's year. A trainer that couldn't coach a hungry pony to walk 10 feet to a bucket of molasses in the beginning of April at Laurel might find himself winning at a 37 percent clip two weeks later at Pimlico. The simple fact is that most stables realistically can't have their stock hitting on all cylinders 24/7, 12 months out of the year. Even the biggest powerhouses in the business, like the Todd Pletcher Racing Stables, hit dry spells and losing steaks.

It's the nature of this competitive business for a training outfit to go through extensive dry spells and then gear up for an approaching meet with well-rested, sound horses. The Formulator Track filter allows the player to isolate the tracks and circuits where a particular trainer performs best. The information is incredibly valuable and may vary considerably from year to year, track to track, and circuit to circuit.

Track Filter: (Use All Tracks), (Use Today's Track), (Use Today's Circuit), (Include Circuit List), (Include Track List).

Every training outfit has either one or a small group of favorite go-to jockeys that have a history of performing well when teamed up with a familiar conditioner. A jockey may have a long-standing partnership with a specific trainer, and ride several hundred races for that outfit during the course of the year. Or, there are circumstances where a jockey may only ride a few select mounts successfully for a specific stable. The jockey/trainer relationships change frequently, but aren't as bad as some of the jockey/agent affairs, which are constantly changing depending on the team's most recent success.

Do you know what jockey/trainer combos are hot at your circuit? If not, you should. The Jockey filter selection, combined with several other filtering options, not only allows the Formulator user the ability to see how the basic jockey/trainer combination performs at the track of choice, but whether or not there is a specific class level, race distance, or surface that may be more conducive to a jockey's individual strength or riding style. Some jockeys excel on the turf as opposed to the dirt. Some have the strength, timing, patience, and stamina to perform better at route races. Some are great gate jocks and have the ability to get a horse quickly to the front. Regardless of the jockey's style and general ability, the filter option will guide you to his or her strengths, but more importantly will expose weaknesses on false favorites where they might be vulnerable. This leads us to the Formulator Jockey Statistics function, which is discussed in greater detail in the next section.

Jockey Statistics

Jockey Filter: (Use All Jockeys), (Use Today's Jockey), (Jockey Change), (Include Jockey List), (Exclude Jockey List).

LET'S TAKE A LOOK at the past performances and assigned jockey on number 11, Mortgage the House, a runner in the eighth race at Gulfstream Park on March 23, 2006.

The 4-year-old filly, trained by Timothy Ritvo, was entered in a $33,000 nonwinners-of-one allowance turf race. Directly below the owner and stable colors, you'll notice that Jeremy Rose was the assigned pilot. His stats appear as follows:

Rose J (253 35 33 36 .13) 2005: (814 179 .22)

```
11   Mortgage the House                     Gr/ro f. 4 (Jan ) OBSMAR04 $60,000                       Life  14 1 3 1  $30,505 79 | D.Fst      5 0 0 0  $2,005 51
     Own: Christopher J. Hall               Sire: Chester House (Mr. Prospector)                     2006   1 0 0 0     $330 49 | Wet (341)  0 0 0 0      $0  -
20-1 Blue, Red BUFFALO in White Ball, Red   Dam:  Fee (Spectacular Bid)                      L 119   2005   6 0 2 0   $9,400 79 | Turf (344) 9 1 3 1 $28,500 79
Rose J (253 35 33 36 .13) 2005:(814 179 .22) Br:  Mr. & Mrs. Theodore Kuster(Ky)                     GP(T)  1 0 0 0     $330 49 | Dist (353) 7 1 2 1 $24,300 73
                                            Tr:   Ritvo Timothy (71 7 5 5 .09) 2005:(516 67 .13)
15Feb06-8GP fm 1 1/16(T):232 :471 1:103 1:40 4↑(F)Alw 33000N1X    49 2 1212 1211 1211 1015 10 17½ Olivero C A  L119f 21.70 73-12 Stormina119 2½ List Price119 4¼ The End Is Clear119½  Outrun 12
23Dec05-5Crc fm 1 1/16(T):223 :47 1:11 1:404 3↑(F)Alw 20000N2L   73 6 64¾ 64½ 75 36 25¼ Aguilar M  L120f 32.60 87-13 JstLttlJt120 5¼ MrttHs120½ Ssprsstr 120 1¾  No match, up for 2nd 8
4Dec05-5Crc fm 1 (T):231 :471 1:104 1:352 3↑(F)Alw 20000N1X      61 1 74¾ 72¾ 1110 911 99¾ Toribio A R  L117f 6.10 83-12 LngThghts117¾ Irrcbl120 1½ JstLttlJt 117nk  Saved grnd, faltered 12
21Nov05-7Crc gd 1 (T):241 :482 1:124 1:374 3↑(F)OC 16k/N1X -N    79 8 75 75½ 75 31½ 2½ Toribio A R  L117f 9.70 80-18 Zltk120½ MortggthHous117¾ EMIPt120nk  Rail, gaining slowly 10
11Nov05-5Crc fm 1 1/16(T):23 :464 1:104 1:424 3↑(F)Alw 24000N1X   69 4 66½ 79½ 98¼ 65¾ 45¾ Aguilar M  L117f 13.30 76-18 KtPrncss 120 3¾ CozzyCt110½ RrTrsr120 1½  In tight leaving bkstr 11
17Oct05-4Crc fst 1 1/16⊗:25 :50 1:151 1:493 3↑(F)Alw 24000N1X    27 5 56½ 58 58 512 520½ Bracho R A  L117f 8.60 49-24 TrggrFshLn117 2¼ FrMssGrc117nk PnnntDncr120 5¼  No factor 6
1Jan05-10Crc gd 1 1/16(T):222 :472 1:112 1:42 (F)TrPOaks100k       72 11 1112 105¾ 106¾ 77¼ 65 Cruz M R  L114 59.40 81-10 DnsttLht118nk DnmtLss116nk SlrSt116no  Passed tired rivals 11
   Previously trained by Ritvo Kathy 2004(as of 12/9):(65 9 5 12 0.14)
9Dec04-8Crc fm 1 1/16(T):224 :472 1:12 1:443 (F)Md Sp Wt 20k     60 4 67½ 55½ 52¾ 62¼ 2½ Cruz M R  L118 *2.00 75-18 [D]Ndsh118½ MrtggthHs118¾ TttlCrk1184  Blocked str, gaining 8
   Placed first through disqualification.
15Nov04-2Crc fst 1 1/16⊗:244 :501 1:152 1:502 (F)Md Sp Wt 23k    34 2 75¾ 63¼ 66 65¾ 814 Cruz M R  L118 3.80 46-31 Cmnl1182 MstrsLht118nk BrjttLht118 2½  Saved grnd, faltered 10
   Previously trained by Ritvo Timothy 2004(as of 10/17):(432 43 48 52 0.10)
17Oct04-7Crc fm 1 1/16(T):23 :491 1:134 1:463 (F)Md Sp Wt 29k    58 8 99¾ 104 64½ 56½ 32 Boulanger G  L118 *1.30 64-29 Unplggd113 1¼ TttlCrk118¾ MrtggthHs118 3¾  3 wd, belated rally 10
WORKS: Mar15 Crc 5f fst 1:054 Bg 18/18  Feb8 Crc 5f fst 1:033 B 6/18
TRAINER: 2Off45-180 (51 .10 $0.80) 31-60Days (90 .12 $1.56) Turf (148 .09 $1.76) Routes (271 .07 $1.24) Alw (58 .09 $1.74)   J/T 2005-06 GP (34 .12 $3.15) J/T 2005-06 (34 .12 $3.15)
```

From the general numbers displayed, you can easily see the total starts (253), wins (35), seconds (33), thirds (36), and win percentage (13) for the current year. In addition you can see his number of starts (814), wins (179), and win percentage (22) for 2005. What if you were interested in seeing if Rose excelled at a specific distance and surface, or if you wanted to check his past success and compatibility when riding horses for Ritvo? One option would be to examine the Jockey/Trainer combination listed on the bottom right-hand corner of the past performance. It reads:

J/T 2005–06 GP (34 .12 $3.15) J/T 2005–06 (34 .12 $3.15)

Reading from left to right, you can clearly see that Rose has ridden 34 mounts for Ritvo in 2005 and 2006 at Gulfstream Park (GP). His win percentage is 12 with a return on investment (ROI) of $3.15 for every $2 wagered. The next group of numbers indicates that the overall jockey/trainer statistics are exactly the same, meaning that South Florida was the only location where Rose and Ritvo had teamed up.

The second option is to examine the credentials for Jeremy Rose by clicking on the Jockey Statistics using the Formulator program. By clicking on his name you'll be forwarded to the following stats. ("W/S" means "wins out of starts.")

Jockey Statistics

Starts	1st	2nd	3rd	%Win	%ITM	Avg. Win Pay Off	Sprint W/S
253	35	33	36	13.8%	41.1%	$14.47	16/104

Route W/S	Turf	Main W/S	M/C W/S	Other W/S
19/149	11/86	24/167	28/187	7/66

30-Day Streak	10-Day Streak
11/111	3/24

Trainer/Jockey Combination

With Trainer	Starts	1st	2nd	3rd	Avg. Win Payoff
Ritvo Timothy	34	4	3	2	$26.80

The in-depth Formulator program paints a complete picture of jockey Jeremy Rose and presents all of his mounts in a neatly packaged statistical breakdown. It exposes how Rose performs on the main track, the turf, riding sprints, routes, and whether he's been hot or cold in the last month or 10 days. It's a fabulous and helpful upgrade when attempting to decipher the strengths and weaknesses of a jockey.

CHART OPTION:

I'd like to deviate slightly from discussing some of the Formulator trainer and jockey functions and deal briefly with the Race Chart function. The Formulator program allows the user to display a variety of *Daily Racing Form* race charts for a specific event. From any past performance, you can display not only the result chart for a specific race, but also, using the Chart View option, you can drill down to the past performances of other runners your horse has competed against. For example purposes, let's return to the past performances of Mortgage the House on page 30.

If you click on Race Date, highlighted in blue on the Formulator screen, you'll display the filly's last racing date. It was race 8 at Gulfstream Park on February 15, 2006. Race charts are available only for the last three starts. In the case of Mortgage the House, it would be February 15, 2006; December 23, 2005; and December 4. The standard Chart View is displayed and you can display any race chart that is available on the DRF web site.

From here you can perform the following actions from the Chart View:

1. Navigate to a different race in the chart by using the Race arrows in the tool bar or the drop-down list.
2. Click on an entry in the Last Raced column of a horse within the Chart View. This displays the chart for each horse's last race.
3. Use the Chart Lookup dialogue box to display a results chart.
4. Click on a horse's name to display the latest past performance of each horse.
5. Return to the past performances by selecting the icon from the tool bar.

Eighth Race
Gulfstream
February 15,2006

1 1/16 Miles. (Turf) ALLOWANCE. Purse $33,000 FOR FILLIES AND MARES FOUR YEARS OLD AND UPWARD WHICH HAVE NEVER WON A RACE OTHER THAN MAIDEN, CLAIMING OR STARTER OR WHICH HAVE NEVER WON TWO RACES. Weight, 123 lbs. Non-winners of a race other than Claiming at a mile or over since January 16 Allowed 2lbs. Such a race since December 17 Allowed 4 lbs. (Condition Eligibility). (If deemed inadvisable to run this race over the Turf course, it will be run on the main track at One Mile) (Rail at 24 feet).

Value of Race: $33,000 Winner $19,800; second $6,270; third $2,970; fourth $1,320; fifth $330; sixth $330; seventh $330; eighth $330; ninth $330; tenth $330; eleventh $330; twelfth $0. Mutuel Pool $330,000 Exacta Pool $265,047 Superfecta Pool $75,892 Trifecta Pool $208,878

LastRaced	Horse	M/Eqt	.A.	Wt	PP	St	1/4	1/2	3/4	Str	Fin	Jockey	Odds $1
27Oct05 8BEL 5	Stormina	L	4	119	5	7	4½	3hd	32	1hd	1 2½	Velazquez J R	2.00
21Jan06 6GP 8	**List Price**	L	4	119	8	4	13	12	11	22½	2 4¼	Guidry M	6.10
13Jan06 7GP 3	The End Is Clear	L	4	119	6	5	21	21	2½	32	3½	Castellano J J	6.10
28Jul05 7SAR 9	Baradore (IRE)	L	4	119	11	11	7½	71½	4hd	42	4nk	Castro E	4.80
24Apr05 7KEE 5	Racee (BRZ)	Lb	5	119	1	2	9½	8hd	9½	61	5nk	Bejarano R	11.90
04Sep05 9ELP 8	**Patty Seattle**	Lf	4	119	7	6	81	9hd	102	72	6¾	Velasquez C	14.50
01Oct04 8BEL 4	Christmas Card	L	5	119	12	12	10½	102½	8½	51	71	Douglas R R	17.60
13Jan06 4GP 4	Vanillazuela	Lbf	4	119	9	10	112½	112½	114	8hd	8 3¼	Bridgmohan S X	36.30
27Jan06 8GP 9	**Speedy Music**	Lbf	4	119	3	3	61	6hd	6½	95	9 4¾	Trujillo E	111.90
23Dec05 5CRC 2	**Mortgage the House**	Lf	4	119	2	8	12	12	12	10½	10 4½	Olivero C A	21.70
21Jan06 6GP 7	Miss Kenai	L	5	119	10	9	51½	5½	7½	113	117	Blanc B	45.00
07Jan06 1GP 4	Promoted Deputy	L	4	119	4	1	3½	41	5hd	12	12	Prado E S	8.90

OFF AT 4:15 Start Good, Won Driving. Track Firm.

TIME :23², :47¹, 1:10⁴, 1:34, 1:40 (:23.57, :47.21, 1:10.79, 1:34.12, 1:40.11)

$2 Mutuel Prices:				
	5--STORMINA	6.00	3.80	3.00
	8--LIST PRICE		6.20	4.60
	6--THE END IS CLEAR			4.40

$1 EXACTA 5-8 PAID $20.20 $1 SUPERFECTA 5-8-6-11 PAID $415.40

$1 TRIFECTA 5-8-6 PAID $131.00

Filly Dark Bay or Brown; 2002; Gulch-Brooklyn's Storm (Storm Cat) Bred By:Wertheimer & Frere (Kentucky)

STORMINA stalked the pace three wide, rallied to take over at the eighth pole and drew clear under urging. LIST PRICE sprinted to a clear lead along the rail, made the pace into the stretch, then couldn't stay with the winner while clearly second best. THE END IS CLEAR chased the pace into the stretch and tired. BARADORE (IRE) rated off the pace, advanced three wide around the far turn to reach contention, then flattened out. RACEE (BRZ) failed to menace. PATTY SEATTLE allowed to settle, improved her position without threatening. CHRISTMAS CARD unhurried after hitting the gate at the start, advanced three wide around the far turn to reach contention, then flattened out. VANILLAZUELA outrun after being steadied in the early going, swung wide for the stretch run and never threatened. SPEEDY MUSIC rated off the pace after being steadied on the first turn, tired in the drive. MORTGAGE THE HOUSE was outrun. MISS KENAI tracked the pace, raced four wide on the far turn and faltered. PROMOTED DEPUTY tracked the pace into the far turn and faded.

Owners--1, Wertheimer and Frere; 2, Glen Hill Farm; 3, Hough Stanley M and Carusone,; 4, Live Oak Plantation; 5, Team Victory; 6, Broaddus E, Hiles, E and Hough; 7, Evans Edward P; 8, Mount Joy Stables Inc; 9, Perez Robert; 10, Hall Christopher J; 11, Croley Thomas L; 12, Darley Stable

Trainers--1, Pletcher Todd A; 2, Proctor Thomas F; 3, Hough Stanley M; 4, Clement Christophe; 5, Pitts Helen; 6, Hiles Rick; 7, Hennig Mark; 8, Stutts Bennie F Jr; 9, Corredor Enrique; 10, Ritvo Timothy; 11, Hills Timothy A; 12, Harty Eoin

Scratched--Holden Champagne(27Jan06 8GP 4),Miss Audrey(27Jan06 8GP 11)

The horses that are listed in bold—List Price, Patty Seattle, Speedy Music, and our sample horse, Mortgage the House—are all entered in today's event. The horses not in bold are not entered in today's event, but the user still has the ability to click on any of the entrants and pull up their individual past performances.

CHANGING THE CHART VIEW

THE FORMULATOR USER CAN change the Chart View by selecting the View Menu and choosing any of the following Chart Views:

a. Standard Chart View: The default view, showing the standard race-results chart for the specific race you selected.

b. Next Race View: Shows the race chart for the next race in which the horse ran.

c. Beyer Figures View: Shows the horse's Beyer Speed Figures for the next race the horse ran in, the Chart race, and for past races. The Beyers are not available for any starts that are less than 10 days old. The chart would look as follows:

Eighth Race
Gulfstream
February 15, 2006

1 1/16 Miles. (Turf) ALLOWANCE. Purse $33,000 FOR FILLIES AND MARES FOUR YEARS OLD AND UPWARD WHICH HAVE NEVER WON A RACE OTHER THAN MAIDEN, CLAIMING OR STARTER OR WHICH HAVE NEVER WON TWO RACES. Weight, 123 lbs. Non-winners of a race other than Claiming at a mile or over since January 16 Allowed 2lbs. Such a race since December 17 Allowed 4 lbs. (Condition Eligibility). (If deemed inadvisable to run this race over the Turf course, it will be run on the main track at One Mile) (Rail at 24 feet).

Value of Race: $33,000 Winner $19,800; second $6,270; third $2,970; fourth $1,320; fifth $330; sixth $330; seventh $330; eighth $330; ninth $330; tenth $330; eleventh $330; twelfth $0. Mutuel Pool $330,000 Exacta Pool $265,047 Superfecta Pool $75,892 Trifecta Pool $208,878

LastRaced	Horse	Next Chart	1 Bk	2 Bk	3 Bk	4 Bk	5 Bk	6 Bk	7 Bk	8 Bk	9 Bk	10 Bk	Odds $1
27Oct05 8BEL 5	Stormina		88	57	—	—	—	—	—	—	—	—	2.00
21Jan06 6GP 8	List Price		82	60	75	—	—	—	—	—	—	—	6.10
13Jan06 7GP 3	The End Is Clear		73	71	73	71	68	68	66	67	38	38	43	6.10
28Jul05 7SAR 5	Baradore (IRE)	NA	72	77	84	82	78	63	—	—	—	—	4.80
24Apr05 7KEE 5	Racee (BRZ)	NA	71	61	—	—	—	—	—	—	—	—	11.90
04Sep05 9ELP 8	Patty Seattle		71	59	76	74	70	77	72	61	69	66	68	14.50
01Oct04 8BEL 4	Christmas Card	NA	69	83	84	79	76	62	50	58	29	—	—	17.60
13Jan06 4GP 4	Vanillazuela	54	67	63	64	77	53	58	74	65	78	59	58	36.30
27Jan06 8GP 9	Speedy Music		60	33	63	69	—	—	—	—	—	—	111.90
23Dec05 5CRC 2	Mortgage the House		49	73	61	79	69	27	72	60	34	58	65	21.70
21Jan06 6GP 7	Miss Kenai		40	65	59	69	48	74	47	69	76	71	63	45.00
07Jan06 1GP 4	Promoted Deputy		24	54	—	—	—	—	—	—	—	—	8.90

OFF AT 4:15 Start Good, Won Driving. Track Firm.
TIME :23², :47¹, 1:10⁴, 1:34, 1:40 (:23.57, :47.21, 1:10.79, 1:34.12, 1:40.11)

$2 Mutuel Prices:

5--STORMINA	6.00	3.80	3.00
8--LIST PRICE		6.20	4.60
6--THE END IS CLEAR			4.40

$1 EXACTA 5-8 PAID $20.20 $1 SUPERFECTA 5-8-6-11 PAID $415.40
$1 TRIFECTA 5-8-6 PAID $131.00

Filly Dark Bay or Brown; 2002; Gulch-Brooklyn's Storm (Storm Cat) Bred By: Wertheimer & Frere (Kentucky)

STORMINA stalked the pace three wide, rallied to take over at the eighth pole and drew clear under urging. LIST PRICE sprinted to a clear lead along the rail, made the pace into the stretch, then couldn't stay with the winner while clearly second best. THE END IS CLEAR chased the pace into the stretch and tired. BARADORE (IRE) rated off the pace, advanced three wide around the far turn to reach contention, then flattened out. RACEE (BRZ) failed to menace. PATTY SEATTLE allowed to settle, improved her position without threatening. CHRISTMAS CARD unhurried after hitting the gate at the start, advanced three wide around the far turn to reach contention, then flattened out. VANILLAZUELA outrun after being steadied in the early going, swung wide for the stretch run and never threatened. SPEEDY MUSIC rated off the pace after being steadied on the first turn, tired in the drive. MORTGAGE THE HOUSE was outrun. MISS KENAI tracked the pace, raced four wide on the far turn and faltered. PROMOTED DEPUTY tracked the pace into the far turn and faded.

Owners--1, Wertheimer and Frere; 2, Glen Hill Farm; 3, Hough Stanley M and Carusone,; 4, Live Oak Plantation; 5, Team Victory; 6, Broaddus E, Hiles, E and Hough; 7, Evans Edward P; 8, Mount Joy Stables Inc; 9, Perez Robert; 10, Hall Christopher J; 11, Croley Thomas L; 12, Darley Stable

Trainers--1, Pletcher Todd A; 2, Proctor Thomas F; 3, Hough Stanley M; 4, Clement Christophe; 5, Pitts Helen; 6, Hiles Rick; 7, Hennig Mark; 8, Stutts Bennie F Jr; 9, Corredor Enrique; 10, Ritvo Timothy; 11, Hills Timothy A; 12, Harty Eoin

Scratched--Holden Champagne(27Jan06 8GP 4),Miss Audrey(27Jan06 8GP 11)

d. Incremental Pace View: Shows the split times for each individual horse in the race.

e. Elapsed Times View: Shows the elapsed time for each individual horse in the race.

f. Race Comments View: Illustrates the *Daily Racing Form* comment line for each horse in the race.

g. Trip Notes View: Shows any trip notes entered for any horse in the race.

You can also choose a Chart View by clicking on an icon in the tool bar.

Wrapping It Up

THERE ARE LITERALLY HUNDREDS of other functions within the Formulator software program that we haven't yet touched on in this introductory chapter. The process of going through all of them one by one would be a daunting and unproductive exercise. The goal was to give you a general overview of what parts of the program we will be focusing on most, and some of the reasons why. As I mentioned at the beginning of the chapter, the basic Formulator functions are covered in the program tutorial and explained in great detail through the software's Help function. If you've just started using the program, I'd recommend that you start there.

My objective is to cover most of the trainer-related operations throughout the text of the book, and show how each function, when combined with general trainer-angle maneuvers and techniques, results in live horses at generous odds.

3

CLAIM TO FAME

WHEN I WAS A teenager, and in my early twenties, there were two outstanding claiming trainers sizzling up the New York tracks: Oscar Barrera, whose striking hot-pink silks were a familiar sight to racegoers, and the very talented Gasper Moschera, who was a star of the Big Apple training scene for more than a decade. He was the New York Racing Association's leading trainer for six straight years in the 1990s, and routinely won more than 100 races a year. Moschera was leading trainer at Aqueduct for 10 seasons and won two titles at Belmont Park. A few years before the Gasper Moschera claiming era, Oscar Barrera hit the NYRA circuit with his windstorm of success.

While there were nine Barrera brothers, the ones who were best known in New York were Luis, Laz, and Oscar. Hall of Fame trainer Laz had his greatest successes with 1978 Triple Crown victor Affirmed, and Kentucky Derby and Belmont Stakes winner Bold Forbes in 1976. The talent and expert horsemanship that encompassed the entire Barrera family could not be denied, and Oscar was able to find his niche within the claiming game.

Although he never had the same quality of horses as brother Laz, Oscar was New York's leading trainer four times and one of the most successful claiming trainers on the grounds. His skill at the claiming box was nothing short of magical. He frequently snatched cheap horses and seemingly, overnight, turned them into near-champions—or at the very least, competitive allowance runners. It wasn't uncommon for Barrera to grab a horse out of a $10,000 or $15,000 claiming event, run him three or four days later for $75,000 or $100,000, and win convincingly. The pattern was repeated week in and week out.

One interesting fact, however, is that Oscar Barrera had all of his success on the dirt. He did not have one single turf-race victory. This was truly remarkable, considering he averaged about 400 starts per year during his training heyday. For those crafty handicappers tracking trainer patterns at the time, it became obvious that Barrera was using the turf course to condition his horses. He was making little effort to win purses when starting runners on the green. Despite his poor success on the turf, many fans only recognized his highly publicized miracles off the claim, and would unknowingly throw money away by betting Barrera's turf horses. If there was ever a time we needed Trainer Form or Formulator, it was back in 1985!

FIRST AND SECOND AFTER CLAIM

ALTHOUGH THEIR TRAINING TECHNIQUES and resources have changed considerably over the past 20 to 25 years, there is still a select group of trainers today that continue to have great success when acquiring a horse from the claim box. The ability to turn an unattractive, prolific loser into an immediate, consistent performer who rattles off three straight victories in another stable still exits. Therefore, I consider the training stats for a horse's first and second starts after a claim to be one of the most crucial and profitable trainer angles available. I believe the trainers listed on pages 39-40 (along with their attractive win percentages and juicy ROI's), and some others highlighted throughout the text, are probably worth the price of this book alone. When combined with the trainer filters and Formulator program, the results of some of these conditioners are even more rewarding.

These talented individuals use their training expertise to spot horses that are sound or starting to cycle up to a peak performance. If the physical condition of the potential claim is, in fact, *not* on the upward swing, then at the very least, these trainers have proven the ability to greatly improve the claimer's form. In some situations it only takes a move to the proper class level or racing circuit, change in racing surface, jockey switch, or medication addition, or perhaps some other positive training maneuver not so readily available to the public eye. In the grand scheme of things, as it relates to betting lucrative training angles, the reason for an improved performance is secondary. We're just interested in the conditioners that have had previous success, and are likely to continue to have good fortune with the angle.

The following DRF trainer stats were taken from the beginning of 2003 to the end of March 2006. As with any statistical study, the results are constantly changing. Therefore, it's imperative that your analysis is continuously updated and maintained for accuracy. The beauty of utilizing the Formulator program, as opposed to just keeping your own regular stats or evaluating only the DRF Trainer Form numbers, is that you're always dealing with statistics that are current and up-to-date. In doing so, this ensures both solid and reliable handicapping data.

The trainer charts listed below and throughout the text are arranged from the highest ROI (return on investment) to the lowest, and are based on a minimum of five wins for each category. The minimum of five wins is a strong enough sample to make certain that the angle is one a trainer consistently and successfully exercises. However, although these statistics are compelling, they are no comparison to using up-to-date Formulator Trainer Form statistics. At face value, these general Trainer Form statistics can be deceptive, and we'll examine how and why that's the case throughout each chapter.

TRAINER STATS FOR 1stAfterClm

Name	Starts	Wins	Win Percentage	ROI (Based on $2.00 to Win)
Lalman, Dennis S	7	5	0.714	$16.30
Montgomery, Gary	18	11	0.611	$16.10
Liu, Raymond	7	5	0.714	$12.70
Pollara, Frank L	11	5	0.455	$11.20
Sowle, Scott	8	6	0.750	$10.90

Ward, Ronnie P	16	5	0.313	$10.80
Eff, Joseph A	21	6	0.286	$10.50
Fix, Jr., Henry G	15	5	0.333	$ 9.48
McArthur, Jerry	29	13	0.448	$ 8.86
Mehok, William L	18	5	0.278	$ 8.68
Wilensky, Herman	15	6	0.400	$ 8.61
Keller, Caryn	25	6	0.240	$ 8.56
Nemett, George S	14	7	0.500	$ 8.46
Kube, Harry	22	9	0.409	$ 8.25
Kamps, Richard	19	10	0.526	$ 8.14
Gilker, Robert	10	6	0.600	$ 8.11
De Jesus, Juan	18	7	0.389	$ 8.00
Million, William N	17	6	0.353	$ 7.53
Cox, Amalia B	28	6	0.214	$ 7.30
Minard, Richard D	23	7	0.304	$ 6.96
Nix, C. L.	25	7	0.280	$ 6.91
Guciardo, Robert	28	5	0.179	$ 6.50
Cappellucci, Robert A	13	10	0.769	$ 6.43
Walper, Deanna	29	8	0.276	$ 5.95
Perry, Stephen J	12	6	0.500	$ 5.80

Let's take a look at some examples using the first-after-claim angle, and the different ways the trainer information provided can be assessed to provide optimum results. Some of the trainers used in our examples are listed in our Top 25 grouping, while others have been randomly selected to show how the Formulator application can be employed.

The 4-year-old gelding Sheba's Charm, trained by Anthony Pecoraro, returns to the Tampa Bay circuit after nearly a 13-month layoff. At first glance, the "1stClaim" stats (33 .27 $2.92) for Pecoraro are quite lucrative, but common sense tells us that there must have been some physical ailment to force this maiden winner to the sidelines. Today, he returns for a reduced $7,500 claiming tag with a lengthy and suspiciously spotty work tab. His last two works are consistently spaced, but nothing to get overly excited about.

By clicking on Anthony Pecoraro's name in the Formulator program, we get the following Default Query results. In the past five years, Pecoraro is 1 for 2, or a 50 percent winner, with horses that have been claimed from the last start and are returning from a >180 day layoff. The $2 ROI is $3.70, with a median pay of $7.40. The Default Query results are nothing to get your handicapping juices flowing, considering the minimal sample for such a training maneuver. Where do we go from here? The next logical step is to modify the Formulator Trainer Pattern stats and see how Pecoraro performs without the extended layoff. If we were to run just his first-off-the-claim stats for the past five years, we'd get the following results:

Trainer:	Anthony Pecoraro
Filter	Options
Time Frame:	Past Five Years
Trainer Changes:	First After Claimed By

Horses	Starts	Wins	ITM	Win%	ITM%	$2ROI	Median Payoff
107	114	22	52	19%	46%	$1.84	$8.70

Once again, the results are not very useful and will likely require some more massaging and creativity. The 19 percent win ratio is far below his 1st Claim stats for 2006 listed in the daily paper, thus indicating that perhaps Pecoraro has only recently gotten hot at the claim box. Once we change the general time-frame option from the five-year mark to the past year, his win percentage escalates to 30 percent with a positive ROI of $3.39.

Horses	Starts	Wins	ITM	Win%	ITM%	$2ROI	Median Payoff
26	27	8	13	30%	48%	$3.39	$10.00

This is a classic example of what I call "What have you done for me lately?" in trainer statistics. Not only is it imperative to have enough race samples and scenarios to come to an educated guess about whether a trainer excels in a certain category, but it's also important that the sample remains fresh. By simply adjusting the time-frame option, we get completely different results.

Unfortunately, the betting public jumped on the Sheba's Charm bandwagon, making him second choice at 2.60–1 despite the lengthy layoff. After showing good early speed, he quickly hit an imaginary wall and finished last, beaten more than 20 lengths. The moral of the story is that not all Trainer Form angles are good bets, especially at short odds. At 7–1 or more, Sheba's Charm might have been worth a wager. Throughout this book, my goal is not to show you 100 examples tailored to winning scores and giant paydays based on trainer data; it is to get you working and familiar with the Formulator software program. I promise the winners will come later!

THIRD RACE

Tampa Bay

MARCH 28, 2006

6 FURLONGS. (1.09) CLAIMING . Purse $8,800 FOR FOUR YEAR OLDS AND UPWARD WHICH HAVE NEVER WON TWO RACES. Weight, 122 lbs. Non–winners of a race since February 28 Allowed 2 lbs. A race since January 28 Allowed 4 lbs. Claiming Price $7,500.

Value of Race: $8,800 Winner $5,280; second $1,584; third $968; fourth $440; fifth $88; sixth $88; seventh $88; eighth $88; ninth $88; tenth $88. Mutuel Pool $96,215.00 Quinella Pool $7,242.00 Exacta Pool $113,191.00 Superfecta Pool $43,868.00

Last Raced	Horse	M/Eqt. A. Wt	PP	St	¼	½	Str	Fin	Jockey	Cl'g Pr	Odds $1
7Jan06 4GP12	Bones Ferrone	L bf 4 118	9	1	3¹	1½	1⁵	1⁹	Bell D C	7500	1.10
23Mar06 2Tam9	Slew's Temper	L 6 120	10	8	10	4½	4½	2½	Bracho J G	7500	81.90
16Mar06 4Tam4	Keep Bill in Front	L b 4 118	8	2	5½	3hd	2hd	31½	Centeno D E	7500	21.30
10Mar06 4Tam10	C. Soldier Field	L 4 118	2	7	9¹	9¹	7½	41½	Jellison J A	7500	67.30
16Mar06 4Tam2	Cover Me Lover	L b 5 111	6	9	7³	8½	3¹	5hd	Rice J⁷	7500	5.80
16Mar06 4Tam7	Rupert's Hazaam	L b 5 119	5	3	6¹	6¹	83½	6¹	Bush W V	7500	15.40
10ct05 12Crc8	Bold Irishman	L b 6 118	3	10	8½	7¹	5½	75½	Thompson W A	7500	6.60
27Jan06 6Tam10	Crooked Tail	L bf 6 108	4	6	4hd	10	10	8hd	Martin G10	7500	42.00
16Mar06 4Tam3	Roaring Reach	L b 4 118	7	5	2¹½	2¹½	6½	9²	Faine C	7500	18.20
6Mar05 3Tam1	Sheba's Charm	f 4 118	1	4	1½	5¹	9½	10	Umana J L	7500	2.60

OFF AT 1:30 Start Good. Won ridden out. Track fast.

TIME :22⁴, :46⁴, :59³, 1:12⁴ (:22.98, :46.95, :59.68, 1:12.95)

$2 Mutuel Prices:

9 – BONES FERRONE	4.20	3.40	3.20
10 – SLEW'S TEMPER		33.00	12.60
8 – KEEP BILL IN FRONT			8.40

$2 QUINELLA 9–10 PAID $120.60 $2 EXACTA 9–10 PAID $186.40
$2 SUPERFECTA 9–10–8–2 PAID $32,506.00

Ch. c, (May), by Crafty Friend – Murfreesboro , by Wavering Monarch . Trainer Rice Linda. Bred by Centennial Farms Mgmt Co & William S Farish Jr (Ky).

BONES FERRONE stalked the early pace outside, bid three wide after three furlongs to gain command then drew off smartly while ridden out. SLEW'S TEMPER made a four wide middle move then was up for the place late. KEEP BILL IN FRONT chased the leaders from the outset, couldn't gain after a half and weakened late. C. SOLDIER FIELD passed tiring rivals. COVER ME LOVER raced evenly. RUPERT'S HAZAAM also turned in an even effort. BOLD IRISHMAN was taken up at the break, made a middle move to the stretch then finished evenly while in traffic. CROOKED TAIL stopped. ROARING REACH pressed the pace for a half then faltered. SHEBA'S CHARM stopped.

Owners– 1, Margulies Sigmund; 2, Amoedo Javier; 3, Bakerman Robert; 4, Dimarzo Joseph; 5, March Carla Shang Sr Donald E and Hastings Robert; 6, Bramante Bernard; 7, Hall Lester A; 8, Broussard Martine; 9, Mann Patricia A; 10, Pecoraro Racing Stable

Trainers– 1, Rice Linda; 2, Dye Steven; 3, Wasiluk Peter Jr; 4, Raymond Robert A; 5, March William; 6, Bramante Bernard; 7, Charoo Wellesley; 8, Broussard Mitchell; 9, Hall Calvin; 10, Pecoraro Anthony

For our next example, let's go out to Aqueduct for the opening of the main track on March 29, 2006. The first race was a $20,000 maiden-claiming event for 3-year-olds and upward going one mile. The Aqueduct opener was the first of five maiden events scheduled on the card, but it didn't matter. At a balmy 61 degrees, all was well on Rockaway Boulevard. The number 9, Furious Pride, was a recent Robert Klesaris claim. It was an angle that Klesaris had used successfully in the past, according to the printed Trainer Form numbers. They read: 1stClaim (63 .17 $1.16). There was a losing ROI, but a halfway decent 17 percent on the win end.

9 Furious Pride		B. c. 3 (Apr)		Life	2 M 0 0	$593 50	D.Fst	1 0 0 0	$83 49

(race past-performance data block for Furious Pride, No. 9)

Sire: Honour and Glory (Relaunch) $12,500
Dam: Sweet City Gal (Kingmambo)
Own: EF and J Stables $20,000 Br: Kinsman Farm(Fla)
6–1 Red, Black Yoke and 'FCS,' Red and   Tr: Klesaris Robert P (–) 2005:(390 63 .16)
Kaenel K (–) 2005:(669 112 .17)

L 118

Life 2 M 0 0 $593 50 D.Fst 1 0 0 0 $83 49
2006 2 M 0 0 $593 50 Wet (364) 1 0 0 0 $510 50
2005 0 M 0 0 $0 – Turf (292) 0 0 0 0 $0 –
Aqu 0 0 0 0 $0 – Dist (362) 0 0 0 0 $0 –

5Feb06–3Aqu gd 1⅛ ⊡:231 :47 1:12 1:45 Md c-25000 50 2 2½ 31 43 59½ 513½Kaenel K5 L115fb 10.90 72-14 ChfSpd 1206 HdOfthChrls 1201¼ StrMr1153 Chased outside, tired 8
   Claimed from Kinsman Stable for $25,000, Domino Carl J Trainer 2005:(80 4 8 16 0.05)
21Jan06–4Aquf st 6f ⊡:222 :461 :583 1:113 Md 50000(50-40) 49 610 1110 810 915101 12½Kaenel K5 115fb 62.50 69-14 ClosingBll 1204½ Mudsh1204 RpprsDlit1201 Off slowly, wide trip 11
WORKS: Mar22 Bel tr.t 4f fst :52 B 42/44 Feb21 Bel tr.t 4f fst :504 B 17/27 Jan16 Bel tr.t 5f fst 1:024 Bg 3/10 Jan9 Bel tr.t 5f fst 1:03 B 11/15
TRAINER: 1stClaim (63 .17 $1.16) 31–60Days (111 .15 $1.97) Dirt (370 .17 $1.30) Routes (216 .15 $1.89) MdnClm (35 .09 $3.41)   J/T 2005-06 AQU(20 .20 $2.14) J/T 2005-06(28 .25 $2.53)

The DRF "Closer Look" analysis hinted at the success of Klesaris off the claim: *"Drops in claiming price after almost 2 months off for new barn; he had speed in his 1st Lasix run in a decent event that spawned 2 next-out winners; barn has a high success rate winning off the claim; must consider."* The handicapper's insight was correct, but a little Formulator detective work painted a completely different picture. After sifting through a few Formulator options, the Klesaris first-off-the-claim angle wasn't all that promising.

By clicking on Robert Klesaris's name in the Formulator program, we got the following Default Query results. The 17 percent number wasn't completely accurate under today's conditions when the time-frame option was extended to five years and the days between starts were adjusted to 31–60 days.

Trainer:	Robert P. Klesaris
Filter	Options
Time Frame:	**Past Five Years**
Days/Starts:	**31–60 Days**
Trainer Changes:	First After Claimed By

Horses	Starts	Wins	ITM	Win%	ITM%	$2ROI	Median Payoff
90	99	13	47	13%	46%	$1.08	$6.00

Even an attempt to keep the sample fresh and adjusting the time-frame option to the past year didn't help the results. In fact, the outcome remained somewhat the same with a 13 percent win clip, lower ROI, and slightly higher median payoff.

Filter	Options
Time Frame:	**Past Year**
Days/Starts:	31–60 Days
Trainer Changes:	First After Claimed By

Horses	Starts	Wins	ITM	Win%	ITM%	$2ROI	Median Payoff
16	16	2	8	13%	50%	$0.79	$6.30

The results continued to dwindle when we included the main-dirt-track Surface function. The original 1st Claim angle that once stood at 17 percent was now down to an unappealing 11 percent after implementing additional data filters. If we took it one step further and added Klesaris's success with today's one-mile route events, using all of the above filters, he was now holding an 0-for-5 goose egg.

Filter	Options
Time Frame:	Past Year
Days/Starts:	31–60 Days
Surface:	**Main Dirt**
Trainer Changes:	First After Claimed By

Horses	Starts	Wins	ITM	Win%	ITM%	$2ROI	Median Payoff
9	9	1	4	11%	44%	$0.67	$6.00

Filter	Options
Time Frame:	Past Year
Days/Starts:	31–60 Days
Distance:	Route
Surface:	**Main Dirt**
Trainer Changes:	First After Claimed By

Horses	Starts	Wins	ITM	Win%	ITM%	$2ROI	Median Payoff
5	5	0	0	N/A	N/A	N/A	N/A

The truth of the matter is that we could have continued to filter and spin the Formulator data in a hundred different directions. This is an easy trap to fall victim to, and it's important that you don't get lost in a statistical maze.

11 Stephen Got Lucky Own: Lalman, Dennis, S.

15–1 Orange, Green Triangular Panel, Orange $25,000

Garcia Alan (22 7 2 2 .31) 2006:(268 39 .15)

Dk. b or br c. 4 (Mar)

Sire: Stephen Got Even (A.P. Indy) $25,000

Dam: Dr. Distinctive (Distinctive Pro)

Br: Belle Meadows Farm(Ky)

Tr: Lalman Dennis (–) 2006:(3 0 .00)

L 118

Life	23	2	3	6	$70,449	83	
2006	4	0	0	1	$5,240	76	
2005	11	2	2	2	$50,740	83	
Aqu	6	1	2	2	$21,200	68	

D.Fst	12	2	1	2	$46,946	83
Wet (320)	9	0	2	4	$22,171	76
Turf (158)	2	0	0	0	$1,332	75
Dist (347)	5	1	1	1	$32,840	83

15Mar06-7Aqufst 1 ⊡:243 :483 1:132 1:384 4↑Clm c- (20-18) 36 4 31½ 41¾ 69½ 624 628½ Migliore R L120b 5.50 60-21 Hngkng120½ CngrssnlRn1203¼ PAttntn1204½ 3 wide trip, tired 6

Claimed from Belle Meadows Farm for $20,000, Cedano Heriberto Trainer 2005:(101 11 15 7 0.11)

20Feb06-3Aqufst 6f ⊡:224 :46 :58 1:103 Clm 25000 76 6 3 78 79½ 610 58½ Morales P5 L113fb 25.00 77-26 SirGllnt1185 Alrmed1183¼ PlsntPttr120nk Inside trip, no rally 7

27Jan06-1Aqufst 1 1/16 ⊡:232 :472 1:114 1:441 Clm 40000(40-35) 56 5 33 32½ 47½ 616 721¼ Samyn J L L120b 16.00 68-13 Drgoonr1154¾ LndMn1214½ DlJwls1202 Chased outside, tired 7

5Jan06-5Aqugd 170 ⊡:234 :473 1:124 1:432 Clm 25000 76 1 33 41½ 42½ 34 33 Samyn J L L118b *2.10 80-17 BrW120nk WldVcr1132¾ StpGtLc1186½ Steadied into 1st turn 5

10Dec05-5Aqugd 170 ⊡:233 :47 1:113 1:42 Clm 25000 71 1 42½ 32½ 31½ 26 26½ Samyn J L L118b 16.00 81-14 Nph1206½ StphGtLc1181¾ MrSppt1141 Awkward start, inside 10

23Nov05-7Aqufst 6½f :224 :454 1:104 1:172 Clm 45000(45-35) 57 4 7 74¾ 98¾ 910 812 Samyn J L L118b 23.10 79-15 Dynergy1151¼ SirGllnt118no MgicAlphbet1151½ Outrun inside 9

9Jly05-5Bel fst 1 ⊗:232 :47 1:12 1:374 3↑Alw 46000N1X –0 4 21½ 22½ 618 726 750¾ Migliore R L116b 8.00 21-28 POffT116½ Grbsh1167¼ MbMnstrl1162¾ Chased outside, tired 7

23Jun05-5Bel fm 1 1/16 Ⓣ:233 :47 1:104 1:412 Clm 40000(40-35) 75 8 32 33½ 31 33 52¾ Samyn J L L120b 13.70 83-11 MplPrc120¾ BlpCt120hd ItstKss1201¼ Chased outside, no bid 9

22May05-7Bel gd 1⅛ :473 1:114 1:364 1:494 3↑Alw 46000N1X 53 9 42 53¼ 78¾ 823 724 Migliore R L118b 12.90 58-24 FirstWord1185 Watchmon118¾ Elements1182 4 wide trip, tired 10

5May05-3Bel fst 1 :231 :46 1:104 1:37 Alw 50000s 83 2 23 21 2hd 11 13 Migliore R L118b 11.60 76-24 StphGtLc1183 SpthMld1183 Ttrhdr1201¼ When roused, clear 5

WORKS: ●Mar9 Bel tr.t 3f fst :354 H *1/18* Feb11 Bel tr.t 3f fst :38 B *21/36* Jan17 Bel tr.t 3f fst :364 B *8/44*

TRAINER: 1stClaim (1 1.00 $10.20) Dirt (12 .17 $2.08) Claim (6 .00 $0.00) J/T 2005-06 AQU (3 .33 $4.93) J/T 2005-06 (3 .33 $4.93)

One of the most potent first-off-the-claim trainers and number one on our Trainer Form list is New York and New Jersey conditioner Dennis Lalman. This low-profile trainer only averages about 14 starts a year, but what he lacks in quantity he certainly makes up for in quality when it comes to mastering the claiming game. Lalman entered number 11, Stephen Got Lucky, in the $25,000 claimer finale at Aqueduct on Wood Memorial Day, Saturday, April 8. Three weeks before that, he plucked the 4-year-old colt for $20,000. After Stephen Got Lucky ran a disappointing sixth while three-wide and was beaten nearly 30 lengths in a dismal performance, one could easily question Lalman's judgment about the prospect of this colt moving forward in his next start.

Lalman's Trainer Form stats in the daily paper appeared as follows: 1stClaim (1 1.00 $10.20). For a closer and more accurate assessment, however, we turned to our trusty Formulator software. When we clicked on Lalman's name in Stephen Got Lucky's past performances, we got the astounding results shown below, thus leaving no reason to rummage around or modify any of the trainer data. Everything we needed to see was staring us right in the face. Even more amazing than the incredible win percentage accumulated by Lalman off the claim were the generous odds of all his winners (Ain't No Sunshine, 8–1; Kent Hall, 13–1; Live Doppler, 14–1; and Perfect Look, 4–1).

Trainer:	Dennis Lalman
Filter	Options
Time Frame:	Past Five Years
Surface:	Dirt
Trainer Changes:	First After Claimed By

Horses	Starts	Wins	ITM	Win%	ITM%	$2ROI	Median Payoff
6	6	4	5	66%	83%	$12.26	$23.00

Stephen Got Lucky was not able to add another score to the Lalman claiming brigade, but he did finish a nice third at 14–1 on the sloppy surface.

ELEVENTH RACE
Aqueduct
APRIL 8, 2006

1 MILE. (1.32²) CLAIMING . Purse $20,000 FOR FOUR YEAR OLDS AND UPWARD WHICH HAVE NEVER WON THREE RACES. Weight, 123 lbs. Non-winners of two races at a mile or over since February 8 Allowed 3 lbs. A race since then Allowed 5 lbs. Claiming Price $25,000 (Races where entered for $15,000 or less not considered).

Value of Race: $20,000 Winner $12,000; second $4,000; third $2,000; fourth $1,000; fifth $600; sixth $100; seventh $100; eighth $100; ninth $100. Mutuel Pool $560,027.00 Exacta Pool $433,241.00 Superfecta Pool $145,519.00 Trifecta Pool $349,584.00

Last Raced	Horse	M/Eqt. A. Wt	PP	St	¼	½	¾	Str	Fin	Jockey	Cl'g Pr	Odds $1
24Feb06 9Aqu⁷	My Kinda Town	L 5 118	9	2	1½	1hd	13½	17	14¾	Smith M E	25000	5.80
29Mar06 9Aqu³	Speed Rouser	L 4 118	1	8	4hd	43	41	4hd	2hd	Dominguez R A	25000	2.50
15Mar06 7Aqu⁶	Stephen Got Lucky	L bf 4 118	8	1	7²	7²½	63½	51½	3¹	Garcia Alan	25000	14.30
2Apr06 3Aqu⁶	Olydar	L b 4 118	6	6	8⁸	86	5½	3hd	42½	Lopez C C	25000	12.20
1Mar06 8Aqu⁶	Preminger	L bf 4 118	7	3	3¹½	3hd	2½	2hd	58¾	Coa E M	25000	2.15
18Mar06 6Aqu³	Midas Gold	L b 4 118	5	5	2hd	22½	31	65	6nk	Espinoza J L	25000	6.60
5Mar06 9Aqu³	Run Along Sonny	L bf 6 118	3	7	5½	5hd	71½	71	7¾	Kaenel K	25000	23.90
18Mar06 6Aqu⁴	Western Galaxy	L 4 118	2	9	9	9	9	9	8¾	Arroyo N Jr	25000	15.00
19Mar06 6Aqu³	Schultzie	L bf 4 118	4	4	6½	6hd	83	81	9	Hill C	25000	15.40

OFF AT 6:12 Start Good. Won ridden out. Track sloppy (Sealed).
TIME :23, :46, 1:11², 1:37⁴ (:23.04, :46.04, 1:11.42, 1:37.92).

$2 Mutuel Prices:	12 – MY KINDA TOWN	13.60	6.50	4.30
	2 – SPEED ROUSER		4.80	3.90
	11 – STEPHEN GOT LUCKY			5.80

$2 EXACTA 12–2 PAID $56.50 $2 SUPERFECTA 12–2–11–9 PAID $3,417.00
$2 TRIFECTA 12–2–11 PAID $497.50

B. g, (Mar), by Williamstown – Mine Tonight , by Upper Nile . Trainer Jerkens James A. Bred by Edition Farm (NY).

MY KINDA TOWN quickly showed in front, set the pace while in hand, drew away when roused and was ridden out to the wire. SPEED ROUSER raced close up along the inside, came wide for the drive and rallied to get the place. STEPHEN GOT LUCKY was outrun early, raced four wide and offered a mild rally outside. OLYDAR was outrun early, raced inside and had no rally. PREMINGER chased the pace from the outside and tired in the stretch. MIDAS GOLD contested the pace along the inside and tired in the stretch. RUN ALONG SONNY raced between rivals and tired. WESTERN GALAXY was outrun. SCHULTZIE raced three wide and tired.

Owners– 1, Hemlock Hills Farm and Hoffman Stewart; 2, Moss Maggi; 3, Lalman Dennis S; 4, Nupp Christopher; 5, Chevalier Stable; 6, Raiche Timothy and Chatterpaul Naipaul; 7, Kaufman Robert Four Fifths Stable and Iselin James H; 8, Team West Side Stables; 9, Blue Stork Stables

Trainers– 1, Jerkens James A; 2, Contessa Gary C; 3, Lalman Dennis; 4, Araya Rene A; 5, Levine Bruce N; 6, Barker Edward R; 7, Stoklosa Richard; 8, Arroyo Enrique; 9, Sedlacek Roy

Scratched– I'm All In (18Mar06 6Aqu⁶) , Sahm Iahm (26Mar06 9Aqu¹) , Mountain Fox (30Mar06 4Aqu⁴)

$2 Pick Three (2–3–12) Paid $1,732.00 ; Pick Three Pool $89,679 .
$2 Pick Three (2–5–12) Paid $294.50 .
$2 Pick Six (4–5–7–2–3/5–12) 5 Correct Paid $335.50 ; Pick Six Pool $110,847 ; Carryover Pool $70,522.
$2 Daily Double (3–12) Paid $241.50 ; Daily Double Pool $199,690 .
$2 Daily Double (5–12) Paid $36.20 .

Aqueduct Attendance: 6,636 Mutuel Pool: $1,722,249.00 ITW Mutuel Pool: $4,097,034.00 ISW Mutuel Pool: $11,823,397.00

SECOND CHANCE AT GLORY

IN SOME CASES IT takes a trainer a race or two to figure out the persona of his new acquisition before that horse starts producing dividends on the racetrack. It may require a surface change from turf to dirt, a drop in class, the addition of Lasix, or a stretch-out in distance to find the winner's circle. For other horsemen, the success never comes and the claim turns out to be a bankroll bust. The new purchase may be unsound or just plain slow. It's quite common that the horse simply has minimal potential despite the superiority of its conditioner. In this scenario, the new trainer may look to unload his lemon at the nearest claiming fire sale. The horse will be dropped below the original claiming price in an attempt to recoup some money.

The following trainer stats for "second race after a claim" for the last three years are listed below. These conditioners have had great success with new additions to their stable, and frequently find a way to score once the recent acquisition gets a race under his belt.

TRAINER STATS FOR 2ndAfterClm

Name	Starts	Wins	Win Percentage	ROI (Based on $2.00 to Win)
Grimm, Margaret E	12	8	0.667	$ 13.10
Allinson, Vernon J	6	5	0.833	$ 12.40
Azpurua, Manuel J	9	6	0.667	$ 12.00
Olijar, Curtis	6	6	1.000	$ 11.10
Shears, Simon	6	5	0.833	$ 10.60
Pierce, Jr., Joseph	15	6	0.400	$ 10.20
Bankuti, Alex	23	9	0.391	$ 10.10
Benson, Harry	16	6	0.375	$ 9.50
Flores, Ramon	24	10	0.417	$ 8.66
Shilling, J. E.	9	5	0.556	$ 7.64
Luna, Daniel G	25	14	0.560	$ 7.43
Hall, Dennis	7	5	0.714	$ 7.34
Beattie, Ryan	10	5	0.500	$ 7.12
Witthauer, John K	19	9	0.474	$ 6.78
DeSouza, Norman	18	6	0.333	$ 6.76
Welsh, Gary	53	7	0.132	$ 6.69
Oran, John T	17	7	0.412	$ 6.29

Guillot, Eric J	16	6	0.375	$ 6.14
Harrington, Mike	20	8	0.400	$ 6.08
Neubauer, Michaela	31	8	0.258	$ 6.00
Atkin, Jerry	40	13	0.325	$ 6.00
Snow, Daryl	25	7	0.280	$ 5.95
Johnson, Andrew H	14	5	0.357	$ 5.83
Kopaj, Paul	11	5	0.455	$ 5.75
Maker, Rebecca 1	3	6	0.462	$ 5.63

On March 30, 2006, Maryland trainer John Alecci entered a
3-year-old maiden claimer named Quoit a Bet in the fifth race at
Laurel Park. As you can see from the past performances below,
Alecci had snagged the filly a month earlier on February 26, moved
her up $10,000 in claiming price, added Lasix, and entered her in
a race where she finished a well-beaten third after pressing the pace
for the first three furlongs.

Today's event, which falls 19 days later, was a class drop back to
the $25,000 level, and we were able to retrieve the following Default
Query results when we ran Alecci through the Formulator program.

Trainer:	John V. Alecci
Filter	Options
Time Frame:	Past Five Years
Distance:	Sprints (<1 Mile)
Surface:	Dirt

Horses	Starts	Wins	ITM	Win%	ITM%	$2ROI	Median Payoff
90	449	104	248	24%	56%	$2.24	$6.90

The next logical step would be to modify the Trainer Pattern filter to see how Alecci performs the second time off the claim. This type of Trainer Form data is *not* printed in the daily paper, but is worth spending the time to research regardless of the end result. You never know what a little research will uncover. There just might be a trainer-data gold nugget waiting to be snatched for those handicappers willing to spend the extra time digging. *Remember: Any training angle that's not easily accessible to the general racing public is always worth researching.* In this case, we would be pleasantly surprised to uncover a winning and profitable angle for the stable. Once we add the Second After Claimed By filter, Alecci's win percentage climbs to 35 percent, with a $5.04 ROI and a median payoff of $7.40. This is a substantial and noteworthy jump from the original 24 percent we started with.

Filter	Options
Time Frame:	Past Five Years
Distance:	Sprints (<1 Mile)
Surface:	Dirt
Trainer Changes:	**Second After Claimed By**

Horses	Starts	Wins	ITM	Win%	ITM%	$2ROI	Median Payoff
31	31	11	22	35%	71%	$5.04	$7.40

To take the Formulator filtering process even further, we can add the Second Time Lasix angle to Alecci's trainer statistics. (See next page.) We'll discuss the medication trainer-angle factor at greater length in Chapter 6, but it's worth a short look now. Although the results become too filtered with a minimal sample to make a meaningful analysis, a win and a second-place finish from two previous starts by Alecci's runners Count The Money and Flypasser make the angle worth researching for a potential live horse. The end result was that Quoit a Bet finished a disappointing fifth at nearly 8–1, but was definitely worth a flier at decent odds based on the positive Second After Claimed By numbers.

Filter	Options
Time Frame:	Past Five Years
Distance:	Sprints (<1 Mile)
Lasix:	**Second Time Lasix**
Surface:	Dirt
Trainer Changes:	Second After Claimed By

Horses	Starts	Wins	ITM	Win%	ITM%	$2ROI	Median Payoff
2	2	1	2	50%	100%	$1.60	$3.20

Our final example in this chapter for the second-after-claim angle takes us to Oaklawn Park and conditioner Thomas Amoss in April 2006. Amoss represents the new generation of horse trainers. He's articulate, ambitious, and knowledgeable. The New Orleans native had been successfully plying his trade at the Louisiana tracks before deciding to expand his horizons several years ago, adding Keeneland , Churchill Downs, Oaklawn Park, and Saratoga to his annual circuit while relocating his home base to Louisville, Kentucky. The most prominent horses he has trained so far are Heritage of Gold, who was the early front-runner for champion handicap mare in 2000, and Tamwheel, the fourth-place finisher in the Breeders' Cup Distaff in 2004 after running a bang-up second to Azeri in the Spinster. The problem with evaluating and betting a talented trainer like Amoss is that he has a flattering reputation and strong fan base. Furthermore, Amoss has the hard results to back his reputation. Basically, his stable wins a high percentage of races, and a high-win-percentage outfit usually generates low mutuel prices.

On April 8, 2006, the national racing spotlight was shining on the Wood Memorial and the Santa Anita Derby, two major Kentucky Derby preps on opposite coasts on the same afternoon. Our attention, however, focuses on another race the same day for a group of less than promising 3-, 4- and 5-year-olds. It was a $20,000 maiden-claiming sprint on the dirt, and the highly regarded Amoss stable had the morning-line 2–1 favorite in number 6, Lynn O.

6 **Lynn O**	B. f. 3 (Jan)		Life	4 M 2 1	$5,280 48	D.Fst	2 0 1 1	$2,990 42
	Sire: Labeeb*GB (Lear Fan) $3,530							
Own: Thomas E. & Laurie A. Lapas	Dam: Susana (Theatrical*Ire)		2006	1 M 1 0	$2,140 48	Wet (333)	1 0 1 0	$2,140 48
2–1 White, Black 'T&L' on White Horsehead $20,000	Br: James T. Hines Jr.(Ky)	L 118	2005	3 M 1 1	$3,140 42	Turf (337)	1 0 0 0	$150 34
Quinonez B (163 11 13 19 .06) 2006:(211 14 .07)	Tr: Amoss Thomas (45 7 8 7 .15) 2006:(105 14 .13)		OP	1 0 1 0	$2,140 48	Dist (284)	1 0 1 0	$2,140 48

22Mar06–6OP gd 6f	:22⁴ :47²1:00²1:13¹	ⒻMd 15000	48 2 4	2ʰᵈ 2ʰᵈ 2ʰᵈ 2¹¼ Graham J	L121b *1.80 75–19 MissSktd121¹½ LynnO121ⁿᵏ FmsMyGm121⁴	Vied, held place 8
21Sep05–4TP fst 1 ✧:24⁴ :49²1:15⁴1:43⁴	ⒻMd c– (15–10)	42 3 3ⁿᵏ 1ʰᵈ 3¼ 22½ 22½ McKee J	L121b *1.40 — — YYSnshn121²½ LnnO121⁵¼ KlsGtl121⁸¾	Steadied after start 6
Claimed from Estate of James T. Hines, Jr. for $15,000, Holthus Robert E Trainer 2005(as of 9/21):(341 56 47 52 0.16)					
24Aug05–1EIP fst 7f	:22⁴ :46³1:12¹1:25⁴	ⒻMd 30000(30–25)	36 4 6	41¾ 42¾ 49 3 14¾McKee J	L120b *2.40 62–20 StrofWhitny116⁷¼ AlohthGrt116⁷¼ LynnO120³	Drft,bmp start 7
4Aug05–3EIP fm 1 ①:23⁴ :48 1:12²1:37¹	ⒻMd Sp Wt 17k	34 7 86½ 86 85¼ 88¾ 88¼ McKee J	L120b 4.10 69–22 Lacy Lindsay120½ Double Faced120²½ Sky Patches120¼	Outrun 8

WORKS: Mar14 LaD 6f fst 1:13³ B 1/2   Mar7 LaD 6f fst 1:14⁴ B 3/3   Feb28 LaD 5f fst 1:01³ B 16/32   Feb21 LaD 5f gd 1:02³ H 9/12   Feb14 LaD 4f fst :47¹ B 4/38   Feb7 LaD 3f fst :35³ B 2/6

TRAINER: 2OffOver180 (22 .27 $2.45) Dirt (460 .24 $1.52) Sprint (361 .24 $1.46) MdnClm (59 .20 $1.17)

J/T 2005–06 OP (7 .14 $2.09) J/T 2005–06 (9 .22 $2.49)

After a six-month layoff, the 3-year-old filly Lynn O returned for Amoss and ran a game second, battling the leader while first off the claim and shipping from Louisiana. She earned a 48 Beyer Speed Figure that day, and the expected setup looked fairly promising when Amoss returned his new purchase 17 days later in a relatively weak $20,000 maiden event. We could tell from the Trainer Form stats listed in the daily paper that Amoss was strong the second time off the extended layoff (2OffOver180: 22 .27 $2.45). However, we needed to turn to the Formulator program to filter out the second-after-claim angle and the one that would eventually show us a drastic improvement over what originally met the handicapper's eye.

The Default Query results for Amoss were too all-encompassing to offer any value. Although his 28 percent clip was quite impressive, the median payoff of $5.20 indicated that his talented stable offered little value. They were bet often and heavily.

Trainer:	Thomas Amoss
Filter	Options
Time Frame:	Past Five Years
Surface:	Dirt

Horses	**Starts**	**Wins**	**ITM**	**Win%**	**ITM%**	**$2ROI**	**Median Payoff**
533	1666	468	1033	28	62	$1.86	$5.20

Would it be possible to make Amoss a trainer-angle play? By modifying just two more filters and adding the sprint and second-after-layoff options, the results improved substantially. In fact, this trainer jumped from a negative ROI to a small but profitable $2.13.

Trainer:	Thomas Amoss
Filter	Options
Time Frame:	Past Five Years
Days/Starts:	**2nd After Layoff**
Distance:	**Sprints (<1 Mile)**
Surface:	Dirt

Horses	Starts	Wins	ITM	Win%	ITM%	$2ROI	Median
117	138	49	91	36	66	$2.13	$5.40

In the final example, we'll focus our attention on the main trainer maneuver taking place in this scenario. By adding the Second After Claimed By results for Amoss to the rest of the filter options we discussed above, we're able to uncover these favorable statistics. Although the sample becomes small, the encouraging results cannot be denied. Lynn O is positioned to score and is part of a winning move for the stable. It's a trainer angle we wouldn't have uncovered without utilizing the Formulator software. Oddly enough, she paid $5.80 to win and was within 60 cents of the median payoff for today's trainer filters and options.

Trainer:	Thomas Amoss
Filter	Options
Time Frame:	Past Five Years
Days/Starts:	2nd After Layoff
Distance:	Sprints (<1 Mile)
Surface:	Dirt
Trainer Changes:	**Second After Claimed By**

Horses	Starts	Wins	ITM	Win%	ITM%	$2ROI	Median
13	13	6	10	46	77	$2.34	$5.20

FOURTH RACE
Oaklawn
APRIL 8, 2006

6 FURLONGS. (1.074) MAIDEN CLAIMING . Purse $14,500 (includes $3,600 Other Sources) FOR MAIDENS, FILLIES AND MARES THREE, FOUR, AND FIVE YEARS OLD. Three Year Olds, 118 lbs.; Older, 124 lbs. Claiming Price $20,000.

Value of Race: $14,500 Winner $8,700; second $2,900; third $1,450; fourth $870; fifth $580. Mutuel Pool $141,322.00 Exacta Pool $96,896.00 Trifecta Pool $69,000.00 Superfecta Pool $33,206.00

Last Raced	Horse	M/Eqt. A. Wt	PP	St	¼	½	Str	Fin	Jockey	Cl'g Pr	Odds $1
22Mar06 6OP2	Lynn O	L b 3 118	6	4	3½	1hd	13½	12¼	Quinonez B	20000	1.90
	Silently Mighty	L 3 118	2	3	6⁴	5½	2½1	27½	Thompson T J	20000	14.50
	Phantom Punch	L 3 118	5	6	52½	4hd	41½	32½	Carmouche K	20000	7.90
10Mar06 4OP11	Oriental Beauty	L bf 3 118	3	2	1hd	2²	3⁴	41½	Berry M C	20000	2.90
17Mar06 1OP6	Powder River	L b 3 118	7	5	42½	63½	6⁴	52½	Meche D J	20000	4.30
25Mar06 3OP6	Princess Sharkey	L 3 118	8	8	7¹	74½	5hd	62¾	Burningham J	20000	41.30
	Keep Looking	L 4 119	4	7	8	8	8	7³	Lejeune J K	20000	37.00
17Mar06 1OP7	Free Phantom	L b 3 118	1	1	2hd	3¹	7hd	8	Doocy T T	20000	3.80

OFF AT 2:36 Start Good For All But PRINCESS SHARKEY. Won driving. Track fast.
TIME :22⁴, :47², 1:00², 1:13² (:22.82, :47.46, 1:00.44, 1:13.58)

$2 Mutuel Prices:

6 – LYNN O.	5.80	3.80	2.80
2 – SILENTLY MIGHTY.		8.60	5.80
5 – PHANTOM PUNCH.			4.00

$2 EXACTA 6–2 PAID $79.00 $1 TRIFECTA 6–2–5 PAID $190.70
$1 SUPERFECTA 6–2–5–3 PAID $563.10

B. f, (Jan), by Labeeb–GB – Susana , by Theatrical–Ire . Trainer Amoss Thomas. Bred by James T Hines Jr (Ky).

LYNN O moved up to contest the pace three wide into the turn, disposed of the other speed turning for home, kicked well clear. SILENTLY MIGHTY lacked early foot, moved outside, drifted out a bit upper stretch, could do little with the winner late, well clear of the others. PHANTOM PUNCH raced off the inside, proved no threat to the top two in the drive. ORIENTAL BEAUTY with the pace early while between foes, dueled late turn, faltered in the drive. POWDER RIVER four wide while prompting the pace into the lane, had little left for the drive. PRINCESS SHARKEY dwelt at the start, remained back. KEEP LOOKING remained always back. FREE PHANTOM early speed along the inside, stopped.

Owners– 1, Lapas Laurie A and Thomas E; 2, Poindexter Thoroughbreds LLC; 3, Martin Gerald A and Ye Weila; 4, Jayaraman Kalarikkal K and Vilasini D; 5, Thunderhead Farms; 6, Vasilescu Octavian; 7, Holt John E; 8, Cresran LLC

Trainers– 1, Amoss Thomas; 2, Chleborad Lynn; 3, Peitz Daniel C; 4, Norman Cole; 5, Von Hemel Kelly; 6, Ashauer Norman; 7, Biddle Glen E; 8, Hobby Steve

Silently Mighty was claimed by Calabrese Frank C; trainer, Wiggins Lon,
Phantom Punch was claimed by Ramsey Kenneth L and Sarah K; trainer, Werner Ronny.

4

LAST RACING DATE

ONE OF THE MOST constantly changing and controversial handicapping factors is evaluating the importance of the number of days between a horse's last start and today's event. When I was in high school and a proud, dim-witted, frivolous handicapper, I often sent away for any horse-racing book, magazine, or get-rich Thoroughbred or harness system I could get my hands on. If your introduction to handicapping was similar to my own, you probably remember how these handicapping articles often stressed the significance of days between each start.

I remember an article in an old *American Turf Monthly* that actually assigned a graded point system depending on how many days it had been since a specific entrant's last race. In fact, I think I even went so far as to integrate some version of this formula into a mechanical system of my own that I created for Atlantic City Racecourse during the summer of 1984. If I remember correctly, it went something like this: Add 5 points for a horse that last started 7 to 14 days ago, 3 points for a horse that last started 15 to 22 days ago, 2 points for a horse that started 23 to 30 days ago, and subtract 1 for any horse that started more than 30 days ago. Sound familiar?

Twenty years ago I thought this nonsensical point system was equiv-
alent to uncovering some type of secret code or map to a lost Egypt-
ian treasure. In the 1980s it was standard handicapping practice that
horses that hadn't started in the last two to three weeks were often
eliminated as potential win threats.

Today, factors such as year-round racing, improved training
methods, and the use of many types of medications have allowed
horses to readily win from anywhere between three to 300 days since
their last racing date. This known fact has driven away and somewhat quieted handicapping theorists looking to find a handicapping
gem hidden in the "last racing day" angle. Fifteen to 20 years ago
it was even considered a negative sign to have a horse coming off
an extended layoff, and the general consensus was that a runner
returning within a week or two could be considered sound, fit, and
likely to run well. But the times have changed—or have they?

Daily Racing Form veteran handicapper Jim Kachulis had this to
add about the importance of layoff runners and discovering proven
winning trainer patterns:

"Trainer patterns have many subtleties as far as handicapping
goes, but among them is the spacing of a horse's race. A classic case
is the versatile New York-bred sprinter Unswept, who has been
under the care of top conditioner Gary Contessa more than once.
The 6-year-old gelding had his usual excellent winter meet at Aqueduct in 2006. The key fact, however, is that Contessa realized that
his runner does his best with exactly one month between races.
Running the Formulator program allows us to see the lifetime history of Unswept. He earned his first 90-plus Beyer when winning
on February 20, 2003, exactly a month after failing to score in the
Fred Capossela Stakes. After several barn changes, trainer Frank
Laboccetta claimed this horse on New Year's Day of 2005. A month
later, he had the sprinter ready to win despite a sharp jump in claiming price. Contessa re-claimed the horse in September of 2005, and
on December 10 (a month after finishing out of the money for a
40-grand price tag), Unswept found the winner's circle again. Studying the gaps between races (especially of an older, hard-hitting
claimer) can often unearth similar gems."

Unswept
Own: Winning Move Stable

Dk. b or b. g. 6 (Jan)
Sire: End Sweep (Forty Niner) $34,980
Dam: Dress (Topsider)
Br: Dr. Jerry Bilinski, Martin Zaretsky & Marc Roberts (NY)
Tr: Contessa Gary C(0 0 0 0 .00) 2006:(262 55 .21)

Life	36	9	7	4	$312,692	100	D.Fst	31	7	5	4	$252,812	92
2006	5	1	1	1	$39,440	100	Wet(363)	4	2	2	0	$59,132	100
2005	12	4	2	2	$106,590	92	Turf(273)	1	0	0	0	$748	78
	0	0	0	0	$0	-	Dst(0)	0	0	0	0	$0	-

29Mar06-7Aqu	fst	6f		:22	:444	:5641	:092	4↑Clm 50000(50-40)	82	3	5	21½	1hd	31	54½	Dominguez R A	L120 fb	2.55	86-16	Tenthirteen115nk Papua1201¾ Lucky Gamble1182	Vied outside, tired	8
10Mar06-8Aqu	fst	6f	⊡	:223	:46	:574	1:094	4↑OC 35k/n2x-N	82	5	4	51¼	51¼	54	45	Arroyo N Jr	L118 fb	3.50	85-13	Rathor1181¾ Introspect1182 Melodeeman1231¼	Came wide, no rally	8
18Feb06-7Aqu	fst	6f	⊡	:233	:473	:594	1:122	4↑Alw 47000n2x	90	8	2	1hd	1½	1hd	2nk	Arroyo N Jr	L118 fb	3.75	77-25	RoyalMoment118nk Unswept1182¾ Callmetony1181¾	Dug in gamely inside	9
11Jan06-7Aqu	fst	6f	⊡	:223	:454	:573	1:094	4↑Hcp 25000s	90	2	4	51¼	4¾	31½	32½	Arroyo N Jr	L116 fb	2.55	87-13	The Student1201 RedCrusader1211½ Unswept1164½	Between foes, no rally	7
1Jan06-3Aqu	my5	6f	⊡	:221	:451	:571	1:094	4↑Clm 35000(35-30)	100	3	2	2½	2hd	2hd	13½	Arroyo N Jr	L122 fb	4.90	90-17	Unswept1223½ *Heart of Jules*1221 Mighty Gulch1201	Vied outside, drew clr	7
10Dec05-3Aqu	gd	6f	⊡	:222	:45	:57	1:101	3↑Clm 35000(35-30)	92	6	1	51¼	2½	22	1hd	Arroyo N Jr	L120 fb	3.75e	88-16	*Unswept*120hd HeartofJules1213¼ NebraskMoon120hd	Determined outside	8
11Nov05-5Aqu	fst	6f		:222	:454	:58	1:102	3↑Clm 40000(50-40)	74	2	1	32	52	64¼	69	Arroyo N Jr	L119 b	18.50	77-20	Fines Creek1142 Stetter Jr1221¾ Exploit Lad121no	Inside trip, tired	6
19Oct05-7Bel	fst	6f		:221	:452	:572	1:10	3↑Clm 45000(50-40)	84	2	2	64	64¼	65½	65	Morales P7	L113 fb	12.10	84-15	Jet Prospector121nk Stetter Jr1222¼ *Stonewood*1211½	Came wide, no rally	7
24Sep05-1Bel	fst	7f		:223	:453	1:103	1:234	3↑[S]Alw 25000s	83	6	3	31	3½	2½	21¼	Arroyo N Jr	L124 fb	2.80	80-20	TakingtheRedeye1241¼ Unswept1244 WildVicr1181¾	Speed 3 wide, gamely	7
5Sep05-2Sar	fst	6f		:223	:46	:581	1:111	3↑Clm c-(35-30)	77	1	4	4¾	41½	32½	21	Migliore R	L121 fb	3.45	83-12	Maybry's Boy1211 Unswept121¾ Only the Best1215¼	Game finish outside	6
Claimed from Valente Roddy J. for $35,000, Levine Bruce N Trainer 2005(as of 9/5): (283 75 54 39 0.27)																						
8Jun05-2Bel	fst	7f		:23	:454	1:092	1:214	4↑Hcp 20000s	68	2	1	41¾	31	37	46¾	Luzzi M J	L124 fb	2.60	84-10	Legislature1226½ Sherpa Guide115nk Dylans Destiny116hd	3 wide, no rally	5
14May05-3Bel	fst	6f		:22	:45	:57	1:093	4↑Clm 50000(50-40)	92	5	5	62¾	4¾	41	43	Luzzi M J	L120 fb	2.30	88-14	MomboLoco120no *PhiladelphiJim*1202 RedCrusder1201	4 wide move, faded	6
14Apr05-3Aqu	fst	6f		:221	:443	:564	1:093	4↑Clm 60000(65-55)	91	1	1	42½	41¼	41	31¼	Arroyo N Jr	L119 fb	*1.75	89-21	Sure You Can120¾ Crafty Player113½ Unswept1191	Buried inside stretch	5
26Mar05-6Aqu	fst	6½f		:223	:444	1:094	1:162	4↑[R]Hcp 35000s	84	6	2	73¼	65½	51¼	32¼	Migliore R	L122 fb	*2.10	94-10	*Legislature*1151¼ *Karakorum Tuxedo*1141 Unswept1221	Good finish inside	8
6Mar05-2Aqu	fst	6f	⊡	:22	:45	:572	1:101	4↑Clm 45000(50-40)	92	4	3	51¼	2hd	12	12	Arroyo N Jr	L119 fb	3.50	88-18	Unswept1192 *D C's Thunder*1205 Special Judge1141	Came wide, drew clear	7
2Feb05-1Aqu	fst	6f	⊡	:223	:452	:572	1:10	4↑Clm 35000(35-30)	91	7	1	32	32½	31½	1nk	Arroyo N Jr	L122 fb	2.60	89-14	*Unswept*122nk Robynthegold1221 Tonic Nights122¾	Determined outside	7
1Jan05-5Aqu	fst	6f	⊡	:223	:462	:582	1:111	4↑Clm c-(25-22.5)	90	9	1	33	1½	12½	12	Arroyo N Jr	L120 b	*2.20	83-19	*Unswept*1202 Mister Stip1202¼ Fighting Roy Kelly118hd	3 wide move, clear	9
Claimed from Chapman, Laz K., Gordon, Hilton and Wexler, Avers for $25,000, Laboccetta Frank Jr Trainer 2004: (155 32 24 29 0.21)																						
27Nov04-10Aqu	fst	6f		:213	:442	:564	1:093	3↑Clm c-(20-18)	88	3	8	62¾	73¾	42½	2½	Arroyo N Jr	L120 fb	*2.80	89-08	Platitude120½ *Unswept*1201½ Lott116½	Game finish outside	10
Claimed from Robbins Sanford H. for $20,000, Galluscio Dominic G Trainer 2004(as of 11/27): (274 32 35 37 0.12)																						
10Nov04-5Aqu	fst	6f		:214	:443	:564	1:10	3↑Clm c-(16-14)	89	8	1	31	3nk	1hd	1¾	Arroyo N Jr	L120 fb	4.10	88-16	[D]Unswept120¾ *Smokieisabandit*120nk Tarakan1161½	Came in stretch	8
Claimed from Andrew Farm and Cassidy, David for $16,000, Contessa Gary C Trainer 2004(as of 11/10): (537 75 91 60 0.14) Disqualified and placed 5th																						
15Sep04-5Bel	fst	7f		:222	:453	1:103	1:233	3↑Clm 25000(25-22.5)	82	5	4	51¼	21	32½	43½	Velasquez C	L121 b	12.10	78-12	FinesCreek122nk ForLovendHonor1211¾ Pltitude1211½	Lugged in stretch	11
28Aug04-6FL	sly	6f		:214	:45	:573	1:111	3↑[S]Alw 20600n3r	82	2	3	44	34½	34½	2¾	Grabowski J A	L120 b	1.80	92-11	*Karakorum Dixie*122¾ Unswept1203½ *No I Can't*1202¼	Good energy	4
11Jly04-8Mth	fst	6f		:22	:444	:571	1:10	3↑Alw 43460n2x	61	2	5	42¼	52¾	65¼	511	Lopez C C	L118 b	2.00	79-14	Bookmaster1182¼ Hey Chub122¾ Bold Trick1181¾	Outside bid turn,empty	6
30May04-8Bel	gd	7f	Ⓣ	:222	:453	1:092	1:221	3↑Jaipur-G3	78	5	3	64¾	52½	89½	810¼	Arroyo N Jr	L112 b	67.25	79-11	Multiple Choice113½ Dedication1141½ *Geronimo*118hd	Steadied 1/4 pole	8
24Apr04-3Aqu	fst	7f		:223	:46	1:101	1:222	4↑Alw 44100n2x	74	5	2	43	42½	510	513¾	Migliore R	L115 b	4.90	79-17	PrettyWild1186½ BuzzysGold1184¾ HeirDTwin1112¼	Chased outside, tired	5
20Mar04-8Aqu	gd	7f		:223	:451	1:093	1:23	4↑Alw 45000n2x	87	4	3	41¾	1hd	1½	21½	Migliore R	L115 b	8.00	88-17	HoustonsPryer1121½ Unswpt1152¼ HognsSpirit1171½	Vied 3 wide, gamely	7
15Feb04-8Aqu	fst	6f	⊡	:231	:46	:58	1:102	3↑[S]HlieHughsH80k	89	3	3	43	45½	45½	43¾	Arroyo N Jr	L114 b	15.80	83-22	Papua122nk A One Rocket113¾ Love Less1132¾	Bumped after start	6
1Jan04-7Aqu	fst	6f	⊡	:224	:454	:574	1:11	4↑Alw 45000n2x	82	7	2	3½	32½	56¾	55	Gryder A T	L117 b	7.00	79-22	[DH]Black Silk113 [DH]*Secret Run*1231¼ Epic1181	Chased 3 wide, tired	7
21Dec03-7Aqu	fst	6f	⊡	:221	:452	:574	1:112	3↑Alw 43000n1x	82	9	1	31	3nk	11	13¼	Gryder A T	L115 b	*1.70	87-12	Unswept1153¼ Champion Ri113½ *Johnny Box*120½	Bid 3 wide, driving	9
11Nov03-9Aqu	fst	6f		:214	:451	:573	1:104	3↑Alw 47000n1x	77	12	3	2½	1hd	27	48¼	Gryder A T	L115 b	4.60	78-17	*Key Deputy*1187¾ Auto City120½ Grand Lucenci113hd	Vied 3 wide, tired	12
5Apr03-9Haw	fst	6f		:22	:461	:582	1:11	LstCodBrCp101k	71	3	3	21½	2hd	44½	411½	Migliore R	L120 b	1.60	76-25	Coach Jimi Lee1245¼ *Iceplosion*1143½ My Calabrese1182¾	Tired	5
20Feb03-7Aqu	fst	6f	⊡	:224	:46	:58	1:103	3↑[S]Alw 45000n2x	92	3	5	11	12	16	14	Gryder A T	L114 b	*.70e	91-16	Unswept1144 Smart Tap118hd *Look Out Evan*117nk	Pace, ridden out	8
20Jan03-8Aqu	fst	6f	⊡	:221	:46	:582	1:111	FCapossela79k	86	3	3	21	1hd	32	35½	Gryder A T	L116 b	2.85	82-22	Alysweep1161½ Philadelphia Jim1204 *Unswept*11616	Between rivals, tired	5
15Dec02-8Aqu	fst	1 1/16	⊡	:232	:471	1:121	1:441	[S]DamonRunyn82k	83	1	12	11½	11	21	23¾	Lopez C C	L116 b	*.90	81-16	*Grey Comet*1223¾ Unswept116½ *Go Rockin' Robin*11615½	Hit rail midstretch	8
29Nov02-7Aqu	fst	6f		:222	:46	:574	1:104	[S]Alw 45000n1x	87	6	2	11	11	16	17½	Gryder A T	L118 b	*2.15	83-20	Unswept1187½ Look Out Evan1221¼ Go Rockin' Robin1222¼	Handily	8
29Sep02-8Bel	fst	7f		:223	:454	1:102	1:224	[S]BFBongard83k	66	1	9	5¾	42	615	617¼	Prado E S	L117 b	5.60	72-18	*FunnyCide*1179 SpitetheDevil1172 InfiniteJustic122nk	Chased inside, tired	10
31Aug02-1Sar	fst	5½f		:223	:461	:582	1:044	[S]Md Sp Wt 41k	88	4	3	32	1hd	2hd	11¾	Day P	118 b	11.40	92-13	Unswept1181¾ War Paint118½ *J. B. Hood*1183¼	Vigorous hand ride	9

WORKS: Mar4 Aqu⊡ 3f fst :37 B *2/8* Feb2 Aqu⊡ 4f fst :482 B *2/17*

TRAINER: Dirt/Turf(31 .06 $0.56) Turf(94 .11 $0.97) Sprint(488 .16 $1.80) Stakes(65 .05 $0.28)

NO REST FOR THE WEARY

FOR THE MOST PART, the modern handicapper now recognizes that an extended layoff in today's Thoroughbred game is no longer an automatic disadvantage. Still, there are many trainers that continue to have enormous success with horses returning off a short break. It's imperative that you know who these individuals are and whether they frequently participate at your local circuit or favorite simulcast-betting signals. The success of these quick "wheel-back" trainers substantiates the fact that individual training habits and proven success are what is most important. The time between races and its overall value depends on the conditioner we have placed under the microscope. There would be no convincing trainer James Berry (5 for 5) or Robert Bowman (11 for 16) that the best plan of attack comes from layoff runners (see chart on next page). These two horsemen have racked up favorable statistics when returning their stock off a week's rest, or even less.

The 25 trainers listed below have had a tremendous amount of success with the "1–7 days since last racing date" angle. I've also included four additional charts in this chapter that cover trainers who specialize in runners that are returning off two- or three-month vacations and making their second start after these extended layoffs. I recommend that you add some of them to your on-line DRF Trainer Watch list, or at the very least give them an extra look if one of them turns up in today's past performances with a highly successful last-racing-date angle.

TRAINER STATS FOR 1–7 DAYS SINCE LAST RACING DATE

Name	Starts	Wins	Win Percentage	ROI (Based on $2.00 to Win)
Berry, James F	5	5	1.000	$ 17.60
Kennedy, Richard W	12	6	0.500	$ 13.40
England, Phillip	14	6	0.429	$ 11.00
Smith, Danny L	22	9	0.409	$ 10.50
Gonzalez, Jose L	16	5	0.313	$ 10.20
Kromann, Lloyd N	15	7	0.467	$ 9.87
Meeks, Karl W	8	6	0.750	$ 9.25
Silva, Paul P	16	5	0.313	$ 8.60
Norton, Norbert	39	18	0.462	$ 8.49
Cuprill, Charles A	40	11	0.275	$ 7.93
Arroyo, Roberto	18	8	0.444	$ 7.79
Evans, Suzanne G	41	13	0.317	$ 7.77
Bell, Charles R	23	6	0.261	$ 7.69
Progno, Michael I	35	5	0.143	$ 7.21
Hall, W. M.	15	6	0.400	$ 7.15
Baird, J. M.	11	5	0.455	$ 6.96
Oxman, Carol	17	6	0.353	$ 6.91
Bowman, Robert	16	11	0.688	$ 6.61
Andrade, Pablo	24	10	0.417	$ 6.58
Rojas, Murray L	20	5	0.250	$ 6.44
Hertler, John O	11	6	0.545	$ 6.42
Pruett, Connie	36	8	0.222	$ 6.42
Khalsa, G. D.	10	5	0.500	$ 6.40
Woolley, Jr., Bennie L	43	15	0.349	$ 6.34
Farro, Patricia	35	9	0.257	$ 6.34

THE LAKE EFFECT

TRAINER SCOTT LAKE ROSE to the top of American racing in a relatively short period. The 41-year-old conditioner started training in 1991 with a one-horse stable. He went from saddling $5,000 claimers at Penn National Race Course to a national powerhouse almost overnight. His stock now competes in the richest races across the world, including Dubai, and his stable includes more than 160 horses. In September 2006, he had already exceeded 400 victories for the year, and was on course to set a record for total wins in one season.

Some of the top horses trained by Lake include multiple graded stakes winner Shake You Down, the winner of the 2003 True North Breeders' Cup and Smile Sprint Handicap, and Thunderello, the runner-up at 48–1 in the 2002 Breeders' Cup Sprint. He also took over the training duties of, and won several races with, the talented sprinter Don Six.

About 90 percent of Scott Lake's stable consists of claiming horses, many of which have been stepped up to win their share of middle-of-the-road allowance and minor stakes events. The gutsy group of consistent claimers that fill his highly successful barn have helped him achieve the title of nation's leading trainer in wins multiple times while setting records in Maryland, Pennsylvania, Delaware, and New York. Whether you love him or hate him, Lake must be considered a serious win threat every time he turns up in the entry box. More importantly, if his magnitude of starters doesn't blow up your Formulator software program while sifting through his percentages, he is often an entertaining trainer to test a magnitude of different filters on. He has many horses at many levels, and the trainer angles appear to be never-ending.

In April 2006, when Lake's 0-for-10 Unbridled's Song maiden Top Secret Speed drew in from the also-eligible list at Aqueduct on only seven days' rest, it was worth some further investigation.

14 Top Secret Speed — Maroon
Own: Gewirtz Evan Klafter Mitchell
Black, Yellow Ball, Black 'Eg,' Two — $25,000
KAENEL K (15 0 0 2 .00) 2006: (370 44 .12)

Gr/ro. c. 4 (Mar)
Sire: Unbridled's Song (Unbridled) $150,000
Dam: Questelavie (Conquistador Cielo)
Br: Paraneck Stallions (NY)
Tr: Lake Scott A(24 6 3 3 .25) 2006:(532 141 .27)

L 124

Life	10	M	3	3	$38,840	75	
2006	7	M	2	3	$32,110	66	
2005	3	M	1	0	$6,730	75	
Aqu	2	0	0	1	$6,200	65	
D.Fst	6	0	1	2	$21,090	66	
Wet(385)	4	0	2	1	$17,750	75	
Turf(285)	0	0	0	0	$0	–	
Dst(380)	3	0	1	1	$14,350	65	

8Apr06–4Aqu slyS 6f :23 :464 :591 1:122 3↑ⓈMd Sp Wt 41k 65 4 3 12½ 1½ 21½ 34 Kaenel K L124 fb 2.50 72– 18 LimeKing1181¼ OurBrveHobbit1242¾ TopSecretSped1241 Ducked in start 9

25Mar06–2Aqu fst 5½f ⊡ :224 :47 :591 1:053 3↑ⓈMd Sp Wt 41k 52 2 3 1½ 1hd 33½ 37½ Kaenel K L123 fb 2.80 83– 18 ToughtoFollow1161 MjorDeegn1236½ TopSecretSped123nk Set pace, tired 7

12Mar06–5Aqu gd 6f ⊡ :23 :464 :593 1:132 4↑ⓈMd Sp Wt 41k 50 2 4 52 310 37 24¾ Garcia Alan L121 f 3.05 67– 23 MjstcKrkorum1164¾ TopScrtSpd1212½ WstrnAccnt121hd Rallied for place 11

Previously trained by Krebs Steven 2005: (251 52 41 32 0.21)

25Feb06–6Aqu fst 5½f ⊡ :222 :46 :59 1:054 4↑ⓈMd Sp Wt 41k 53 3 3 61¾ 64¾ 43½ 21¾ Garcia Alan L122 f 5.80 88– 10 Incorporttim1171¾ TopScrtSpd1221½ WstrnAccnt122¾ Game finish on rail 8

18Feb06–2Aqu fst 1 ⊡ :231 :482 1:151 1:414 4↑ⓈMd Sp Wt 42k 40 7 13 12 52½ 510 515¾ Kaenel K5 L117 fb *1.15 58– 25 NorthrnStorm12211¾ HrsYSovnr122hd LcknthCt122¾ Bobbled start, tired 8

Previously trained by Lake Scott A 2005: (1796 417 328 239 0.23)

16Jan06–6Aqu fst 170 ⊡ :232 :474 1:131 1:44 4↑ⓈMd Sp Wt 42k 66 7 15½ 11½ 1½ 2hd 37¼ Kaenel K5 L117 fb 4.20 73– 25 JumpingJackLouie1223 *Tommsi*1224¼ TopSecretSpeed117¾ Set pace, tired 9

2Jan06–6Aqu gd 6f ⊡ :223 :462 :591 1:121 4↑ⓈMd Sp Wt 41k 62 9 3 32 33½ 34½ 46½ Morales P5 L117 fb 3.95 71– 19 *LittleSulymn*1225½ ASongforHop122no *HrculsOnTop*1221 Brushed into lane 11

16Dec05–4Aqu my 170 ⊡ :234 :484 1:142 1:453 3↑ⓈMd c-25000 75 8 13 11½ 12½ 12½ 2nk Garcia Alan L121 f *1.70 70– 33 Easy Spur116nk Top Secret Speed1215¼ *Dr. Isom*1167¾ Set pace, caught 10

Claimed from Paraneck Stable for $25,000, Pedersen Jennifer Trainer 2005(as of 12/16): (353 28 38 34 0.08)

1Dec05–1Aqu fst 5½f ⊡ :223 :47 :592 1:054 3↑ⓈMd Sp Wt 41k 56 2 4 3½ 31½ 52¼ 53¾ Hill C5 115 f *.85 - - ThirteenMil120¾ ForthReding1151¼ TrtdWood120¾ Stumbled start, inside 8

17Nov05–6Aqu fst 1 :234 :48 1:141 1:403 3↑ⓈMd Sp Wt 42k 54 1 1½ 1½ 1½ 3½ 48½ Morales P5 115 2.60 53– 40 *Drizzly*1202 Fishs Eddy1202½ *Easy Spur*1154 Set pace, tired 10

WORKS: Feb7 Bel tr.t 4f fst :492 B *30/55*

TRAINER: 1-7Days(47 .28 $1.69) Dirt(2228 .24 $1.62) Sprint(1784 .26 $1.77) MdnClm(178 .26 $1.52) J/T 2005-06 AQU(12 .08 $0.42) J/T 2005-06(12 .08 $0.42)

Lake specializes in winning as many races as frequently as possible, and Top Secret Speed was no exception. This 4-year-old colt was taking the most significant class drop in racing, going from maiden special weight to the maiden-claiming ranks. Lake was producing his consistently good numbers with all of his Aqueduct starters (24 6 3 3 .25), and was doing slightly better with the short turnaround angle 1–7 Days (47 .28 $1.69). I ran a general Default Query on him and got the following results. His win percentage over the last five years for the 1–7 Day angle was slightly better at 30 percent than the two-year query printed in the *Form*, but the ROI was still showing a flat-bet loss. I was curious to see if we could make Lake's maiden runner a possible play when fitted to today's exact conditions. As with any other trainer who consistently wins a lot of races at a lot of different levels, finding value can be troublesome.

Trainer:	Scott A. Lake
Time Frame:	Past Five Years
Days/Starts:	1 to 7 Days
Surface:	Dirt

Horses	Starts	Wins	ITM	Win%	ITM%	$2ROI	Median Payoff
124	138	41	90	30%	65%	$1.94	$5.60

Since today's event was restricted to New York-breds, I added that often-profitable angle to today's Formulator query. I also included the Distance filter to the query. To my surprise, his results substantially deteriorated. Lake's percentage dropped to 15 percent on the win end and the ROI plummeted to an unpleasant $1.20.

Trainer:	Scott A. Lake
Time Frame:	Past Five Years
Class:	**State—All Maidens**
Distance:	**Sprints (<1 Mile)**
Days/Starts:	1 to 7 Days
Surface:	Dirt

Horses	Starts	Wins	ITM	Win%	ITM%	$2ROI	Median Payoff
42	95	14	31	15%	33%	$1.20	$6.55

Fortunately, by changing just one Class option from all statebred maiden starters to today's maiden-claiming level, the results sky-rocketed back up to a winning maneuver. At 38 percent and an ROI of $2.14, the 1 to 7 Days angle became a lucrative one with the addition of a few other filters. A little Formulator filter creativity is all that is sometimes needed to expose a winning angle.

Trainer:	Scott A. Lake
Time Frame:	Past Five Years
Class:	**State—Maiden Claiming**
Distance:	Sprints (<1 Mile)
Days/Starts:	1 to 7 Days
Surface:	Dirt

Horses	Starts	Wins	ITM	Win%	ITM%	$2ROI	Median Payoff
6	8	3	5	38%	63%	$2.14	$6.00

SECOND AND THIRD TIME'S THE CHARM

THE BEAUTY OF THE Formulator program is that not only does it provide the user with 12 filter ranges in the "days between starts" option, but it also includes the "second and third after layoff" feature. Statistics for the second race off a layoff are included in the print version of *Daily Racing Form*, but those for the third attempt after a layoff are not. In the last 10 years, it has become a standard handicapping assumption that a majority of horses cycle up to their premium effort when making their second or third start back from an extended layoff. In fact, I would confidently say that a majority of these types of runners receive far more daily support at the betting windows than may actually be warranted based on an individual horse's overall ability or how he stacks up against today's rivals and race conditions. If you're a firm believer in this hypothesis, as I am, then there's a lot to be said for finding trainers that fire their best shot immediately off the layoff line. That's not to say that second- or third-start-back horses are *always* overbet and undervalued. The key is to know your individual trainer's strengths and weaknesses.

TRAINER STATS FOR 2ND START AFTER 45–180+ DAY LAYOFF

Name	Starts	Wins	Win Percentage	ROI (Based on $2.00 to Win)
Ericson, Tiffany	14	5	0.357	$ 22.30
Hicks, Morris	13	7	0.538	$ 14.90
Arrigo, Dan W	6	5	0.833	$ 12.40
Stephens, James A	7	5	0.714	$ 12.30
Blake, Albert E	5	5	1.000	$ 11.40
Barney, Edward H	17	5	0.294	$ 11.30
Clark, Sharon B	6	5	0.833	$ 11.00
Rarick, Todd A	25	15	0.600	$ 9.84
Guidos, John	11	6	0.545	$ 9.75
Caddell, Teddy D	9	5	0.556	$ 9.33
Azpurua, Sr., Eduardo	12	6	0.500	$ 9.13
Lake, Charles M	45	6	0.133	$ 9.08
Damm, Raymond C	6	5	0.833	$ 9.07
Gillam, Jeremy J	22	5	0.227	$ 8.91
Welsh, Gary	67	11	0.164	$ 8.42
Gass, II, Michael A	43	11	0.256	$ 8.26
Saavedra, Anthony K	23	6	0.261	$ 8.15
Loter, Betty	33	6	0.182	$ 8.11
Bayley, Cynthia K	45	6	0.133	$ 8.05
Gonzalez, Jose R	18	8	0.444	$ 7.87
Loney, A. R.	28	10	0.357	$ 7.69
Cenicola, Lewis A	24	5	0.208	$ 7.68
Peitz, Daniel C	79	19	0.241	$ 7.50
Watermeier, Ann	51	5	0.098	$ 7.36
Cefalo, Alfred E	16	6	0.375	$ 7.31

TRAINER STATS FOR 2ND START AFTER 180+ DAY LAYOFF

Name	Starts	Wins	Win Percentage	ROI (Based on $2.00 to Win)
Hughes, Mary J	6	5	0.833	$ 14.20
Billingsley, Sid M	10	6	0.600	$ 11.60
Johnston, Marion	8	5	0.625	$ 9.75
Burns, John M	16	6	0.375	$ 9.50
Wever, Cynthia S	20	9	0.450	$ 9.31
McCann, Sr., Elwood D	14	9	0.643	$ 9.13
Rust, Blake	9	5	0.556	$ 8.22
Lobo, Paulo H	38	9	0.237	$ 7.81
Martinez, Joey A	15	6	0.400	$ 6.96
Lay, Larry	10	5	0.500	$ 6.94
Schooler, Fred A	8	6	0.750	$ 6.73
Sam, Thomas W	27	7	0.259	$ 6.64
Edelman, George	15	5	0.333	$ 6.62
Hartlage, Gary G	32	12	0.375	$ 6.59
Pascual, Maria V	25	8	0.320	$ 6.48
Ortiz, Sr., Manuel	17	6	0.353	$ 6.44
Leavitt, Clifford N	25	5	0.200	$ 6.42
Puhich, Michael	18	7	0.389	$ 6.38
Sacco, Gregory D	23	6	0.261	$ 6.37
McLean, Donald	11	5	0.455	$ 6.35
Williams, J. A.	15	5	0.333	$ 6.32
Grace, John R	21	5	0.238	$ 6.26
Webb, Samuel E	43	12	0.279	$ 6.16
Gruwell, Bessie S	20	6	0.300	$ 6.04
Hartley, James E	9	5	0.556	$ 5.93

A huge opportunity occasionally materializes when you can confidently bet against a shaky favorite that emerges second or third off the bench when the trainer layoff stats are sternly against this type of move. One such example occurred in the opener on a Thursday-afternoon card late in the Gulfsteam Park meet during April 2006.

Number 6, Spiritual Drift, was returning for her third start off the bench routing on the grass for the talented Peter Walder stable. Walder, who frequently sends a solid string of runners to the Sunshine State during the winter months and returns to Monmouth Park during the summer, was having another worthwhile winter break. He was winning with one-third of his starters (52 16 6 5 .30). Spiritual Drift's last two efforts showed a slowly increasing Beyer Speed Figure line of 69 to 71 while routing on the turf. Combined with today's class drop from the $50,000 to $32,000 level, all indications were that the best from this veteran mare was yet to come. Or had we already seen it?

6 Spiritual Drift				

(Daily Racing Form past-performance chart for Spiritual Drift, $32,000, L 121, Own: Marco Bommarito, 3–1 White, White Marco in Green Star, Lezcano J. Sire: Magabird (Storm Bird), Dam: Country Lover (Country Pine), Br: Eddy Behrens (Fla), Tr: Walder Peter R (52 16 6 5 .30) 2006: (53 16 .30). Life 34 7 8 8 $201,794 87. Past-performance lines from 20Mar06 through 31Mar05.)

WORKS: Feb18 GP 5f fst 1:03 B 17/18 Jan28 GP 4f fst :49² B 31/54

TRAINER: Turf (50 .20 $1.43) Routes (140 .26 $1.64) Claim (178 .29 $1.71)

J/T 2005–06 (7 .29 $2.37)

The Formulator Default Query for trainer Peter Walder supplied the following data:

Trainer:	Peter R. Walder
Time Frame:	Past Five Years
Distance:	Routes (>= 1 Mile)
Surface:	Turf

Horses	Starts	Wins	ITM	Win%	ITM%	$2ROI	Median Payoff
34	104	21	57	20%	55%	$1.77	$7.30

Walder's mediocre 20 percent win average with general turf-route runners came in significantly lower than his 30 percent general stats for the meet. This wasn't a positive scenario, but certainly not horrific enough to make him an automatic toss. In this situation it seemed helpful to take a step back and see what Walder's record might look like if we were to add the 1st After Layoff (+45) Days Between Starts option to the current sample. After doing so, the results remained comparable. The overall win percentage decreased slightly to 19 and the ROI dipped about 16 cents.

Trainer:	Peter R. Walder
Time Frame:	Past Five Years
Days/Starts:	**1st After Layoff (+45)**
Distance:	Routes (>= 1 Mile)
Surface:	Turf

Horses	Starts	Wins	ITM	Win%	ITM%	$2ROI	Median Payoff
22	42	8	22	19%	52%	$1.61	$8.80

Now here's where the layoff angle gets interesting and gets your Formulator juices flowing. What happens when we add the 2nd After Layoff filter to the equation? The results increase dramatically and climb back up to a 30 percent level with a positive $2.47 ROI. It becomes apparent that Walder's grass horses perform considerably better second off the bench.

Trainer:	Peter R. Walder
Time Frame:	Past Five Years
Days/Starts:	**2nd After Layoff**
Distance:	Routes (>= 1 Mile)
Surface:	Turf

Horses	Starts	Wins	ITM	Win%	ITM%	$2ROI	Median Payoff
17	23	7	14	30%	61%	$2.47	$7.30

For today's actual race scenario, we're interested on focusing on Walder's 3rd After Layoff stats for turf routes. It's here that we discover his weakness and recognize a downward spiral once again. If it weren't for the score by the now-retired Chim Chimney back in 2002 at nearly 12–1, the $2.35 ROI would have been severely depleted as well, to go along with the 15 percent ratio in the win column. As the 1.70–1 lukewarm favorite, Spiritual Drift was a risky betting proposition.

Trainer:	Peter R. Walder
Time Frame:	Past Five Years
Days/Starts:	**3rd After Layoff**
Distance:	Routes (>= 1 Mile)
Surface:	Turf

Horses	Starts	Wins	ITM	Win%	ITM%	$2ROI	Median Payoff
12	13	2	6	15%	46%	$2.35	$15.30

In summary, the Walder layoff pattern went from 19 percent (1st After Layoff) to 30 percent (2nd After Layoff), and back to down to 15 percent for today's (3rd After Layoff) race conditions. With leading Tampa Bay Downs rider Jose Lezcano in for the afternoon mount today, Spiritual Drift was pulled up and eased on the backside.

FIRST RACE

Gulfstream

APRIL 13, 2006

1¹⁄₁₆ MILES. (Turf) (1.38) CLAIMING . Purse $21,000 FOR FILLIES AND MARES FOUR YEARS OLD AND UPWARD. Weight, 123 lbs. Non–winners of a race at a mile or over since March 14 Allowed 2 lbs. Claiming Price $32,000, For Each $1,000 To $30,000 1 lb. (Maiden and Claiming races for $25,000 or less not considered) (Preference to horses that have not started for less than $25,000 in their last 5 starts). (If deemed inadvisable to run this race over the Turf course, it will be run on the main track at One Mile) (Rail at 60 feet). (Clear. 76.)

Value of Race: $21,000 Winner $12,600; second $4,620; third $2,310; fourth $1,050; fifth $210; sixth $210. Mutuel Pool $87,912.00 Exacta Pool $82,068.00 Trifecta Pool $61,085.00

Last Raced	Horse	M/Eqt.	A.	Wt	PP	St	¼	½	¾	Str	Fin	Jockey	Cl'g Pr	Odds $1
27Feb06 4GP5	Out of Pride	L f	7	121	4	2	1²	1¹	1¹	1¹½	1¹½	Castro E	32000	2.40
16Mar06 7GP6	Twilight Gallop	L	5	121	3	4	4¹½	2½	2½	3ʰᵈ	2¹	Castellano A Jr	32000	12.30
16Mar06 7GP3	Lisa the Great	L b	4	121	2	3	5½	5¹½	4¹½	44	3¹¾	King E L Jr	32000	4.10
27Feb06 4GP2	Potnia	L b	5	121	1	1	3ʰᵈ	3ʰᵈ	3½	2ʰᵈ	4³½	Aguilar M	32000	3.60
16Aug05 8Crc3	Shesadorabull	L f	5	121	5	5	2ʰᵈ	41	5	5	5	Delgado J J	32000	22.50
20Mar06 3GP5	Spiritual Drift	L bf	6	121	6	6	6	6	—	—	—	Lezcano J	32000	1.70

OFF AT 12:50 Start Good. Won driving. Course firm.

TIME :24, :48⁴, 1:13¹, 1:36¹, 1:42 (:24.10, :48.83, 1:13.33, 1:36.20, 1:42.09)

$2 Mutuel Prices:

4 – OUT OF PRIDE	6.80	4.40	3.40
3 – TWILIGHT GALLOP		9.40	3.20
2 – LISA THE GREAT			3.00

$1 EXACTA 4–3 PAID $31.80 $1 TRIFECTA 4–3–2 PAID $115.60

Gr/ro. m, (May), by Out of Place – I'm Proud , by Proud Truth . Trainer Pilotti Larry. Bred by Newport Farm (Fla).

OUT OF PRIDE set a comfortable pace, responded when roused, shook clear and held on well late, driving. TWILIGHT GALLOP stalked three wide early, then outside a rival, rallied between rivals entering the stretch and was gaining slowly late. LISA THE GREAT raced off the pace outside a rival, rallied three wide past the quarter pole and was outfinished. POTNIA raced close up inside and had no rally. SHESADORABULL raced close up between rivals and tired. SPIRITUAL DRIFT was pulled up and eased on the backside.

Owners– 1, Serafini Michael A; 2, Gumpster Stable LLC; 3, Dwoskin Steven; 4, Cunningham Timothy; 5, Silver Diamond Thoroughbreds Inc; 6, Bommarito Marco

Trainers– 1, Pilotti Larry; 2, Hull Michael D; 3, Dwoskin Steven; 4, Petro Michael P; 5, Criollo Manuel; 6, Walder Peter R

Lisa the Great was claimed by Keller Marc; trainer, Gleaves Philip A.

When trainer Mario Morales showed up with Heavy On the Roses in a $10,000 claiming route on April 19, the second start off a 45–180 day break, the encouraging Trainer Form stats were listed for all to see. In this example, a thorough Formulator filter investigation wasn't necessary, and goes to show that a wealth of trainer data isn't always a search-and-rescue mission for the handicapper.

6 **Heavy On the Roses**
Black
Own: Marcela Stable & Alfonso Arosemena
Royal Blue, Red Side Ball, Royal Blue
$10,000
LEZCANO J (20 1 1 2 .05) 2006: (305 79 .26)

B. g. 5 (May)
Sire: Sky Classic (Nijinsky II) $12,500
Dam: Inlay (Miswaki)
Br: Richard Lenihan & Patricia Lenihan (Ky)
Tr: Morales Mario(11 1 1 3 .09) 2006:(25 3 .12)

L 123

Life	23	2	0	7	$18,630	78	D.Fst	16	2	0	6	$16,750	78
2006	3	0	0	1	$1,270	57	Wet(366)	6	0	0	1	$1,785	63
2005	14	1	0	5	$11,485	78	Turf(315)	1	0	0	0	$95	45
GP	6	0	0	3	$3,540	61	Dst(339)	1	0	0	1	$990	52

2Apr06-2GP fst 6f :224 :46 :582 1:112 4↑ Clm 10000N3L 57 4 5 32 31 32 32½ Cruz M R L124 b 24.40 84-13 FlighttoEdn124nk SnorNicky1142¼ HvyOnthRoss1241 Checked turn & late 7
4Feb06-4Tam gd 7f :232 :473 1:14 1:271 4↑ Clm 7500N3L 31 6 5 73¾ 98 109 1016 Villa-Gomez H 118 fb 11.00 59-21 *RightHndMn*118hd BgNnsBoy1185¾ Spongbobhorspnts1182½ Through early 10
17Jan06-4Tam fst 6f :221 :452 :584 1:13 4↑ Clm 7500N3L 36 9 4 74¼ 88¼ 88 86¾ Villa-Gomez H 118 f 5.30 78-16 Manish Water118½ Gotta Have Magic118½ Mr. Bawin118¾ Showed little 10
29Dec05-7Crc fst 5½f :224 :47 :591 1:054 3↑ Clm 10000B 53 3 6 45½ 55 56 69¾ Millwood C10 113 fb 20.90 82-16 Crazybrook1204¾ Flight to Eden120½ Sea Chest1202 Rail trip, faltered 6
10Sep05-12Crc gd 5½f :221 :461 :591 1:06 3↑ Clm 10000B 63 4 6 76½ 66½ 64¼ 66 Freites A7 L116 fb 19.20 85-18 Saye's118¾ Sugarcane Road1182¾ *Parisian Cowboy*1181 No factor 7
21Aug05-2Crc fst 5½f :221 :462 :59 1:054 3↑ Clm 10000B 57 1 6 65½ 66½ 56½ 67¾ Lopez J D5 L118 fb 2.40 84-15 Ice Skating1181¾ Parisian Cowboy118½ *Saye's*1185¼ Failed to menace 8
30Jly05-4Crc sly 6f :221 :461 :591 1:124 3↑ Clm 16000B 50 6 6 76¼ 66 58 410¾ Lopez J D7 L116 b 8.00 73-14 Musical Beat123no Painter Gabe1181¾ Rompburger1189 No factor 7
2Jly05-10Crc fst 7f :223 :454 1:113 1:253 3↑ Clm 10000B 78 3 5 11 11½ 12½ 31 Lopez J D7 L116 fb 7.20 84-13 *Sir Socrates*123¾ Goldini118nk Heavy On the Roses1164 Gave way late 7
17Jun05-4Crc slyS 6½f :224 :462 1:123 1:193 3↑ Clm 16000B 56 3 7 5½ 43 34 56¾ Lopez J D7 L116 b 29.00 74-14 Plenilunio123nk BlindRiverFox1183½ Investigt1231¾ Bumped backstretch 9
23May05-2Crc fst 5½f :23 :472 1:001 1:072 3↑ Clm 10000B 63 4 8 87½ 79½ 48½ 33½ Clemente A V L123 fb 3.80 80-18 Amtodd1232¼ *JudithsMinstr*1181¼ HvyOnthRoss123hd Slow st, belated rally 8
7May05-2Crc fst 7f :223 :461 1:131 1:274 3↑ Clm 10000N2L 56 5 2 2hd 11½ 14 1½ Morales P7 L116 b *.80 74-17 HevyOntheRoses116½ FmousRich1133¾ FtherJo118¾ Bumped turn, lasted 8
25Apr05-4Crc fst 5f :223 :47 1:001 3↑ Clm 10000N2L 61 3 7 64 66½ 34 33¼ Bello J M L123 f *2.60 84-19 JudithsMinister1161 *Amtodd*1232¼ *HevyOntheRoses*1232 Off rail, gained 3rd 11

WORKS: Mar23 PmM 4f fst :50 B *16/26* Feb21 PmM 4f fst :503 Bg *17/25*
TRAINER: 2Off45-180(8 .25 $6.18) Sprint/Route(11 .00 $0.00) 2Sprints/Route(1 .00 $0.00) Dirt(98 .13 $2.69) Routes(21 .14 $2.76) Claim(42 .17 $2.80) J/T 2005-06 GP(2 .00 $0.00) J/T 2005-06(5 .40 $7.12)

Although the listed sample was small (8 .25 $6.18), there was good reason to be optimistic that this 5-year-old gelding was primed for a move forward. After a decent third 17 days earlier with a troubled trip, Heavy On the Roses was worth a wager at an overlaid 9–1. The generous odds were substantially higher than his 4–1 morning line, and jockey Lezcano took it to this weak group of midpriced claimers with a front-running score. (See chart, next page.)

Afterward, a little massaging in the Formulator time-frame option from five years to two years resulted in the following data, which included the April 19 victory. The win percentage stood at 27 percent, but more importantly, the three Morales winners were 14–1, 14–1 and 9–1, and three others hit the board at generous odds.

These types of layoff runners that are making a second and third attempt after a two- or three-month break turn up in the past performances every day. Fortunately, the value continues to be there for the handicapper looking to capitalize on them.

Trainer: Mario Morales
Time Frame: Past Two Years
Days/Starts: **2nd After Layoff (+45)**
Surface: Dirt

Horses	Starts	Wins	ITM	Win%	ITM%	$2ROI	Median Payoff
8	11	3	7	27%	64%	$7.45	$30.00

FOURTH RACE
Gulfstream
APRIL 19, 2006

1 MILE. (1.34) CLAIMING . Purse $10,000 FOR THREE YEAR OLDS AND UPWARD WHICH HAVE NEVER WON THREE RACES. Three Year Olds, 116 lbs.; Older, 123 lbs. Claiming Price $10,000.

Value of Race: $10,000 Winner $6,000; second $2,200; third $1,100; fourth $500; fifth $100; sixth $100. Mutuel Pool $101,029.00 Exacta Pool $95,936.00 Trifecta Pool $90,302.00

Last Raced	Horse	M/Eqt.	A.	Wt	PP	St	¼	½	¾	Str	Fin	Jockey	Cl'g Pr	Odds $1
2Apr06 2GP3	Heavy On the Roses	L b	5	123	5	2	12½	15	13	12	12¼	Lezcano J	10000	9.30
24Mar06 5GP3	Avie's d'Light	L bf	4	123	6	4	22½	22	25	24	25¼	Maragh R	10000	0.50
5Mar06 6Tam8	Club Fed	L f	3	116	1	5	51	6	32	32½	35¾	Cruz M R	10000	11.20
30Mar06 3GP2	Petesamassbred	L b	5	118	3	3	6	5hd	51	45	49	Sanchez J5	10000	3.90
6Apr06 2GP5	Big John G	L b	3	116	2	6	3hd	32	4hd	52	51¾	Bain G W	10000	9.00
10Mar06 1GP3	Kwik Bullet	L f	3	116	4	1	4hd	41½	6	6	6	Castellano A Jr	10000	14.60

OFF AT 2:22 Start Good. Won driving. Track fast.
TIME :23⁴, :46³, 1:11¹, 1:37² (:23.95, :46.67, 1:11.21, 1:37.52)

$2 Mutuel Prices:

6 – HEAVY ON THE ROSES.............. 20.60	5.80	3.20
7 – AVIE'S D'LIGHT....................	2.60	2.10
1 – CLUB FED........................		2.80

$1 EXACTA 6–7 PAID $21.10 $1 TRIFECTA 6–7–1 PAID $129.40

B. g, (May), by Sky Classic – Inlay , by Miswaki . Trainer Morales Mario. Bred by Richard Lenihan & Patricia Lenihan (Ky).

HEAVY ON THE ROSES sprinted to a clear lead along the rail, responded when set down for the drive and remained clear to the wire under steady urging. AVIE'S D'LIGHT chased the winner throughout, made a run to loom a threat in the stretch but couldn't gain late. CLUB FED reserved early, advanced into contention along the rail around the turn but lacked a late response. PETESAMASSBRED was not a factor. BIG JOHN G well placed early after being taken up for close quarters at the start, faltered on the turn. KWIK BULLET was done early.

Owners– 1, Marcela Stable and Arosemena Alfonso; 2, Meltzer Elaine J; 3, Marable S Esposito S and J Calascibetta Racing Stable Inc et al; 4, Fuller Peter D; 5, Arnold Richard P Jr; 6, Hurtak Daniel C

Trainers– 1, Morales Mario; 2, Walder Peter R; 3, Calascibetta Joseph; 4, Fuller- Catalano A; 5, Arnold Richard P Jr; 6, Hurtak Daniel C

Avie's d'Light was claimed by Got It Now Stable; trainer, Homeister Rosemary.
Scratched– Dark Snow (22Dec05 4Crc6)

$1 Pick Three (3–2–6) Paid $569.60 ; Pick Three Pool $17,090 .

NEW KID ON THE BLOCK

CHRIS BLOCK RECEIVED HIS training apprenticeship under Hall of Fame horseman Bill Mott. If there's one thing Block learned from his mentor, it is how to get a runner ready off an extended layoff. Block regularly races his talented stock on the Illinois circuit, but has had just as much success when venturing outside his home base. Block's patience and undeniable skill at placing his layoff runners where they are competitive is probably his greatest attribute. When his talented 7-year-old veteran mare Lighthouse Lil showed up to make her 2006 grass debut in a one-mile optional claimer, all systems looked like a go.

3 Lighthouse Lil
Own: Hussar Racing Stable, LLC
7-2 RED, blue stripes, blue cap $100,000
Razo E Jr (162 38 14 22 .23) 2006:(169 38 .22)

Ch. m. 7 (Mar)
Sire: Hold for Gold (Red Ransom) $5,000
Dam: Danceforthechips (Gate Dancer)
Br: D. Mike Campbell(Ill)
Tr: Block Chris M (25 5 3 4 .20) 2006:(37 6 .16)

	Life	24 8 3 5	$230,156	84	D.Fst	4 1 0 1	$11,120	49
	2005	7 2 1 1	$70,942	82	Wet (339)	1 0 0 0	$0	34
L 117	2004	3 2 0 1	$80,230	84	Turf (285)	19 7 3 4	$219,036	84
	Haw ⊕	5 3 1 0	$81,760	82	Dist (339)	9 3 2 2	$89,474	82

9Nov05-3Hawfm 1¹⁄₁₆ ⊕:24⁴ :50¹ 1:15² 1:47² 3↑ⒻOC 35k/N3X   77 5 65½ 65½ 42½ 11½ 12½ Razo E Jr   L122   *1.30 62-37 LghthsLl122²½ Mdjdj 119¹ ChqrdLv115ⁿᵏ   5 wide turn, drew off 7
19Oct05-7Hawfm 1 ⊕:22⁴ :45² 1:10¹ 1:35² 3↑ⒻOC 35k/N3X   82 7 81² 71⁴ 71³ 38 2¹¾ Razo E Jr   L122   2.90 92-06 MssPFrt122¹¾ LhthsLl 122¹½ ArsA122ⁿᵏ   Off rail, second best 9
15Sep05-3AP fm *1¼⊕:24³ :49 1:14³ 1:44³ 3↑ⒻClm 50000(50-40)   77 5 77½ 76 64½ 74½ 42½ Razo E Jr   L122   3.60 86-10 Itun122² Suvtr122ʰᵈ UnusulSyndrom122ⁿᵏ   Improved position 7
14Aug05-6AP yl *1 ⊕:24⁴ :49⁴ 1:15³ 1:40³ 3↑ⒻClm 50000(50-40)   82 5 79 77¾ 65½ 63 1ⁿᵒ Razo E Jr   L122   3.60 76-32 LhthsLl122ⁿᵒ Vdlct122¹ UnslSndr122ʰᵈ   Off rail, up last jump 7
13Jly05-8AP gd *1¹⁄₁₆⊕:24² :49⁴ 1:15⁴ 1:47 3↑ⒻOC 62k/N3X   79 1 81⁷ 81² 71¹ 410 38 Guidry M   L122   2.80 68-32 ChcDncr 122⁷ Vdlocty124¹ LghthosLl 122¹   Angled out, belatedly 8
25Jun05-6AP fm 1¹⁄₁₆⊕:23² :47⁴1:13¹1:43 3↑ⒻⓈLNClnHrtgH88k   77 711¹²119 105½ 84½ 72 Marquez C H Jr   L120   *2.00ₑ 92-07 BHppy115ⁿᵒ ArsnAnn116¾ CshmrMss117ʰᵈ   Improved position 12
29May05-8AP gd *1 ⊕:24³ :48 1:13²1:38 3↑ⒻRluctntGst42k   77 5 911 911 99½ 86½ 74 Marquez C H Jr   L120   5.70 85-10 VtmnBg120½ GhostlyGt122¹½ Ms.Lydon124¹½   No speed, outrun 9
Run in divisions

26Jun04-6AP gd 1¹⁄₁₆⊕:23¹ :48 1:12³1:44¹ 3↑ⒻⓈLNClnHrtgH85k   84 910¹⁷10¹³ 98 54½ 1ⁿᵏ Marquez C H Jr   L118   *1.90 88-14 LghthsLl118ⁿᵏ ICnFnFn118½ SmnthB119¹½   6 wide 1/4, driving 10
29May04-6AP yl *1 ⊕:25³ :51³1:18¹1:43¹ 3↑ⒻOC 62k/N3X -N   80 6 10⁹²10⁷½ 108½ 74¾ 32½ Marquez C H Jr   L122   *3.00 61-38 SmnthB.119² GoldenTrevlly120ⁿᵏ LighthouseLil 122¹½   Belatedly 10
26Apr04-9Hawfm 1 ⊕:22⁴ :46 1:11³1:37⁴ 3↑ Alw 39180N2X   80 4 10¹⁷10²¹ 9¹³ 51½ 1½ Marquez C H Jr   L121   *3.10 82-21 Lighthouse Lil121½ Sunset Kisses 121ʰᵈ BarrelRacer116¾   Driving 10

WORKS: Apr15 Haw 5f fst 1:02³ B 10/43   Apr9 Haw 5f fst 1:03² B 11/18   Apr2 Haw 5f fst 1:03 B 12/29   Mar27 Haw 4f fst :54⁴ B 29/33
TRAINER: 61-180Days (33 .27 $2.75)   WonLastStart (57 .32 $2.33)   Turf (155 .23 $2.53)   Routes (250 .22 $2.16)   Claim (92 .22 $1.67)   Alw (112 .15J/T 2005-06 HAW(69 .20 $1.81) J/T 2005-06 (156 .22 $1.67)

The Trainer Form stats listed in *Daily Racing Form* proved the conditioner's skill with layoffs (61–180Days 33 .27 $2.75). In addition, Block's ability to keep his runners in shape and sound after a sharp effort was clearly evident with the next trainer angle listed. He was clicking at 32 percent with horses coming off a score (WonLastStart 57 .32 $2.33). The Formulator Default Query not only proved Block's adeptness with the layoff, but also provided an even better win percentage and ROI when combining the Winner Last Out and 61–80 Days stats. At a 40 percent win clip and $4.39 ROI, what was there not to like?

Trainer: Chris M. Block
Time Frame: Past Five Years
Days/Starts: 61–180 Days
Winners, Etc: Winner Last Out

Horses	Starts	Wins	ITM	Win%	ITM%	$2ROI	Median Payoff
18	20	8	12	40	60%	$4.39	$5.50

THIRD RACE
Hawthorne
APRIL 23, 2006

1 MILE. (Turf) (1.33²) ALLOWANCE OPTIONAL CLAIMING . Purse $35,000 (plus $12,600 IOA – IL Registered Own Award) FOR FILLIES AND MARES FOUR YEARS OLD AND UPWARD WHICH HAVE NOT WON A RACE OTHER THAN MAIDEN, CLAIMING, OR STARTER IN 2006 OR CLAIMING PRICE $100,000. Weight, 123 lbs. Non–winners Of $22,005 At A Mile Or Over Since November 15 Allowed 2 lbs. $18,600 Twice At A Mile Or Over Since September 1 Allowed 4 lbs. Such A Race Twice Since May 31 Allowed 6 lbs. (Maiden and Claiming Races For $75,000 Or Less Not Considered In Estimating Allowances) (Preference By Condition Eligibility).

Value of Race: $46,200 Winner $29,400; second $9,800; third $3,850; fourth $2,100; fifth $1,050. Mutuel Pool $100,222.00 Exacta Pool $101,072.00

Last Raced	Horse	M/Eqt.	A.	Wt	PP	St	¼	½	¾	Str	Fin	Jockey	Cl'g Pr	Odds $1
9Nov05 3Haw1	Lighthouse Lil	L	7	118	3	7	7	7	7	3hd	11½	Razo E Jr	100000	4.60
14Mar06 4Haw3	Ms. Lydonia	L	5	117	5	6	67	63	61	42	22½	Torres F C		14.20
5Nov05 7Haw3	Chic Dancer	L	5	119	6	5	5½	5½	51½	2hd	31¾	Emigh C A		1.70
2Apr06 4Haw5	Ghostly Gate	L	5	117	1	1	11	1½	31	1hd	41½	Marquez C H Jr		2.80
2Apr06 1Haw2	Tuffted	L	5	117	2	3	2½	21	1½	52	52¾	Perez E E		9.30
23Oct05 8Kee6	Beau Happy	L b	5	117	7	4	31½	3½	2hd	61	61	Campbell J M		5.90
5Nov05 7Haw4	Hug Me Hug Me	L b	5	117	4	2	4½	41½	4½	7	7	Sterling L J Jr		9.50

OFF AT 2:07 Start Good. Won driving. Course firm.

TIME :234, :472, 1:11⁴, 1:24², 1:37 (:23.98, :47.44, 1:11.97, 1:24.55, 1:37.08)

$2 Mutuel Prices:

3 – LIGHTHOUSE LIL	11.20	5.80	3.20
5 – MS. LYDONIA		12.60	6.00
6 – CHIC DANCER			2.60

$2 EXACTA 3–5 PAID $109.20

Ch. m, (Mar), by Hold for Gold – Danceforthechips , by Gate Dancer . Trainer Block Chris M. Bred by D Mike Campbell (Ill).

LIGHTHOUSE LIL lacked speed inside, angled out in the stretch, rallied late and won going away. MS. LYDONIA lacked speed inside, split horses in the stretch while rallying then could not finish with the winner. CHIC DANCER raced off the rail near the middle of the field and rallied to loom a threat but flattened out. GHOSTLY GATE vied for the lead inside and weakened. TUFFTED contested the pace from off the rail and tired. BEAU HAPPY raced close up three wide and gave way. HUG ME HUG ME gave way in the drive.

Owners– 1, Hussar Racing Stable LLC; 2, Lydon William and Carson Springs Farm; 3, S D Brilie Ltd Partnership and Denker J; 4, Jer-Mar Stable LLC; 5, Win Place Show-Me Racing; 6, Quarter B Farm; 7, Vanier Nancy A

Trainers– 1, Block Chris M; 2, Janks Christine K; 3, Janks Christine K; 4, Robertson Hugh H; 5, Williamson Brian; 6, Stidham Michael; 7, Williamson Brian

$2 Pick Three (1/2–2–3) Paid $137.40 ; Pick Three Pool $7,698 .

TOO MUCH OF A GOOD THING: FILTER OVERLOAD

IN THE SCENARIO OF trainer Chris Block and his mare Lighthouse Lil, you have to decide how much more Trainer Form filtering you believe is necessary. The Formulator Default Query for the Block runner was already producing encouraging results, with a solid win percentage and lucrative ROI, and in my opinion, further tinkering probably wasn't necessary.

One of the keys to effectively using the Formulator program is not to exhaust the stats to a point where they become too watered-down. If you do, you'll find yourself with a small and therefore less reliable group of circumstances and races in which to find profitable trainer angles. By playing with the numbers too long, and adding and subtracting a half dozen filters, you'll likely massage your results into either a negative or positive outcome.

At some point in your handicapping process you need to know when to stop filtering and accept the results at face value. The key is not to rely on these stats alone, but to use them as an added resource to your general handicapping regimen. Otherwise, you'll find yourself becoming what I like to call a filter fiend, which is likely to result in two negative Formulator handicapping circumstances: (1) You spend too much time on one horse or one race. (2) You filter the results down to a point where they become erratic, thus resulting in an inaccurate reading.

If we insisted on digging a little further we could add the Distance and Surface filters to the Block equation. We'd then be left with the following results after removing the Winner Last Out filter. Our win percentage dips from 40 to 30 percent, but more importantly, the ROI remains slightly profitable with a $2.17 return.

Trainer:	Chris M. Block
Time Frame:	Past Five Years
Days/Starts:	61 – 180 Days
Distance:	**Routes (>= 1 Mile)**
Surface:	**Turf**

Horses	Starts	Wins	ITM	Win%	ITM%	$2ROI	Median Payoff
31	43	13	23	30	53%	$2.17	$5.60

TRAINER STATS FOR 61–180 DAYS
SINCE LAST RACING DATE

Name	Starts	Wins	Win Percentage	ROI (Based on $2.00 to Win)
Dibben, H. K.	15	7	0.467	$ 24.10
Magnon, III, Joseph C	22	6	0.273	$ 14.80
Crabtree, Lynn	11	6	0.545	$ 13.90
McCarron, Gregg	14	6	0.429	$ 13.90
De Ridder, Karel A	13	5	0.385	$ 12.70
Fenimore, Floyd E	20	10	0.500	$ 11.70
Oliphant, Claude	0	6	0.300	$ 11.60
Bennett, William D	10	5	0.500	$ 10.90
Garcea, Eric	14	5	0.357	$ 10.60
Wallace, Ronnie	23	9	0.391	$ 10.10
Aguirre, Anthony	21	6	0.286	$ 9.41

Delozier, III, Suzanne G	20	7	0.350	$ 8.81
Cox, Greg D	21	5	0.238	$ 8.80
Edelman, Don	30	8	0.267	$ 8.54
Crumley, Jevon	63	14	0.222	$ 8.44
McKellar, Joseph P	35	8	0.229	$ 8.41
Leach, Tony W	26	7	0.269	$ 7.53
Gunter, Michael C	31	6	0.194	$ 7.52
Garvin, John C	11	5	0.455	$ 7.51
Fahey, III, John	15	6	0.400	$ 7.33
Crozier, Thomas A	20	7	0.350	$ 6.99
Moscarelli, Vincent W	36	9	0.250	$ 6.89
Kaplan, William A	24	8	0.333	$ 6.88
Wolfendale, Sue A	15	6	0.400	$ 6.80
Sneed, Dale	16	6	0.375	$ 6.64

CONFLICTING LAYOFF DATA

THE THREE-WEEK SPRING KEENELAND meet offers some of the most competitive racing in the country, and the short circuit's maiden-special-weight races are no exception. Many of the country's top training outfits unleash their strings of regally bred juveniles as well as older starters, which makes it problematic to handicap so many gifted horses and shrewd trainers in one race.

When David Carroll's 4-year-old filly She's a Devil Slew returned from the sidelines on April 14 after a nine-month break, the Trainer Form stats for Carroll printed in *Daily Racing Form* looked promising: +180Days (13 .23 $2.17). DRF's Kentucky handicapper Steve Klein wrote: "She's a Devil Slew finished fifth at Churchill in her debut, then was flattered when the first two finishers both returned to win. Carroll shows 23 percent wins, and a $2.17 ROI with horses returning from breaks of six months and longer." Klein's analysis was correct, and at first clearly offered some solid reasons to bet the highly regarded $800,000 Seattle Slew offspring.

1 She's a Devil Slew

Dk. b or br f. 4 (Apr) KEEAPR04 $800,000
Sire: Seattle Slew (Bold Reasoning) $300,000
Dam: She's a Devil Due (Devil His Due)
Br: Brian Griggs, Mike Goetz & Raymond A. Roncari(h L 122
Tr: Carroll David (–) 2006:(50 7 .14)

Own: Stan E. Fulton
10–1 Lime, white 'F' on blue ball, lime cap
Guidry M (18 2 3 2 .11) 2006:(241 21 .09)

Life	1 M 0 0	$1,140 66	D.Fst	1 0 0 0	$1,140 66
2005	1 M 0 0	$1,140 66	Wet (377)	0 0 0 0	$0 –
2004	0 M 0 0	$0 –	Turf (287)	0 0 0 0	$0 –
Kee	0 0 0 0	$0 –	Dist (360)	1 0 0 0	$1,140 66

10 Jly05 11CD fst 6f :21² :45² :57³ 1:10³ 3↑ⓕMd Sp Wt 40k   66 5 12   8⁶ 86¼ 78¼ 5⁹ Melancon L   L119   6.60 79–13 *Genuine True* 119³¾ *Naughty Is* 119³¼ Glasgow 112¹¾ Inside,no rally 12
WORKS: Apr11 CD 4f fst :49⁴ B *22/39* Apr3 CD 5f gd 1:00¹ B *2/21*
TRAINER: +180Days (13 .23 $2.17) 2ndStart (23 .00 $0.00) Dirt (148 .16 $1.26) Sprint (97 .16 $1.38) MdnSpWt (71 .11 $1.14)

However, what happens when we dig a little deeper into David Carroll's Trainer Profile? The shrewd handicapper uncovers that the initial positive stat is a bit deceptive. For starters, a little clue emerges directly next to the positive +180 Days angle. The listing for 2nd Start (23 .00 $0.00) illustrates a completely different representation of what initially appeared to be a positive Carroll trainer stat. This is a situation that frequently occurs when dealing with trainer stats and constantly changing numbers. The handicapper is faced with conflicting positive and negative trainer data. What is one to do? In this case, it was an ideal time to turn to the Formulator software program and see what we could uncover.

The Formulator Default Query for David Carroll provided very little promising data—a mediocre 10 percent in the win column and a dismal $0.83 ROI.

Trainer:	David Carroll
Time Frame:	Past Five Years
Days/Starts:	Second Career Start

Horses	Starts	Wins	ITM	Win%	ITM%	$2ROI	Median Payoff
81	81	8	26	10%	32%	$0.83	$6.80

My first inclination in such a case is to modify the query and add the +180 Days positive stat to the equation to see if the results continue to hold up, or hopefully improve. Unfortunately and surprisingly, the results worsened and our once bright, promising, and profitable trainer stat became even weaker.

Trainer:	David Carroll
Time Frame:	Past Five Years
Days/Starts:	**>180 Days**

Horses	Starts	Wins	ITM	Win%	ITM%	$2ROI	Median Payoff
38	38	3	12	8%	32%	$0.74	$9.80

At this point it was time to add more race-condition variables to the equation while still remembering to keep the sample specific, but large enough to be effective and accurate. With one simple addition the sample hit rock bottom, making She's a Devil Slew and trainer David Carroll a must-pass today, despite her post-time odds and the eventual race outcome. I included today's main-track (dirt) surface, which resulted in an 0-for-28 tally. I even added today's maiden-special-weight class condition to the sample and Carroll remained winless at 0 for 13. When She's a Devil Slew and Mark Guidry rallied down the speed-favoring Keeneland stretch to catch 3–5 Votecatcher, Carroll ended his winless streak for the category and graduated to 1 for 29. Despite the $9.80 win payoff, our dependable Formulator stats proved that today's trainer stats for Carroll would be a losing proposition over the long haul. I would clearly bet against Carroll again tomorrow, and the following day, if a similar trainer-angle profile presented itself.

Trainer:	David Carroll
Time Frame:	Past Five Years
Class:	**Maiden Special Weight**
Days/Starts:	>180 Days
Surface:	Dirt

Horses	Starts	Wins	ITM	Win%	ITM%	$2ROI	Median Payoff
13	13	0	5	N/A	38%	N/A	N/A

TRAINER STATS FOR 180+ DAYS SINCE LAST RACING DATE

Name	Starts	Wins	Win Percentage	ROI (Based on $2.00 to Win)
Paez, Carlos E	18	6	0.333	$ 13.80
Huffman, William G	26	7	0.269	$ 11.90
Fires, William H	29	5	0.172	$ 10.20
Briley, Lonnie	16	6	0.375	$ 10.10
Caldwell, Delmar R	37	8	0.216	$ 9.06
Combs, Don	18	5	0.278	$ 8.16
DeSouza, Norman	23	8	0.348	$ 7.84
Mason, Larry A	7	7	1.000	$ 7.80
McGill, Harry	13	5	0.385	$ 7.62
Carter, Elmer	42	5	0.119	$ 7.43
Hendrix, Coy	36	8	0.222	$ 7.22
Croft, Barry N	22	6	0.273	$ 6.89
Cox, L. C.	54	14	0.259	$ 8.88
Arnold, II George R	55	8	0.145	$ 6.84
Johnson, Kenneth L	11	5	0.455	$ 6.65

Patterson, Dennis M	17	5	0.294	$ 6.59
McCarron, Gregg	27	8	0.296	$ 6.47
Collazo, Henry	61	7	0.115	$ 6.22
Nicks, Ralph E	19	5	0.263	$ 6.21
Rycroft, Delbert	13	5	0.385	$ 6.14
Taylor, Mike D	32	12	0.375	$ 6.13
Livesay, Charles	25	5	0.200	$ 6.09
Brooks, Clifton D	20	8	0.400	$ 6.03
George, Ernest	18	6	0.333	$ 6.00
Ananas, Edwin	21	5	0.238	$ 5.97

5

IS THE GRASS GREENER?

ONE OF MY FAVORITE turf-racing ovals was the once-lavish one-mile Atlantic City racetrack course, the original home of the United Nations Handicap. The track was sold in 2001, but it was during the late spring of 1998 that live racing became limited to only a handful of days each year. Atlantic City is required to run a small amount of live racing cards to ensure that the facility keeps its year-round simulcast signal. I wasn't around to witness the legendary Dr. Fager or Round Table participate on the Atlantic City grounds, but I was the proud owner of multiple tickets on Sandpit when he won the U.N. back-to-back in 1995 and 1996.

Today, live turf racing at Atlantic City is limited to only four or five days each year, with most of the seven-race turf cards featuring bottom-dwelling claimers, maidens, and New Jersey-bred starter-allowance events. Although the racing is far from Grade 1 quality, and the pools are minimal because there's only on-track handle available, I've still found it to be one of the most profitable afternoons in racing. The reason is twofold. First, the only past performances available are those that can be accessed on-line. The beauty of the mini-meet is that there are only small clusters of the 5,000 track attendees with quality *Daily Racing Form* past-performance lines. This a huge advantage over the competition when you consider that maybe only two dozen individuals on-track have past performances with Beyer Speed Figures, Tomlinson Ratings, and excellent Trainer Form data. I've found the edge to be enormous.

The second factor is that there is a select group of shrewd turf trainers who show up every year and win a handful of the races. These talented trainers from the Mid-Atlantic States arrive looking to make a quick score with older horses that have shown little if any prior turf form. A trainer's universal success on the turf, with horses making their first turf start, and with those going from dirt to turf are extremely important during the limited AC grass onslaught.

The 2006 mini-meet began with a two-day card scheduled the week of April 26, and another two days the following week on May 3 and 4. One of the advantages of the Formulator program, which works ideally for this type of race-day scenario, is the ability to filter your desired surface right from the main racecard. When you're dealing with a fair circuit or a short meet like Atlantic City Racetrack, where all the races are scheduled on one surface, it's simple to set the option at All Turf (or Dirt, depending on the circuit) while specifically looking for past-performance lines of entrants with turf experience. Instantaneously, the software program allows us to produce revamped past performances indicating not only who has run on the grass, but complete and neatly formatted past performances for each runner on the green. To get a better grip on how helpful the Surface function is, let's take a look at the first race from Atlantic City, which was a maiden-special-weight 5½-furlong sprint. Without running the Turf filter option, our past performances would appear as follows:

1 Atlantic City

ⒻⓇMd Sp Wt 15k

5½ Furlongs. (Turf) (1:014) MAIDEN SPECIAL WEIGHT. Purse $15,000 FOR MAIDENS, FILLIES AND MARES THREE YEARS OLD AND UPWARD WHICH HAVE STARTED FOR A CLAIMING PRICE OF $15,000 OR LESS IN 2005–2006. Three Year Olds, 116 lbs.; Older, 123 lbs.

1ST HALF DAILY DOUBLE / EXACTA / TRIFECTA

1 Classic Victory

Own: Sunflower Stable, Inc.
10–1 Light Blue, Yellow Sunflower, Blue
Mello D (-) 2006:(269 32 .12)

Dk. b or br f. 3 (Jan) OBSAPR05 $20,000
Sire: Snuck In (Montbrook) $5,000
Dam: Valid Precision (Valid Appeal)
Br: Glory Days Breeding, Inc.(Fla)
Tr: Begley Earl P Jr (-) 2006:(45 7 .16)

L 116

Life 3 M 0 0 $268 23 | D.Fst 3 0 0 0 $268 23
2006 3 M 0 0 $268 23 | Wet (354) 0 0 0 0 $0 -
2005 0 M 0 0 $0 - | Turf (234) 0 0 0 0 $0 -
Atl Ⓣ 0 0 0 0 $0 - | Dist (334) 0 0 0 0 $0 -

1Apr06-1Tamfst 6f :222 :461 :594 1:131 ⒻMd 7500 23 9 2 22 22 34 511 Bracaloni N D L120fb 6.20 73-12 LnlsLdLc1205 MlItOr120nk GldnEdtn1203 Chased, weakened 11
16Mar06-10Tamfst 6f :23 :47 :594 1:134 ⒻMd 12500 2 3 12 87¾ 98½ 91110 17¼Ferrer J C L120fb 6.40 64-14 FrdFrlc1201¾ *DbsGnShppng* 120½ ShsAppIng1202½ Broke in air 12
3Mar06-4Tamfst 6f :224 :464 1:00 1:131 ⒻMd 12500 15 1 7 1hd 3½ 64½ 812 Castillo O O L120 7.80 72-13 SmmrTrp1203¼ BdgEln120nk MghtChs1203 Hard used, empty 12

WORKS: Mar26 Tam 3f fst :372 Bg *6/23* Feb23 Tam 4f fst :504 Bg *16/30* Feb16 Tam 4f fst :51 B *25/36* Feb11 Tam 4f fst :493 B *11/45*

TRAINER: 1stTurf (7 .00 $0.00) Dirt/Turf (18 .06 $1.23) Turf (39 .08 $1.72) Sprint (82 .20 $1.96) MdnSpWt (18 .11 $0.62)

2 Magic Reign

Own: Meadow Echo Farm
15–1 Hunter Green, White Collar and Diamond
McDaid J (-) 2006:(297 29 .10)

Ch. m. 5 (Feb)
Sire: Reigning King (Cormorant) $1,000
Dam: Mouthing Off (Nijinsky's Secret)
Br: Karen Kohl(Pa)
Tr: Meares Francis (-) 2006:(17 3 .18)

L 123

Life 22 M 3 4 $15,783 56 | D.Fst 8 0 1 0 $2,260 38
2005 11 M 2 4 $11,367 52 | Wet (296*) 2 0 0 2 $2,838 37
2004 11 M 1 0 $4,416 56 | Turf (259) 12 0 2 2 $10,685 56
Atl Ⓣ 0 0 0 0 $0 - | Dist (269) 2 0 0 0 $0 44

26Dec05-1Pha myS6½f :224 :472 1:142 1:213 3↑ⒻⓈMd 7000(8-7) 27 5 10 107½ 87¾ 57½ 35¾ McDaid J L120b 18.70 61-26 Mstcll1211 Whrsmmnhn1224¾ McRn120½ Far back, wide bid 10
13Dec05-3Pha fst 1 :244 :50 1:16 1:422 3↑ⒻMd 7000(8-7) 23 5 95½ 87¼ 910 812 812¾Vaz E L120b 19.50 53-33 LthosBch1202¼ EndlssPowr120½ FrmlGrc120¾ Always outrun 9
26Nov05-10Pha fst 6½f :23 :471 1:134 1:204 3↑ⒻⓈMd 8000(8-7) 20 2 4 42 56 610 611½Pierce J L122b 5.60 59-22 Mggie'sHt1183¾ *IJustWontQuit* 1202 LBSpitfire110¾ Inside, tired 11
12Nov05-1Pha fst 6f :221 :464 1:001 1:142 3↑ⒻMd 8000(8-7) 38 3 5 55 57 37 39¾ Pierce J L122b 3.60 58-26 ⒹMnPowr1205½ *Emmv* 1204¼ MgicRign1226¼ Failed to menace 9
Placed second through disqualification.
25Oct05-4Pha slyS7f :223 :46 1:144 1:284 3↑ⒻMd 15000(15-13) 37 8 2 55½ 47½ 21 34 Joyce J5 L117b 5.10 58-27 MstMlb1221½ FrmlGrc1192½ MgcRgn1171 Rail trip, hung late 8
13Sep05-3Pha fm 1 1/16 Ⓣ:232 :474 1:121 1:434 3↑ⒻⓈMd Sp Wt 21k 50 1 2½ 11½ 22 37 311¼Joyce J5 L117b 15.30 82-05 Ad'sQst1225¾ Gm'sShnng1175½ MgcRgn11710 Set pace, tired 8
20Aug05-1Pen fm 1 1/16 Ⓣ:233 :474 1:123 1:442 3↑ⒻMd 22500(25-22.5) 52 4 911 87¾ 94½ 54¼ 35 Quinones A R L120b 11.60 80-15 Swtoldgirl1224½ BrbiJoJo120¾ MgicRign1201 Wide 2nd turn 12
28Jly05-3Pen sf *1 1/16 Ⓣ:241 :494 1:143 1:48 3↑ⒻMd 7500 31 2 78½ 87¾ 99¾ 79 53 McDaid J5 L117b 3.40 — — LittleTigress117¾ CrftyAn117no YoungDevon1171¾ Mild rally 10
14Jly05-1Pen fm *1 Ⓣ:231 :481 1:13 1:39 3↑ⒻⓈMd 7500 35 2 33½ 33 54¼ 46½ 22¾ McDaid J5 L117b *1.80 — — CsnSr1172¾ MgcRgn1171 Crptflht115½ Bumped late, gaining 9
21Jun05-7Pha fm 5f Ⓣ:214 :45 :572 3↑ⒻMd Sp Wt 21k 44 5 4 95½ 88¾ 98¾ 78½ McDaid J7 L116b 74.70 87-04 Mck'sQn116nk *Ovrcks* 1164½ MssgfMyth1162 Outrun, no factor 9

WORKS: Apr11 Pha 3f fst :37 B *14/21*

TRAINER: 61-180Days (1 .00 $0.00) Dirt/Turf (4 .25 $5.50) Turf (19 .11 $1.84) Sprint (31 .16 $1.32) MdnSpWt (7 .43 $4.06) J/T 2005-06 (28 .07 $1.04)

3 Digger's Star

Own: F. H. S. Stables
9–2 Light Blue, White Circled FHS, White
Rivera L Jr (-) 2006:(130 14 .11)

B. m. 7 (Feb)
Sire: Cold Digger (Tank's Prospect) $1,000
Dam: Star Writer (Star Spangled)
Br: Fred H. Salter Jr.(NJ)
Tr: Farro Patricia (-) 2006:(159 14 .09)

L 123

Life 13 M 1 4 $8,535 43 | D.Fst 9 0 1 3 $6,300 43
2006 6 M 1 2 $4,155 43 | Wet (318) 4 0 0 1 $2,235 41
2005 6 M 0 2 $3,720 41 | Turf (221*) 0 0 0 0 $0 -
Atl Ⓣ 0 0 0 0 $0 - | Dist (216) 0 0 0 0 $0 -

11Apr06-1Pha fst 5½f :222 :461 :584 1:053 4↑ⒻMd 8000(8-7) 34 6 3 3½ 32 24 34½ Rivera L Jr L122b 2.50 80-13 ShlbLgh1224½ Intrg120nk DrsStr1226½ Edged for 2d,easily 3d 7
14Mar06-1Pha myS6f :232 :473 1:012 1:152 4↑ⒻMd 8000(8-7) 31 1 5 42 55½ 54½ 55¼ Rivera L Jr L122b 9.60 58-28 *SphnTms* 1222½ *Whrsnhn* 122hd MVrncRs1201¼ Lacked a solid rally 8
5Mar06-2Pha fst 5½f :23 :47 :592 1:054 4↑ⒻMd 8000(8-7) 43 5 2 3½ 22 22½ 35 Rivera L Jr L122b 3.10 79-16 Envious1224¾ *RebelRouser* 120nk Diggr'sStr1228¾ Outside, faded 7
18Feb06-3Pha fst 5f :232 :483 1:021 4↑ⒻMd 8000(8-7) 36 1 5 53¼ 41¼ 21 2¾ Rivera L Jr L122b 3.00 71-24 BldrsQst122¾ Dggr'sStr1226¾ Lndvr117½ Gradually closed gap 7
24Jan06-2Pha fst 5½f :221 :464 1:001 1:071 4↑ⒻMd 8000(8-7) 26 2 7 85¾ 84¾ 66½ 66½ Pennington F L122b 5.50 70-18 CzyFnn1221½ *Qn'sFlly* 1172¾ Jstsprngflng122½ Failed to menace 11
10Jan06-4Pha fst 5f :223 :462 1:00 4↑ⒻMd 13000(15-13) 37 2 3 65¾ 66½ 57½ 55 Pennington F L120b 6.20 78-16 ImRdnckWmn122hd *BrdL* 1204¼ ShlbLgh122½ Failed to menace 8
Previously trained by Zoppi Joseph 2005(as of 6/24): (18 0 0 1 .00)
24Jun05-9Mthfst 6f :22 :46 :593 1:132 3↑ⒻⓈMd 18000(20-18) 32 11 4 64½ 55 43¾ 54¾ Suckie M C L121b 36.60 68-14 KtCnfdntl1173 **TrrCnths**114½ PrcsInncnc117nk 5-w,no late bid 12
11Jun05-1Mthfst 6f :22 :452 :581 1:12 3↑ⒻⓈMd Sp Wt 46k 26 1 7 63½ 77¾ 610 612¼Suckie M C L122b 31.00 68-12 OtfthLp116no Ppp'sAshlgh1163¾ WhNtTd122¾ Lacked a rally 7
28May05-11Mthfst 6f :22 :46 :59 1:123 3↑ⒻⓈMd Sp Wt 46k 26 3 10 73¼ 78½ 510 511¾Suckie M C L122b 57.00 65-15 SummrSting1165¾ *SoupItUp* 1124 Gtn1221 Bumped start,inside 12
Previously trained by Farro Patricia 2004: (479 80 66 52 0.17)
22Feb05-5Pha gd 6f :222 :462 :582 1:112 4↑ⒻMd 20000(25-20) 20 9 3 3½ 53¾ 712 717¾Rivera L Jr L120fb 9.20 65-14 *StcyBrew* 1228 Jon'sGryBeuty1221 *J.D.'sHrley* 122no Chased, tired 9

WORKS: Feb9 Pha 3f fst :372 B *4/6*

TRAINER: 1stTurf (2 .00 $0.00) Dirt/Turf (29 .17 $1.73) Turf (77 .19 $2.63) Sprint (457 .14 $1.35) MdnSpWt (26 .04 $0.53) J/T 2005-06 (41 .10 $1.32)

4 Terra Cynthus

Own: Mark Tronco & Harold R. Downer
30–1 Black, White Circled HD, White Dots on
Vasquez Rolando (-) 2006:(22 0 .00)

Dk. b or br m. 10 (Jun)
Sire: U. S. Flag (Hoist the Flag) $1,000
Dam: Mapplander (Briartic)
Br: Dana Katselas(NJ)
Tr: Downer Harold R (-) 2006:(1 0 .00)

L 123

Life 28 M 6 3 $45,759 57 | D.Fst 23 0 5 3 $37,242 57
2006 1 M 0 0 $0 25 | Wet (354) 5 0 1 0 $8,517 49
2005 10 M 2 3 $11,030 43 | Turf (203) 0 0 0 0 $0 -
Atl Ⓣ 0 0 0 0 $0 - | Dist (320) 0 0 0 0 $0 -

9Jan06-1Pha fst 6f :22 :464 1:001 1:133 4↑ⒻMd 7000(8-7) 25 2 10 913 96¼ 65½ 69¾ Vasquez RolandL120 11.30 62-20 RpdRvr1222½ BuldrsQust1204 Shngn120¾ Shuffled back start 10
28Nov05-1Pha fst 6f :221 :47 1:004 1:154 3↑ⒻMd 7000(8-7) 32 11 1 108¼ 86¼ 43½ 32¼ Mello D L120 4.70 58-26 *Bll'sJrsy* 120hd Sptlss1202½ TrrCynths120nk Up for 3rd between 12
3Nov05-1Medfst 6f :222 :454 :582 1:114 3↑ⒻMd 10000 41 5 5 56¼ 45½ 35 36 Hill C5 L118 4.30 75-14 YouGo1222¾ WildctPrincess1223¼ TerrCynthus1185 Mild rally 6
19Oct05-2Medfst 6f :222 :454 :582 1:112 3↑ⒻⓈMd 14000(16-14) 37 5 6 78 56 63¾ 55 Hill C5 L116 5.60 78-12 MstrMscr1213¾ MstDrr1211 SrrVst121nk Outside turn,even lane 8
4Oct05-9Medfst 6f :222 :46 :583 1:114 3↑ⒻⓈMd 14000(16-14) 37 3 5 78½ 77¼ 63¼ 51¼ Hill C5 L116 4.10 80-11 Irdn119nk MstyDrmr121hd JrsyDoll121½ Finished well outside 10
11Aug05-1Mthfst 6f :222 :464 1:00 1:133 3↑ⒻⓈMd 18000(20-18) 43 6 6 1014 98½ 52½ 2nk Perez M L7 L114 8.10 72-19 BrftLd119nk TrrCths1143 PrflTPch119¾ Swung 6-w,drifted in 10
3Aug05-9Mthfst 6f :22 :46 :592 1:133 3↑ⒻⓈMd 18000(20-18) 26 11 2 118¾ 88¾ 87¼ 67½ Pizarro J L120 12.20 64-18 DoblyAppIng119hd *BrfootLdy* 1121½ *PcbSx* 1201 6-wide,mild gain 12
20Jly05-1Mthfst 6f :221 :454 :584 1:123 3↑ⒻⓈMd 18000(20-18) 41 4 7 710 711 310 34½ Maragh R L121 4.10 72-15 CpRs108no LbrtsCstl1094½ TrrCts1218¾ Moved 5-wide,gaining 8
24Jun05-9Mthfst 6f :22 :46 :593 1:132 3↑ⒻⓈMd 18000(20-18) 37 11 12 119¾ 1111 1116 23 Podobinski S M7L114 37.10 70-14 KtCfdtl1173 TrrCths114½ PrcsIcc117nk Angled,closed well 12
25Feb05-2Pha gd 7f :232 :471 1:134 1:27 4↑ⒻMd 7000(8-7) 29 5 4 31½ 3½ 42 56¾ Mello D L120 4.10 64-23 FlyngWndwrd122no StGrgGrl122nk Dz'nDx1223¾ 2 wide tired 7

WORKS: Apr18 Pha 3f fst :353 B *4/21* Mar31 Per 3f fst :39 B *1/1*

TRAINER: 61-180Days (2 .00 $0.00) Sprint (13 .00 $0.00) J/T 2005-06 (1 .00 $0.00)

5 A. P. Acorn
Own: Mesenbrink, Jennie and Char
5–2 Green, White PP, Green Cap
Rodriguez A (–) 2006:(64 12 .19)

Ch. f. 4 (Mar)
Sire: Crowd Pleaser (A.P. Indy) $2,500
Dam: My Golden Charm (Fountain of Gold)
Br: Jennie S. Mesenbrink & Charlie Mesenbrink (NJ)
Tr: Mesenbrink Jennie S (–) (–)

L 1167

Life	9 M 0 1	$4,040	54	D.Fst	7 0 0 0	$1,960	11
2005	9 M 0 1	$4,040	54	Wet (287)	1 0 0 0	$320	–
2004	0 M 0 0	$0	–	Turf (267)	1 0 0 1	$1,760	54
Att	0 0 0 0	$0	–	Dist (232)	1 0 0 1	$1,760	54

Previously trained by Nunn Douglas

WORKS: Apr17 Pha 4f fst :48⁴ B 6/12 ● Apr2 Pha 3f fst :36² B 1/5
TRAINER: Sprint (5 .00 $0.00) MdnSpWt (4 .00 $0.00)

6 Duchway
Own: Marlin Zipp
25–1 White, Green and Black Emblem, Green
Bracho J A (–) 2006:(45 5 .11)

Ch. f. 4 (Apr)
Sire: Deposit Ticket (Northern Baby) $2,500
Dam: Roving Duchess (Roving Minstrel)
Br: Marlin Zipp(Pa)
Tr: Gagliardi Jill (–) 2006:(1 0 .00)

L 123

Life	3 M 0 0	$420	9	D.Fst	2 0 0 0	$420	9
2006	2 M 0 0	$420	9	Wet (283)	1 0 0 0	$0	–
2005	1 M 0 0	$0	–	Turf (326)	0 0 0 0	$0	–
Att	0 0 0 0	$0	–	Dist (284)	0 0 0 0	$0	–

Previously trained by Brown Steven A

WORKS: Mar20 Fai 4f fst :50 B (d) .2/4 Feb10 Pen 3f fst :36² H 5/23 Jan26 Pen 4f fst :52⁴ B 41/48
TRAINER: 1stTurf (1 .00 $0.00) Sprint (8 .13 $4.47)

7 Unsinkable Ship
Own: M. S. M. Stable
10–1 White, Multicolored Disk, White Cap
Santagata N (–) 2006:(233 20 .09)

B. f. 4 (Apr) OBSWIN03 $22,000
Sire: Stormy Atlantic (Storm Cat) $20,000
Dam: Gracie Allen (Allen's Prospect)
Br: Ups and Down Farm(Fla)
Tr: Barndollar Sheilagh (–) 2006:(14 2 .14)

L 123

Life	9 M 0 2	$3,650	30	D.Fst	5 0 0 2	$2,746	30
2006	2 M 0 1	$1,256	30	Wet (347)	2 0 0 0	$460	7
2005	7 M 0 1	$2,400	30	Turf (281)	2 0 0 0	$450	14
Att	0 0 0 0	$0	–	Dist (370)	0 0 0 0	$0	–

Previously trained by Monjes Ruben 2005(as of 6/20):(104 11 13 18 0.11)
Previously trained by Olivares Luis 2005(as of 6/20):(104 11 13 18 0.11)

WORKS: Mar14 FFm 4f fst :51 H 2/7 Feb26 FFm 3f fst :39 B 1/1
TRAINER: Dirt/Turf (2 .00 $0.00) Turf (10 .00 $0.00) Sprint (33 .06 $0.36) MdnSpWt (8 .00 $0.00)

8 Lightning Ride
Own: Parapet Stable
25–1 Red, Red FLP on Black Ball, Black
Flores J L (–) 2006:(325 48 .15)

Dk. b or b. f. 4 (May)
Sire: Editor's Note (Forty Niner) $5,000
Dam: Candy Wood (Bandarwood)
Br: Secluded Stables(Pa)
Tr: Pollara Frank L (–) 2006:(2 0 .11)

L 123

Life	11 M 0 0	$1,275	26	D.Fst	9 0 0 0	$1,275	26
2006	5 M 0 0	$1,275	26	Wet (315)	2 0 0 0	$0	22
2005	6 M 0 0	$0	–	Turf (244)	0 0 0 0	$0	–
Att	0 0 0 0	$0	–	Dist (307)	0 0 0 0	$0	–

Previously trained by Helmetag Robert W 2005(as of 8/9):(64 2 3 4 0.03)

WORKS: Apr25 Pha 4f fst :51 B 31/39
TRAINER: 1stTurf (1 .00 $0.00) Dirt/Turf (3 .00 $0.00) 31–60Days (5 .00 $0.00) Turf (8 .00 $0.00) Sprint (45 .11 $1.40) MdnSpWt (7 .14 $0.86)

9 Pass the Sword
Own: Sharon Neilli-Doyle
10–1 Pink, Purple Diamond Framed S, Purple
Flores L (–) 2006:(156 10 .06)

Ch. f. 4 (Mar)
Sire: Imaginary Sword (Crusader Sword)
Dam: Passé (El Raggaas)
Br: James K. Doyle(NJ)
Tr: Auwarter Edward K (–) 2006:(19 1 .00)

L 123

Life	9 M 0 1	$4,145	39	D.Fst	7 0 0 1	$3,765	39
2006	3 M 0 1	$510	19	Wet (265*)	2 0 0 0	$360	18
2005	6 M 0 0	$3,635	39	Turf (218*)	0 0 0 0	$0	–
Att	0 0 0 0	$0	–	Dist (283*)	0 0 0 0	$0	–

WORKS: Apr4 Pha 3f fst :36³ B 2/8
TRAINER: 20ff(45–180 (14 .00 $0.00) 1stTurf (4 .00 $0.00) Dirt/Turf (6 .17 $2.63) Turf (14 .00 $1.13) Sprint (98 .04 $0.82) MdnSpWt (10 .00 $0.00)

10 Ashley'ssummergold
Own: Robert P. Helmetag
12–1 Blue, Turquoise Belt, Turquoise
Caln N (–) 2006:(99 4 .04)

Dk. b or br. m. 5 (Apr)
Sire: Camille's Passer (Dynaformer)
Dam: Golden Key (Slew o' Gold)
Br: James C. Flaherty(NJ)
Tr: Helmetag Robert W (–) 2006:(19 0 .00)

L 113¹⁰

Life	23 M 3 0	$8,430	33	D.Fst	21 0 3 0	$8,430	33
2006	3 M 0 0	$510	15	Wet (320*)	2 0 0 0	$0	6
2005	14 M 2 0	$5,820	33	Turf (271)	0 0 0 0	$0	–
Att	0 0 0 0	$0	–	Dist (164)	0 0 0 0	$0	–

WORKS: Apr4 Pha 3f fst :37³ B 12/17
TRAINER: 61–180Days (14 .00 $0.00) 1stTurf (1 .00 $0.00) Dirt/Turf (4 .00 $0.00) Turf (4 .00 $0.00) Sprint (79 .03 $0.80) MdnSpWt (16 .00 $0.00)

11 Immediate Access
Own: Joel A. Klingman
3–1 Turquoise, Black Diamond Frame, Black
Pimental J (–) 2006:(145 16 .11)

Gr/ro f. 4 (Mar)
Sire: Robins (Fappiano) $10,000
Dam: Zerra (Silent Fox)
Br: M. LaDona Hudson(Ky)
Tr: Ryerson James T (–) 2006:(63 9 .14)

L 123

Life	4 M 0 1	$2,170	45	D.Fst	2 0 0 0	$240	24
2006	3 M 0 1	$2,170	45	Wet (324)	2 0 0 1	$1,930	45
2004	1 M 0 0	$0	–	Turf (262)	0 0 0 0	$0	–
Att	0 0 0 0	$0	–	Dist (154)	0 0 0 0	$0	–

WORKS: Apr19 Bel 4f fst :47⁴ H 3/26 Apr13 Bel 4f fst :50 B 14/30
TRAINER: +180Days (7 .00 $0.00) 1stTurf (11 .09 $1.96) Dirt/Turf (29 .00 $0.00) Turf (44 .11 $1.07) Sprint (169 .12 $1.71) MdnSpWt (36 .17 $2.56)

12 North Girl
Own: R and L Racing
12–1 Yellow, Red Circle RAL, Red Stripe
Rosario M A (–) 2006:(14 1 .07)

Dk. b or br. m. 5 (Apr)
Sire: Outflanker (Danzig) $7,500
Dam: Northern Danzig (Sejm)
Br: John S. Scott(Fla)
Tr: Estrada Elord (–) 2006:(31 3 .10)

L 113¹⁰

Life	2 M 0 0	$765	16	D.Fst	1 0 0 0	$510	16
2006	2 M 0 0	$765	16	Wet (344)	1 0 0 0	$255	2
2005	0 M 0 0	$0	–	Turf (277)	0 0 0 0	$0	–
Att	0 0 0 0	$0	–	Dist (378)	0 0 0 0	$0	–

WORKS: Mar4 Pha 3f fst :35² B 2/13
TRAINER: Sprint (64 .16 $1.37)

By adding the Turf surface function, the race now transformed into the following:

Despite the fact that there was a full field of 12 older maidens scheduled in the opener, there were only three horses with any prior turf experience. They included number 2, Magic Reign; number 5, A.P. Acorn; and number 7, Unsinkable Ship. Using this Surface filter function for each race, we can easily print out a condensed version of the complete day's card, which will provide *only* the runners in each race with prior turf experience. It's a huge advantage, especially when you have a group of horses that may have hidden turf form that dates back two or even three years. This essential running-line data will not show up in the general 10-line past-performance format. This Surface filter is also helpful on days of muddy and sloppy tracks, when you can print past performances exclusively for horses with experience on off tracks.

The entire Atlantic City racecard offered numerous trainer-betting opportunities. In the first race alone, there were a variety of interesting angles, but one stood out from the rest. Atlantic City course specialist Patricia Farro trained number 3, Digger's Star. At first glance, the Formulator Default Query for "the Digger" and Farro doesn't look all that attractive—a mediocre 14 percent wins with a $2.06 ROI for the first-time turf angle.

Trainer:	Patricia Farro
Time Frame:	Past Five Years
Surface:	First Time Turf

Horses	Starts	Wins	ITM	Win%	ITM%	$2ROI	Median Payoff
14	14	2	6	14%	43%	$2.06	$14.40

However, by changing one simple track filter, Digger's Star went from being a likely pass from a wagering standpoint (based on her lifetime inexperience on the turf) to an excellent betting option. The dirt-to-turf Trainer Form stat (Dirt/Turf 29 .17 $1.73) printed in the past performances gave some clue to Farro's ability and winning intentions over the Atlantic City turf course. It did not, however, provide the entire representation. Once the Trainer Form data was modified to include Today's Track, I uncovered these interesting results. Dating way back to 2001, when Walkthruthevalley first won over the course, Farro not only managed to win two races but hit the board in every start at the track for a perfect 4-for-4 ITM percentage. Her ROI was a soaring $7.20.

Trainer:	Patricia Farro
Time Frame:	Past Five Years
Surface:	First-Time Turf
Track/Circuit:	**Today's Track**

Horses	Starts	Wins	ITM	Win%	ITM%	$2ROI	Median Payoff
4	4	2	4	50%	100%	$7.20	$14.40

Digger's Star was nosed at the wire by Earl Begley's 10–1 shot Classic Victory (also going dirt-to-turf), but did manage to round off a nice $128.80 exacta and was part of the $774.20 trifecta. Easy game. The good news was that Farro had three other starters on the same afternoon and two more the following day. When Nina Marie and Nick Santagata won the fifth race at 8–1 to kick off a $2 trifecta returning a whopping $1,535.20, Farro had been elevated to "automatic" play status in my book, regardless of how overmatched her entrants looked on paper.

FIRST RACE

Atlantic City

APRIL 26, 2006

5½ FURLONGS. (Turf) (1.014) MAIDEN SPECIAL WEIGHT . Purse $15,000 FOR MAIDENS, FILLIES AND MARES THREE YEARS OLD AND UPWARD WHICH HAVE STARTED FOR A CLAIMING PRICE OF $15,000 OR LESS IN 2005–2006. Three Year Olds, 116 lbs.; Older, 123 lbs. (Clear. 60.)

Value of Race: $15,000 Winner $9,000; second $2,850; third $1,500; fourth $600; fifth $150; sixth $150; seventh $150; eighth $150; ninth $150; ninth $150; eleventh $150. Mutuel Pool $5,856.00 Exacta Pool $5,091.00 Trifecta Pool $2,065.00

Last Raced	Horse	M/Eqt.	A.	Wt	PP	St	¼	⅜	Str	Fin	Jockey	Odds $1
1Apr06 ¹Tam⁵	Classic Victory	L bf	3	116	1	6	1²	1²	11½	1no	Mello D	10.80
11Apr06 ¹Pha³	Digger's Star	L b	7	123	3	5	3½	2²	22½	2³	Rivera L Jr	3.50
21Jly05 ⁴Mth⁶	Immediate Access	L	4	123	11	11	10¹	9hd	4¹	32¾	Pimentel J	5.50
26Oct05 ³Lrl⁶	A. P. Acorn	L f	4	116	5	4	4½	3½	3²	4¾	Rodriguez A⁷	2.50
9Jan06 ¹Pha⁶	Terra Cynthus	L	10	123	4	10	9hd	10²	6hd	5no	Vasquez Rolando	17.30
11Apr06 ³Pha⁴	Pass the Sword	L	4	123	9	1	7²	7¹	5½	6nk	Flores L	44.80
26Dec05 ¹Pha³	Magic Reign	L b	5	123	2	9	11	11	9hd	7³	McDaid J	7.60
14Mar06 ¹Pha⁷	Lightning Ride	L b	4	123	8	2	8²	8hd	11	8hd	Flores J L	43.50
11Apr06 ¹Pha⁵	DH Unsinkable Ship	L b	4	123	7	8	6½	51½	7hd	9	Santagata N	6.60
18Feb06 ³Pha⁴	DH Ashleyssummergold	L	6	113	10	3	2hd	4hd	8hd	9¹	Calo N¹⁰	20.30
30Mar06 ¹Pen⁸	Duchway	L	4	123	6	7	5½	6½	10hd	11	Bracho J A	11.90

DH–Dead Heat.

OFF AT 3:00 Start Good. Won driving. Course firm.

TIME :21⁴, :45², :58, 1:04² (:21.83, :45.43, :58.02, 1:04.56)

$2 Mutuel Prices:

1 – CLASSIC VICTORY..................	23.60	8.60	8.00
3 – DIGGER'S STAR.....................		5.00	3.00
11 – IMMEDIATE ACCESS...............			4.40

$2 EXACTA 1–3 PAID $128.80 $1 TRIFECTA 1–3–11 PAID $387.10

Dk. b or br. f, (Jan), by Snuck In – Valid Precision , by Valid Appeal . Trainer Begley Earl P Jr. Bred by Glory Days Breeding Inc (Fla).

CLASSIC VICTORY set pace, driving. DIGGER'S STAR game finish outside. IMMEDIATE ACCESS finished well. A. P. ACORN chased, evenly. TERRA CYNTHUS off rail, mild rally. PASS THE SWORD had no rally. MAGIC REIGN no factor. LIGHTNING RIDE no factor. UNSINKABLE SHIP chased, tired. ASHLEY'SSUMMERGOLD faded. DUCHWAY gave way.

Owners– 1, Sunflower Stable Inc; 2, F H S Stables; 3, Kligman Joel A; 4, Messenbrink Jennie and Char; 5, Downer Harold R and Tronco Mark; 6, Neill-Doyle Sharon; 7, Meadow Echo Farm; 8, Parapet Stable; 9, M S M Stable; 10, Helmetag Robert P; 11, Zipp Marlin

Trainers– 1, Begley Earl P Jr; 2, Farro Patricia; 3, Ryerson James T; 4, Mesenbrink Jennie S; 5, Downer Harold R; 6, Auwarter Edward K; 7, Meares Francis; 8, Pollara Frank L; 9, Barndollar Sheilagh; 10, Helmetag Robert W; 11, Gagliardi Jill

Scratched– North Girl (11Apr06 ¹Pha⁴)

FIFTH RACE
Atlantic City
APRIL 26, 2006

5½ FURLONGS. (Turf) (1.01⁴) STARTER ALLOWANCE . Purse $18,000 FOR FILLIES AND MARES THREE YEARS OLD AND UPWARD WHICH HAVE STARTED FOR A CLAIMING PRICE OF $12,500 OR LESS IN 2005–2006 AND WHICH HAVE NOT WON TWO RACES SINCE NOVEMBER 26, 2005. Three Year Olds, 116 lbs.; Older, 123 lbs. Non-winners Of Two Races Since February 26 Allowed 3 lbs. A Race Since Then Allowed 5 lbs. (Races Where Entered For $7,500 Or Less Not Considered In Allowances or Eligibility).

Value of Race: $18,000 Winner $10,800; second $3,420; third $1,980; fourth $720; fifth $180; sixth $180; seventh $180; eighth $180; ninth $180; tenth $180. Mutuel Pool $9,543.00 Exacta Pool $6,777.00 Trifecta Pool $4,094.00

Last Raced	Horse	M/Eqt.	A.	Wt	PP	St	¼	⅜	Str	Fin	Jockey	Odds $1
21Mar06 10Pha6	Nina Marie	L b	7	118	7	4	4½	3½	52½	1hd	Santagata N	8.30
26Sep05 7Pha10	Golden Moon	L b	8	118	3	10	9hd	5hd	4hd	21½	Pennington F	9.40
1Apr06 8Pha8	Stormy GrandBanks	L bf	4	120	2	1	11	12	12	3½	Flores J L	2.20
5Apr06 8OP7	Chinchilla	L bf	3	111	1	9	61½	44	2hd	4¾	Pimentel J	5.90
10Dec05 9CT8	Neigh Highs	L b	5	111	6	7	8½	82	71	5hd	Beltran J M7	4.90
4Feb06 5Pha3	Regal Lexie	L	7	118	5	2	31½	22½	31	61¼	Madrid M	12.40
9Apr06 9Pha2	Pharaway Wedding	L f	5	108	8	8	10	10	83	71¾	Calo N10	17.80
14Apr06 7Lrl13	Six Rings	L	5	118	4	6	71	7hd	95	81	McDaid J	7.00
28Mar06 5Pha2	My Favorite Miss	L bf	4	118	10	3	2hd	6hd	61	91¼	Mello D	9.30
2Apr06 2Pha6	Worth a Dime	L b	8	111	9	5	5hd	92	10	10	Rodriguez A7	26.40

OFF AT 5:00 Start Good. Won driving. Course firm.

TIME :21², :44³, :57², 1:04 (:21.47, :44.75, :57.57, 1:04.17)

$2 Mutuel Prices:				
	8 – NINA MARIE	18.60	12.60	9.80
	3 – GOLDEN MOON		14.00	8.00
	2 – STORMY GRAND BANKS			4.60

$2 EXACTA 8–3 PAID $186.00 $1 TRIFECTA 8–3–2 PAID $767.60

Dk. b or br. m, (Feb), by Hansel – Danielle's Ice , by Tiffany Ice . Trainer Farro Patricia. Bred by Gen Monty Foss & Gen John Moirano (NY).

NINA MARIE rallied three wide, got nod. GOLDEN MOON rail run, missed. STORMY GRAND BANKS set pace, stayed on well. CHINCHILLA bid, outfinished. NEIGH HIGHS closed belatedly. REGAL LEXIE chased, weakened. PHARAWAY WEDDING no factor. SIX RINGS no factor. MY FAVORITE MISS chased, faded. WORTH A DIME outrun.

Owners– 1, My Son My Son Stable LLC; 2, Tootie Racing Stable; 3, Zamensky William J; 4, The Elkstone Group LLC; 5, Pica Frederick J; 6, Kay Gary A; 7, Atlantic Crossing Partnership; 8, P and D Racing; 9, Plumstead Stables; 10, Lattanzi Vicki

Trainers– 1, Farro Patricia; 2, Crowell Susan L; 3, Guerrero Juan Carlos; 4, Pino Michael V; 5, Schoenthal Phil; 6, Kay Gary A; 7, Allen Randy; 8, Day Diane; 9, Seeger Robert J; 10, Carango Anthony

Scratched– Bob's Valentine (22Nov05 1Suf8) , Little Compassion (29Nov05 1Pha10)

On Thursday afternoon Farro nearly dazzled again with her older horse Given to Fly. The 8-year-old ran a determined second at 15–1 after a three-month layoff from Philadelphia Park. He was making the first-turf and obvious dirt-to-turf maneuver. It was at this point that I decided the only regret I had was that the Atlantic City meet could not be extended another two to three months.

7 Given to Fly
15–1 Own: Gumpster Stable LLC
Black, Red Mountain Emblem, Red Bars on
Ortiz F L (–) 2006:(121 10 .08)

Dk. b or br h. 8 (Apr)
Sire: Beau Genius (Bold Ruckus) $6,000
Dam: Misdanger (Miswaki)
Br: Rising Sun Farm, Inc.(NJ)
Tr: Farro Patricia (–) 2006:(159 14 .09)

L 118

Life	51	7	9	9	$177,042	90	D.Fst	41 5 7 9	$122,637 90
2006	1	1	0	0	$5,100	64	Wet (347)	10 2 2 0	$54,405 70
2005	10	0	3	1	$8,570	72	Turf (271)	0 0 0 0	$0 –
Atl Ⓣ	0	0	0	0	$0	–	Dist (354)	0 0 0 0	$0 –

30Jan06–5Pha fst	6½f	:22³ :45³ 1:11¹ 1:17⁴	4↑ Clm 4000N1Y	64	8	2	1hd	1hd	11	12¾	Ortiz F L	L122fb	11.80	86–16	GivntoFly1222¾ MrJtst1221¼ JohnLittl1223¾	Vied, drove clear	9
31Dec05–2Pha gd	7f	:22¹ :45³ 1:12 1:25³	3↑ Clm 4000N1Y	38	3	3	23	44	86¼	913¾	Madrigal R Jr	L122fb	22.60	65–19	GdMtng1221¾ Whph1222¾ SlntPr122nk	Dropped back steadily	11
3Dec05–6Pha fst	6f	:22³ :46 :58³ 1:12¹	3↑ Clm 4000N1Y	48	5	3	44	45	510	512	Madrigal R Jr	L122b	13.10	67–25	Fabulous Fortune122½ *BrendanMac* 1221½ *CrucialHonor* 1229	Tired	7
1Nov05–2Pha fst	7f	:22³ :45² 1:11¹ 1:25	3↑ Clm 4000N1Y	51	7	1	63	51¾	36½	28¼	Joyce J5	L117fb	5.70	73–16	GrntRdg1178¼ GntFl117½ Brnt'sTn1222¼	Very wide, no match	7
11Oct05–4Pha my S	5½f	:22⁴ :47 1:00¹ 1:07¹	3↑ Clm 4000N1Y	29	7	4	56	45½	47	57½	Joyce J5	L117fb	2.80	69–20	LttlCbbG1221¼ LtMBFr1142 CrclHr1221¼	Very wide, no rally	7
4Jun05-10Pha wf	7f	:22² :45³ 1:11 1:24²	3↑ Clm 4000N1Y	45	2	2	22	3nk	57	67¼	Hampshire J F Jr	L123fb	*1.80	77–09	KngofthMount1161¼ MttsPc116¾ EloquntWgr1232	Vied, tired	10
28May05–3Pha fst	5½f	:22¹ :46 :58² 1:04³	3↑ Clm 4000N1Y	53	3	8	51¾	62¾	65½	47¼	Black A S	L124fb	*1.50	83–12	Rpnzl'sKnght1244 RsnWrror117no InEvryPort1193¼	Gave way	9
18Apr05–4Pha fst	7f	:22² :46¹ 1:12 1:25³	4↑ Clm 7500N2Y	72	7	1	1hd	1½	2½	2hd	Ortiz F L	L118fb	17.80	78–25	PrncSlvrrod118hd GvntoFly1181¼ *FmlyBk* 1183	Gamely to wire	8
29Mar05–2Pha sly	6½f	:22³ :46¹ 1:11¹ 1:18	4↑ Clm 4000N1Y	63	2	3	31	32	23	23¼	Ortiz F L	L122fb	8.00	82–14	Trlthfox1223¼ GvntoFly122¾ ⓓWldGoos1151	Lasted for place	11
27Feb05–4Pha fst	7f	:22³ :45⁴ 1:11⁴ 1:25¹	4↑ Clm 4000N1Y	48	7	5	4¾	42½	35	35¼	Ortiz F L	L122fb	2.70	75–15	Hmbrto122½ Cryptomn1224¾ GvntFly1225½	Wide, no late rally	8

WORKS: Apr18 Pha 4f fst :49¹ B *21/39* Mar28 Pha 4f fst :48⁴ B *12/33*

TRAINER: 61–180Days (36 .06 $0.42) 1stTurf (2 .00 $0.00) Dirt/Turf (29 .17 $1.73) WonLastStart (114 .24 $2.64) Turf (77 .19 $2.63) Sprint (457 .14 $1.35) J/T 2005–06(178 .13 $1.08)

FIRST RACE
Atlantic City
APRIL 27, 2006

5½ FURLONGS. (Turf) (1.014) STARTER ALLOWANCE . Purse $17,500 (includes $3,500 NJB – NJ Bred Enhancement) FOR REGISTERED NEW JERSEY–BRED THREE YEAR OLDS AND UPWARD WHICH HAVE STARTED FOR A CLAIMING PRICE OF $10,000 OR LESS IN 2005–2006. Three Year Olds, 116 lbs.; Older, 123 lbs. Non–winners Of Two Races Since February 26 Allowed 3 lbs. A Race Since Then Allowed 5 lbs. (Races Where Entered For $7,500 Or Less Not Considered). (Clear. 70.)

Value of Race: $17,500 Winner $10,500; second $3,325; third $1,925; fourth $700; fifth $175; sixth $175; seventh $175; eighth $175; ninth $175; tenth $175. Mutuel Pool $8,619.00 Exacta Pool $5,436.00 Trifecta Pool $2,322.00

Last Raced	Horse	M/Eqt. A. Wt	PP	St	¼	⅜	Str	Fin	Jockey	Odds $1
4Nov05 ⁴Med⁹	R. Encounter	L b 12 118	8	8	7¹	5½	41½	11¾	Santagata N	1.90
30Jan06 ⁵Pha¹	Given to Fly	L bf 8 118	7	3	2ʰᵈ	3½	3ʰᵈ	2¾	Ortiz F L	15.10
9Jan06 ⁴Pha⁴	Fort Teller	L b 7 118	9	1	3²	2³	2ʰᵈ	3ⁿᵏ	Prado A J	19.20
11Apr06 ⁹Pha⁷	Fort Seattle	L bf 4 118	3	4	4½	4½	5³½	41¾	Rivera L Jr	4.50
9Nov05 ⁶Med²	Stretchin' North	L b 6 118	4	2	1½	1¹	12½	5³	McDaid J	4.00
10Dec05 ¹Aqu¹⁰	Vow	L bf 8 108	1	7	9¹	9½	7½	6¹	Madrid M¹⁰	9.90
19Dec05 ¹Pha¹	Bullettthebluesky	L bf 7 118	2	5	6ʰᵈ	8¹	61½	7²	Flores L	20.70
12Nov05 ⁹Med³	Call an Interview	L bf 6 118	5	9	10	10	9²	8¾	Pennington F	9.50
8Apr06 ⁴Pha⁸	Rolando Furioso	L b 8 118	6	10	8½	7³	8½	93½	Flores J L	38.10
1Apr06 ⁸Pen²	Tempted Spirit	L b 4 118	10	6	5²	6½	10	10	Mello D	7.60

OFF AT 3:00 Start Good. Won driving. Course firm.

TIME :21⁴, :44⁴, :57¹, 1:03³ (:21.82, :44.94, :57.36, 1:03.61)

$2 Mutuel Prices:

8 – R. ENCOUNTER	5.80	5.00	7.00
7 – GIVEN TO FLY		17.20	13.00
9 – FORT TELLER			9.40

$2 EXACTA 8–7 PAID $92.60 $1 TRIFECTA 8–7–9 PAID $348.30

Dk. b or br. g, (May), by Tex R. Rabbit – Faffy G. , by Capital Idea . Trainer Auwarter Edward K. Bred by James Doyle (NJ).

R. ENCOUNTER saved ground off the pace, angled out and rallied late outside. GIVEN TO FLY between foes, gamely. FORT TELLER speed 3 wide, weakened. FORT SEATTLE even effort. STRETCHIN' NORTH set pace, clear, weakened. VOW improved position. BULLETTTHEBLUESKY had no rally. CALL AN INTERVIEW no factor. ROLANDO FURIOSO no factor. TEMPTED SPIRIT faded.

Owners– 1, Neill-Doyle Sharon; 2, Gumpster Stable LLC; 3, Lembo Menotti; 4, Bada Bing Stable; 5, Shaw Timothy J; 6, Presidential Thoroughbreds; 7, Kay Gary A; 8, Thompson Glenn R; 9, Johnkins Genevieve; 10, Rager Clayton

Trainers– 1, Auwarter Edward K; 2, Farro Patricia; 3, Berrios Manuel; 4, Robbins Charles R; 5, Shaw Tim J; 6, Breen Kelly J; 7, Kay Gary A; 8, Thompson Glenn R; 9, Pollara Frank L; 10, Brown Steven R

Below is a list of trainers who have excelled with horses making their first start on the turf. Patricia Farro did not make this exclusive roster, but those who did are worth following and betting when their runners show up on the green at a track near you.

TRAINER STATS FOR 1stTurf

Name	Starts	Wins	Win Percentage	ROI (Based on $2.00 to Win)
Morales, Nabu	14	6	0.429	$20.30
Hofmans, Grant	16	5	0.313	$17.80
DeStasio, Richard A	23	6	0.261	$14.20
Toye, Joe	36	8	0.222	$12.30
Nix, C. L.	30	7	0.233	$11.30
Lawrence, Wray I	28	5	0.179	$10.90

Napier, William J	14	6	0.429	$9.89
Kolarik, Jeanne M	7	5	0.714	$9.46
Anderson, Jann P	17	6	0.353	$9.26
Connelly, William R	32	9	0.281	$8.75
Nuesch, Patrick F	22	5	0.227	$8.65
Smithwick, Jr., D. M.	47	6	0.128	$8.52
Nielsen, Paul	12	5	0.417	$8.47
Morse, Randy L	22	5	0.227	$8.06
Hines, Nicholas J	43	5	0.116	$7.78
Franko, Daniel	40	9	0.225	$7.17
Kintz, S. M.	31	7	0.226	$6.05
Day Phillips, Catherine	31	9	0.290	$6.05
Bindner, Jr., Walter M	43	6	0.140	$5.69
Dollase, Wallace A	18	9	0.500	$5.46
Koriner, Brian J	47	9	0.191	$5.45
Lawrence, II, James L	44	5	0.114	$5.29
Mayo, Larry A	22	5	0.227	$5.24
Register, Alison	22	5	0.227	$5.22
Hall, John L	15	6	0.400	$5.20

The turf-to-dirt and dirt-to-turf trainer maneuvers are among the most widely used and successful angles. During the spring and summer months when grass racing is operating at full throttle throughout the country, it's not uncommon to uncover a handful of daily situations where horses are switching surfaces. There are a multitude of trainers who excel with the surface change. It's not at all unusual for a trainer to take a horse with horrendous form and turn that recent poor performance into a winning race when switching to the new surface. In many cases, the race before the surface change is a mere setup for today's preferred surface. The poor-last-race past-performance line often leaves the general public sniffing around in another direction while simply overlooking the horse and trainer making the preferred surface switch. The end result is usually generous odds producing overlays on live horses making the positive surface change. Despite the availability of updated trainer-pattern data via the Internet, printed *Daily Racing Form* Trainer Form information, and other publicly available trainer-data books, these types of surface-switch runners still manage to escape the public's handicapping eye and pocket.

THE JERKENS MAGIC

NEW YORK-BASED TRAINER Jimmy Jerkens, a son of Hall of Fame trainer Allen Jerkens, is a master of the turf-to-dirt and dirt-to-turf angles, among many other crafty training maneuvers. He earned his first Breeders' Cup victory in 2005 when his talented and classy Grade 1 runner Artie Schiller beat the highly touted race favorite, Leroidesanimaux, in the Mile.

Jerkens's training expertise covers all spectrums of racing's class levels. When his 4-year-old gelding Western Accent returned to the Belmont Park spring meet in a $6^1/_2$-furlong sprint for maidens, all indications were that the son of Western Expression might finally find the winner's circle in his fourth lifetime start. Jerkens's Trainer Form stats in *Daily Racing Form* were very impressive, including a fast-out-of-the-gate overall record at the current Belmont meet (Tr: Jerkens James A 9 3 0 1 .33). His turf-to-dirt (21 .38 $3.21) and route-to-sprint (18 .33 $2.20) numbers and positive ROI were even healthier.

At 6–1 morning-line odds, Western Accent was at least worth a thorough Formulator rundown to see if these initial numbers were accurate and not just a mirage. The Default Query for Jerkens appeared as follows. Without any further number massaging, the gifted trainer had some impressive stats. In fact, you could argue that an automatic bet on the Jerkens turf-to-dirt angle was not entirely illogical if the post-time price was acceptable.

Trainer:	James A. Jerkens
Time Frame:	Past Five Years
Surface:	Turf to Dirt

Horses	Starts	Wins	ITM	Win%	ITM%	$2ROI	Median Payoff
46	65	21	45	32%	69%	$3.16	$10.60

At this point, it would be an intricate task to attempt to further improve these numbers. However, I managed to do so in the win-percentage column by adding the other positive Trainer Form angle already listed in the daily paper: Route to Sprint. Although the ROI and median payoff declined, the overall win percentage soared from 32 to 40 percent. Like the senior Jerkens, who frequently provides apprentices and other up-and-coming jockeys with the opportunity to ride quality horses, Jimmy Jerkens enlisted apprentice Isaac Barahona for the mount on Western Accent.

Trainer:	James A. Jerkens
Time Frame:	Past Five Years
Distance:	**Route to Sprint**
Surface:	Turf to Dirt

Horses	Starts	Wins	ITM	Win%	ITM%	$2ROI	Median Payoff
9	10	4	7	40%	70%	$2.91	$6.00

NORTHERN CALIFORNIA: MASON'S MAGIC

I RARELY PARK MY handicapping tack at Bay Meadows or actively bet and pursue any Northern California racing in general. However, for those of you who choose to follow this circuit, there are a few select trainers that perform extremely well with various angles. One of these trainers is the underrated Lloyd C. Mason. Mason is dynamite with first-time starters and a master on the turf course, showing a very healthy ROI with various dirt-to-turf and first-turf categories. In most cases, his live horses are well hidden with just average five- and six-furlong drills. Mason's horses usually run with Lasix, and it's rare that he doesn't reach out to one of the top 10 riders at the local circuit.

When his 3-year-old filly Penny Power appeared in the Bay Meadows entries on May 11, 2006, I had a hunch it would pay dividends to take notice.

2 Penny Power
Own: Jim Kwong
10–1 White, Turquoise LM on Back,
Martinez L V (–) 2006:(446 69 .15)

$20,000

Ch. f. 3 (Jan) ARZNOV04 $7,500
Sire: Kessem Power*NZ (Kessem)
Dam: Steady Penny (Stanstead)
Br: Jim Wilson(Cal)
Tr: Mason Lloyd C (–) 2006:(85 15 .18)

L 1145

Life	10	1	0	3	$9,178	45	D.Fst	10	1	0	3	$9,178 45
2006	5	1	0	2	$8,288	45	Wet (276*)	0	0	0	0	$0 -
2005	5	M	0	1	$890	34	Turf (355)	0	0	0	0	$0 -
BMⓉ	0	0	0	0	$0	-	Dist (278)	0	0	0	0	$0 -

19Apr06-5GG fst 1 :221 :453 1:124 1:423 ⒻClm 16000(16-14) 40 2 58½ 510 58 43½ 33 Martinez L V5 LB114b 15.20 53-34 ThGrtQstn119no MstBTppr1193 PnnPr1148 Bmpd strt, even late 6
22Mar06-6GG fst 1 1/16 :232 :484 1:14 1:462 ⒻMd 8000 44 9 98 75½ 42½ 21½ 13 Martinez L V5 LB114b 4.90 71-18 PnnyPwr1143 Snd'sPlc1196 FrcflWy114nk Circled 4w, driving 10
Previously trained by Knapp Neil 2005:(165 24 31 29 0.15)
18Feb06-2TuPfst 1 :224 :47 1:113 1:39 Md 8000(8-7) 27 7 714 55 47½ 47½ 414¾ Mawing L A L118b 3.60 58-24 BzzthTr1214¼ *DblCrdt* 12110 *CllctSttl* 121½ 4 wide, far turn,empty 7
21Jan06-5TuPfst 1 :234 :47 1:123 1:412 Md 5000 45 3 52 54 32 32½ 3¾ Mawing L A L118b 7.90 60-26 Mr.Gb121no DixiGntlmn116¾ PnnyPowr1181½ 3-w, late gain 7
10Jan06-3TuPfst 1 :232 :473 1:131 1:40 Md 8000(10-7) 27 9 53¼ 52½ 53½ 65½ 512¼ Kenney K5 L114b 11.30 56-29 *TquilndRoss* 1212¼ *Mr.Gb* 1214¼ BrkoutPowr1213½ Wide, no rally 9
19Dec05-5TuPfst 6f :23 :464 :592 1:123 ⒻMd c-5000 22 10 1 41¼ 3½ 43½ 77¼ Kenney K5 L114b 6.10 67-21 MnTsk1194 *WnnngItAll* 119½ FourWndsNtv119hd 3-4 wide,tired 11
Claimed from Polito Nancy for $5,000, Polito Nancy Trainer 2005(as of 12/19):(68 6 10 4 0.09)
9Dec05-7TuPfst 5f :222 :46 :584 ⒻMd 5000 34 2 2 34½ 44½ 35 36 Kenney K5 L114b 20.60 81-14 FryAtmnHz1194½ AddJ1191½ PnnyPr1143¼ Gaining some late 9
25Nov05-5TuPfst 6f :222 :453 :58 1:112 ⒻMd 12500(16-10.5) –0 9 1 53¼ 56¼ 814 825¼ Packer B R L120b 38.50 55-17 *RivrLn* 120¾ *DvlshDx* 1206¼ SnugglMUp1204½ Outside,weakened 9
Previously trained by Thompson James E 2005(as of 8/1):(30 9 1 0 0.30)
1Aug05-3Yav fst 5½f :224 :451 :573 1:042 ⒻMd Sp Wt 6k –0 6 3 42 53¼ 68¾ 717¼ Hernandez M G L120b 4.70 72-07 Sh'sSttM1201 *AlngCmJns* 1201 DQnRn1209¾ Early factor, tired 8
19Jly05-4Yav fst 4½f :223 :453 :52 Md Sp Wt 6k 11 7 4 33 34½ 47 Oliver R J L124b 2.90 84-07 NdVd1201 *Sh'sSttM* 1172¼ AlngCmJns1173¾ Pace, steadied 3/8 9
WORKS: May4 GG 5f fst 1:002 H *2/18* Apr28 GG 4f fst :492 H *10/33* Apr9 GG 5f gd 1:012 H *9/36* Apr2 GG 4f gd :50 H *24/75* Mar18 GG 4f fst :482 H *7/27* Mar11 GG 5f wf 1:013 H *15/21*
TRAINER: 1stTurf (14 .14 $1.03) Dirt/Turf (27 .33 $5.60) Turf (49 .20 $3.32) Routes (122 .19 $2.98) Claim (149 .19 $2.49) J/T 2005-06 BM(1.00 $0.00) J/T 2005-06(6 .33 $4.63)

Mason had acquired the training duties of this filly from Neil Knapp two races back, and quickly produced a victory on March 22. Penny Power had mediocre turf breeding, and was making her grass debut in her 11th lifetime start after needing nine tries to break her maiden at the bottom claiming level. She had a snappy five-furlong drill at Golden Gate seven days before the race, which was a little out of the ordinary for the Mason camp. Her first start against winners at a mile on April 19 was a decent effort. She closed well after a bumping incident at the start to finish third.

In today's 1 1/16-mile turf event, Penny Power was moving up from $16,000 to $20,000 claimers. More importantly, Mason was making the key dirt-to-turf surface switch as well as the first-turf exchange. Without even running Mason's stats through the Formulator software, a handicapper could determine through the printed Trainer Form data in the daily paper that the filly was probably well-meant. Or could he? Mason's first three Trainer Form stats read: 1stTurf (14 .14 $1.03), Dirt/Turf (27 .33 $5.60), and Turf (49 .20 $3.32). The interesting fact about the Lloyd Mason turf success, however, was that it had occurred within the last 24 months, and running the basic query through the Formulator program was not at all enticing based on the past five years.

Trainer: Lloyd C. Mason
Time Frame: Past Five Years
Surface: First-Time Turf

Horses	Starts	Wins	ITM	Win%	ITM%	$2ROI	Median Payoff
37	37	3	13	8%	32%	$1.35	$6.46

However, when we changed the query from the past five years to the past two years, the win-percentage results improved from 8 percent to 20 percent, with a positive $2.65 ROI. (These numbers include the eventual win by Penny Power.) Some further massaging of the Formulator trainer query options enhanced the results even further. By adding the Dirt to Turf filter and the Routes option, Mason's percentage increased dramatically with a solid 43 percent winners and a tidy $7.92 ROI.

Trainer:	Lloyd C. Mason
Time Frame:	Past Two Years
Distance:	**Routes (>= 1 Mile)**
Surface:	**Dirt to Turf**

Horses	Starts	Wins	ITM	Win%	ITM%	$2ROI	Median Payoff
17	23	10	13	43%	57%	$7.92	$18.90

Having run through some different variables with trainer Lloyd Mason, there's a valuable lesson to be learned regarding trainer-angle handicapping and the timeliness of Trainer Form data. The longer the time-frame Formulator option selected, the larger the sample there will be to review. This is a good thing. The downside to the lengthy time period is that some trainers can be compared to major-league ballplayers in that they are very streaky. A trainer may win with his first turf-to-dirt starters in 2006, and then go 0 for 18 in the next 36 months with the same move. This is not a likely scenario, but it does happen.

In most circumstances trainers have a particular "specialty" or skill that they stick with over the long haul. But that's not always the case. For example, several years ago, New York trainer Nick Zito was horrible with first-time starters. In the last couple years alone his percentage has increased spectacularly with debut runners. Why? Zito changed his training regimen to get his runners more prepared in morning drills as opposed to having them learn from actual racetrack experience. There was a brief period at Saratoga racetrack during the summer of 2004 when the sharp handicapper could have cashed on many bonanza first-time-starter tickets with Zito debut runners.

IS THE GRASS GREENER?

TRAINER STATS FOR DIRT/TURF

Name	Starts	Wins	Win Percentage	ROI (Based on $2.00 to Win)
Wilson, Lorna S	21	8	0.381	$ 31.30
Houle, William	15	7	0.467	$ 27.80
Trujillo, Michael F	15	5	0.333	$ 20.40
King, James W	14	10	0.714	$ 15.60
Smith, Tracie L	22	5	0.227	$ 14.20
Morales, Nabu	20	6	0.300	$ 14.20
Gautreaux, Raymond	12	5	0.417	$ 13.80
Hofmans, Grant	30	9	0.300	$ 11.40
Loney, A. R.	17	6	0.353	$ 10.60
Kasmerski, Len	16	5	0.313	$ 10.30
DeStasio, Richard A	34	7	0.206	$ 10.30
Fout, Paul R	16	7	0.438	$ 10.20
Held, Dieter K	35	5	0.143	$ 9.13
Lawrence, Wray I	36	6	0.167	$ 8.63
Taylor, William D	23	10	0.435	$ 8.40
Mahorney, William	13	5	0.385	$ 7.98
Mayo, Larry A	56	11	0.196	$ 7.74
Smith, W. B.	16	5	0.313	$ 7.73
Nuesch, Patrick F	60	9	0.150	$ 7.61
Herrington, Paul	16	7	0.438	$ 7.25
Neff, Myles I	27	7	0.259	$ 7.19
Crider, Charlotte	49	8	0.163	$ 7.19
Bettis, Charles L	38	6	0.158	$ 7.15
McCarthy, William E	30	6	0.200	$ 7.04
Nielsen, Paul	20	8	0.400	$ 6.96

TRAINER STATS FOR TURF/DIRT

Name	Starts	Wins	Win Percentage	ROI (Based on $2.00 to Win)
Bischoff, Thomas E	9	5	0.556	$ 16.60
Creath, Heather	8	5	0.625	$ 15.30
Bush, Thomas M	32	14	0.438	$ 12.80
Aubrey, J. K.	14	6	0.429	$ 11.50
Fahey, III, John	11	7	0.636	$ 9.31
Bindner, Jr., Walter M	100	22	0.220	$ 7.33
Paulus, David E	28	10	0.357	$ 7.23

Fenimore, Floyd E	29	16	0.552	$ 7.11
Ferraro, James W	84	14	0.167	$ 7.10
Glorioso, Ronald S	19	5	0.263	$ 7.09
Morris, Neil R	26	8	0.308	$ 7.08
Grimm, Margaret E	20	9	0.450	$ 7.06
Gonzalez, Ramon O	18	6	0.333	$ 7.02
Peitz, Daniel C	69	9	0.130	$ 6.72
Tollett, Bill	21	8	0.381	$ 6.25
Bailey, Kelly L	22	6	0.273	$ 6.16
Christmas, William G	32	5	0.156	$ 6.14
Ketterman, Debra J	14	5	0.357	$ 6.14
Crook, W. B.	31	7	0.226	$ 6.06
Calhoun, Karl	14	5	0.357	$ 6.04
Huffman, William G	33	6	0.182	$ 5.95
Faulkner, Rodney C	17	7	0.412	$ 5.94
Delahoussaye, Glenn	29	13	0.448	$ 5.93
Edwards, Dennis S	12	8	0.667	$ 5.93
Morrison, Mike J	16	6	0.375	$ 5.90

THE SHORE'S GREATEST STRETCH

MONMOUTH PARK RECENTLY SPENT $4.5 million upgrading its outdated 1950 turf course. The new course, which sets the track up nicely to host the 2007 Breeders' Cup, allows for four different rail settings—hedge, 12 feet, 24 feet, and 36 feet. In addition, it has a second chute for five and five-and-a-half-furlong races, the latter being a first for Monmouth Park.

In the spring of 2006, with the initial races on the new surface not scheduled to be run for several weeks after opening day, any handicapper interested in playing the Monmouth card was unfortunately stuck with a menu of all-dirt races. The turf-racing devotees interested in only putting their green on the green would have to look elsewhere for betting opportunities. For those of us who were interested in rummaging through opening-day trainer stats at Monmouth Park, however, one excellent betting opportunity did emerge. It was a James Ryerson 3-year-old colt in the sixth race. The colt's name was Tiger D. R. and he was making his second start off a nearly two-month layoff while taking the all-important turf-to-dirt surface change.

1A Tiger D. R.
Own: DR Stable
6–1 Aqua, Pink R and Sash, Yellow Cuffs on $35,000
Garcia Alan (–) 2006:(347 49 .14)

Dk. b or br c. 3 (Mar) OBSMAR05 $60,000
Sire: Tiger Ridge (Storm Cat) $7,500
Dam: Lighting Cielo (Conquistador Cielo)
Br: Pedro Maestre(Fla)
Tr: Ryerson James T (–) 2006:(69 9 .13)

L 118

Life	8	1	0	1	$18,340	67	D.Fst	6	1	0	1	$17,790	67
2006	4	1	0	0	$11,850	67	Wet (365)	0	0	0	0	$0	-
2005	4	M	0	1	$6,490	57	Turf (315)	2	0	0	0	$550	63
Mth	2	0	0	0	$710	57	Dist (389)	2	1	0	0	$11,900	67

13Apr06-7GP fm 1 Ⓣ:222 :452 1:092 1:333 Clm 70000(75-65) 47 4 77¾ 59 89¾ 89¾ 716½ Trujillo E L118b 10.30 72-15 CrtRd1204¼ HsYrHl1201½ MstrPrspct120½ Bumped start, 3 wide 8
19Feb06-1GP fst 1 :242 :473 1:12 1:38 Md 45000 67 7 1½ 1hd 1hd 1hd 11¼ Bejarano R L122b 4.20 81-17 TgrD.R.1221¼ Mr.Mystry122½ RylDmn122nk Edged away late 8
1Feb06-7GP fst 7f :221 :444 1:102 1:231 Md 62500(62.5-57.5) 55 6 2 41 52¼ 44½ 411¼ Bejarano R L122b 7.30 81-09 The Yips1225½ *Shawnee Dancer* 1224 War Scandal1221¾ Tired 9
11Jan06-5GP fm 1 1/16 Ⓣ:221 :453 1:10 1:413 Md 62500(62.5-57.5) 63 7 53 54¼ 51½ 41¼ 52¾ Bejarano R L122b 5.10 80-16 CostlVow122nk SirOso122no UncBubb1202¼ 3 wide, gave way 12
11Nov05-6Medfst 1 :232 :464 1:121 1:384 Md Sp Wt 40k 50 2 31½ 31½ 31½ 32 43¾ Kaenel K5 L114b 2.50 77-14 PrkAvn119hd *CstlVw* 1191½ SrsBsnss1192¼ 3wd bid,leveled out 7
19Oct05-5Medfst 170 :222 :454 1:11 1:404 Md Sp Wt 34k 51 7 11½ 1½ 21 24 311 Rivera L Jr L119b 4.90 74-19 SntAgsts1198½ ThWrrr1122½ TgrD.R.1192 Set pace, weakened 7
25Sep05-2Mthfst 170 :232 :474 1:123 1:43 Md Sp Wt 36k 57 1 11 11 1½ 31½ 56¾ Rivera L Jr L119b 32.70 72-16 *Fgn'sLgcy* 1195 PrkAvn119hd MmbMstr1191 Pace,weakened 1/8 8
6Aug05-5Mthfst 5½f :223 :46 :582 1:044 Md Sp Wt 37k 14 6 8 87½ 88¾ 814 823¼ Baze M C L119b 4.40e 68-12 MstrAlmny1192½ TnGd1191½ *TwnCncl* 1192¼ Away slowly, outrun 8

WORKS: Apr8 PmM 5f fst 1:003 H *3/16* Apr1 PmM 5f fst 1:021 B *9/14* Mar25 PmM 5f fst 1:04 B *32/34*
TRAINER: 2Off45-180 (41 .12 $1.91) Turf/Dirt (17 .24 $1.82) Dirt (290 .13 $1.69) Routes (163 .13 $1.52) Claim (90 .12 $1.24) J/T 2005-06 MTH (1 .00 $0.00) J/T 2005-06 (2 .00 $0.00)

Although the colt had been soundly beaten at Gulfstream Park for a $70,000 tag, he did have a legitimate trouble line in that one-mile turf event. Today he was taking a drastic drop to the $35,000 claiming level, and Ryerson's turf-to-dirt Trainer Form stats (Turf/Dirt 17 .24 $1.82) indicated that he had some prior success with the tactic, further supporting the colt's chances.

Tiger D. R. won easily, and the subsequent Formulator Default Query rundown that includes that victory appeared as follows:

Trainer: James T. Ryerson
Time Frame: Past Five Years
Surface: Turf to Dirt

Horses	Starts	Wins	ITM	Win%	ITM%	$2ROI	Median Payoff
42	63	16	32	25%	51%	$2.46	$9.70

By simply adding the other main Trainer Form layoff stats to the mix, Ryerson's win percentage soared to nearly 40 percent. The main point here is that there are various trainer angles in place that are worth noting and massaging through the Formulator program.

Trainer: James T. Ryerson
Time Frame: Past Five Years
Days/Starts: 2nd After Layoff
Surface: Turf to Dirt

Horses	Starts	Wins	ITM	Win%	ITM%	$2ROI	Median Payoff
7	8	3	4	38%	50%	$4.50	$13.20

In fact, by just using the 50% Claiming Tag Drop option, Ryerson scores with 22 percent of these runners.

TRAINER ANGLES

Trainer:	James T. Ryerson
Time Frame:	Past Five Years
Class Moves:	**50% Claiming Tag Drop**

Horses	Starts	Wins	ITM	Win%	ITM%	$2ROI	Median Payoff
19	23	5	11	22%	48%	$1.99	$10.40

SIXTH RACE
Monmouth
MAY 13, 2006

1 MILE. (1.33⁴) CLAIMING . Purse $30,000 FOR THREE YEAR OLDS OR FOUR YEAR OLDS AND UPWARD WHICH HAVE NEVER WON TWO RACES. Three Year Olds, 120 lbs.; Older, 124 lbs. Non–winners of a race since March 14 Allowed 2 lbs. Claiming Price $35,000, For Each $2,500 To $30,000 1 lb. (Races where entered for $28,000 or less not considered in allowances).

Value of Race: $30,000 Winner $18,000; second $6,000; third $3,300; fourth $1,500; fourth $300; sixth $300; seventh $300; eighth $300. Mutuel Pool $131,096.00 Exacta Pool $128,563.00 Trifecta Pool $79,863.00

Last Raced	Horse	M/Eqt. A. Wt	PP	St	¼	½	¾	Str	Fin	Jockey	Cl'g Pr	Odds $1
13Apr06 7GP7	Tiger D. R.	L b 3 118	7	5	2½	2³	2⁵	2⁴	1²½	Garcia Alan	35000	a-5.60
30Mar06 6GP3	Call the Marines	L bf 4 122	6	4	1½	1½	1½	1½	2⁴½	Chavez J F	35000	2.60
30Mar06 2GP3	Cherokee Breeze	L bf 4 124	1	7	7⁵	7³½	6³	4¹	3½	King E L Jr	35000	8.70
4Mar06 5Aqu3	DH Afleet Tiger	L f 3 118	5	8	8	8	7hd	5²	4	Velez J A Jr	35000	a-5.60
1Apr06 1Aqu3	DH Colonial Silver	L f 4 122	4	1	4hd	3hd	3¹	3²	4¹0¾	Castro E	35000	2.70
4May06 8Atl7	Loquacious Lover	L b 4 122	8	6	3hd	5²	5½	7⁵	6½	Black A S	35000	11.40
6Apr06 1Aqu2	Henry's Appeal	L b 3 118	2	2	6⁴½	6³½	4²	6¹	7¹¹½	Bravo J	35000	*2.60
23Apr06 3GP3	King's Choice	L 4 122	3	3	5¹	4hd	8	8	8	Maragh R	35000	18.00

DH–Dead Heat.
*–Actual Betting Favorite.
a–Coupled: Tiger D. R. and Afleet Tiger.

OFF AT 3:20 Start Good. Won driving. Track fast.
TIME :23⁴, :47³, 1:12³, 1:39² (:23.90, :47.60, 1:12.64, 1:39.42)

$2 Mutuel Prices:

1A– TIGER D. R.(a–entry)	13.20	5.00	3.40
6 – CALL THE MARINES		4.60	3.00
2 – CHEROKEE BREEZE			3.60

$2 EXACTA 1–6 PAID $67.80 $2 TRIFECTA 1–6–2 PAID $395.20

Dk. b or br. g, (Mar), by Tiger Ridge – Lighting Cielo , by Conquistador Cielo . Trainer Ryerson James T. Bred by Pedro Maestre (Fla).

TIGER D. R. rated close to the pace two deep, dug in gamely from the top of the stretch and was inching clear the final seventy yards. CALL THE MARINES rated the pace inside, was pressured for more into the final turn, stayed on with a short advantage from the top of the stretch but began weakening toward the sixteenth pole. CHEROKEE BREEZE settled in toward mid track near the back of the pack, bid widest on the final turn and finished evenly. AFLEET TIGER settled in off the rail after a slow start then finished with energy. COLONIAL SILVER was kept off the pace while off the rail and proved empty in the lane. LOQUACIOUS LOVER gave chase for a half mile then tired. HENRY'S APPEAL was outrun. KING'S CHOICE was through after half.

Owners– 1, D R Stable; 2, Phantom House Farm; 3, Robinson J Mack; 4, Potash Edward C; 5, C D and G Stable; 6, Bardaro Anthony J and Pierce Jr Joseph H; 7, Silly Goose Racing Stable; 8, Iwin 02

Trainers– 1, Ryerson James T; 2, Forbes John H; 3, Croll William E; 4, Ryerson James T; 5, Klesaris Robert P; 6, Pierce Joseph H Jr; 7, Breen Kelly J; 8, Lee Garry F

$2 Pick Three (1–6–1) Paid $1,343.80 ; Pick Three Pool $12,543 .

CREATURES OF HABIT

TRAINER ANGLES ARE AMONG the most useful and important handicapping factors for one single reason: Trainers are creatures of habit. If they find an angle or maneuver that has produced some success in the past, they are likely to keep using it. However, in some unique circumstances, a trainer will continue to plug along and utilize a training tactic despite dismal results. Under these conditions, the Formulator program can be used as an excellent source to eliminate bad bets instead of finding potential winners. One such example occurred in the fourth race at Hollywood Park on May 27, 2006, a one-mile maiden-special-weight turf event. Trainer Jack Van Berg entered his 3-year-old colt A Big To'do. Van Berg was off to an excellent Hollywood Park meet, clicking with 22 percent of his entries (22 5 1 1 .22), which was far above his 10 percent overall 2006 record.

2 A Big To'do
Own: Robert Kruger
Pink, black '$' emblem on back, black
Baze T C (96 13 5 15 .13) 2006:(444 48 .11)

B. c. 3 (Feb)
Sire: Wild Event (Wild Again) $7,500
Dam: Wool Princess*Fr (Direct Flight)
Br: Marilyn Fazio Seltzer(Fla)
Tr: Van Berg Jack C (22 5 1 1 .22) 2006:(99 10 .10)

Blinkers ON
L 116

Life	4	M	0	0	$3,960	69	D.Fst	1	0	0	0	$400	43
2006	3	M	0	0	$3,560	69	Wet (302)	0	0	0	0	$0	-
2005	1	M	0	0	$400	43	Turf (324)	3	0	0	0	$3,560	69
Hol (T)	0	0	0	0	$0	-	Dist (283)	2	0	0	0	$3,160	69

16Apr06-9SA fm 1⅛ (T):461 1:112 1:363 1:483 Md Sp Wt 52k 59 2 78 87¼ 74 95¾ 89½ John K LB121f 52.00 76-14 Ppnn1211¼ LmnLw 121hd Ptmnyrwll121nk Saved ground, no rally 12
30Mar06-6SA fm 1 (T):243 :491 1:132 1:37 Md Sp Wt 52k 62 2 43 73¾ 64½ 78 67¾ John K LB120f 16.50 70-22 CryCnty 120¾ Brnsfld1201 Cmsd1202¼ Saved ground, weakened 10
11Jan06-4SA fm 1 (T):233 :483 1:131 1:372 Md Sp Wt 48k 69 5 32 41½ 41¼ 41¾ 42¾ Emigh C A LB122 48.80 73-24 PtrndZo122¾ VctorySgn1221 Brnsfld1221 Steadied,in tight late 11
3Dec05-5Hol fst 6½f :214 :443 1:094 1:163 Md Sp Wt 43k 43 10 8 95¼ 109¼ 1313 1315¼ Farina T B120 103.00 72-10 PcChnt1203¼ DndScr1201 RcCrPss1202¼ 3wd btwn,weakened 13

WORKS: May17 Hol 5f fst 1:014 H 10/18 Apr8 Hol 5f fst 1:021 H 44/63 Mar26 Hol 5f fst 1:041 H 34/36 Mar12 Hol 5f fst 1:051 H 36/37

TRAINER: 1stBlink (16 .13 $1.35) BlinkOn (17 .12 $1.27) 31-60Days (45 .04 $0.54) Turf (59 .07 $1.59) Routes (98 .09 $2.57) MdnSpWt (50 .06 $J/T 2005-06 HOL (14 .14 $1.84) J/T 2005-06 (34 .12 $5.60)

The colt was making his fourth start on the turf for the year after three consecutive subpar efforts, but would race with blinkers this time. Perhaps the addition of shades and the jockey switch to Tyler Baze would be the wake-up call the colt required for an improved performance. The DRF Trainer Form stats for 1st Blink (16 .13 $1.35) and BlinkOn (17 .12 $1.27) were not awful, but were a far cry from what would be revealed with the Formulator software. The Default Query appeared as follows:

Trainer:	Jack C. Van Berg
Time Frame:	Past Five Years
Blinkers:	**Blinkers On**

Horses	Starts	Wins	ITM	Win%	ITM%	$2ROI	Median Payoff
84	363	17	70	5%	19%	$0.76	$10.20

At a 5 percent win ratio, the results were obviously very discouraging. Any reasonable handicapper could have easily justified making an automatic toss based on these dismal numbers. It seemed almost impossible that Van Berg's percentage could get any worse until you added today's surface to the mix. At 1 for 72 and barely a quarter ROI for every $2 wagered, this 22 percent trainer appeared to have landed A Big To'do in an impossible spot. The question that immediately comes to mind is, why would Van Berg continue to place his runners in these types of hapless situations? Your guess is as good as mine. As handicappers and believers of trainer stats, we have to follow the numbers and leave the "why" and "how" to someone else. A Big To'do ran to his expectations, finishing eighth at 39–1.

Trainer:	Jack C. Van Berg
Time Frame:	Past Five Years
Blinkers:	Blinkers On
Surface:	**Turf**

Horses	Starts	Wins	ITM	Win%	ITM%	$2ROI	Median Payoff
24	72	1	11	1%	15%	$0.24	$17.40

FOURTH RACE
Hollywood

1 MILE. (Turf) (1.32³) MAIDEN SPECIAL WEIGHT . Purse $46,000 (plus $13,800 CBOIF – CA Bred Owner Fund) FOR MAIDENS, THREE YEAR OLDS AND UPWARD. Three Year Olds, 116 lbs.; Older, 124 lbs.

MAY 27, 2006

Value of Race: $48,400 Winner $27,600; second $9,200; third $5,520; fourth $2,760; fifth $920; sixth $400; seventh $400; eighth $400; ninth $400; tenth $400; eleventh $400. Mutuel Pool $466,266.00 Exacta Pool $307,778.00 Quinella Pool $19,803.00 Trifecta Pool $269,002.00 Superfecta Pool $166,395.00

Last Raced	Horse	M/Eqt.	A.	Wt	PP	St	¼	½	¾	Str	Fin	Jockey	Odds $1
30Mar06 6SA²	Bransfield	LB	3	116	9	9	8½	8½	7½	6¹	1no	Espinoza V	2.40
16Apr06 9SA⁴	Camisado-FR	LB b	3	116	4	2	22½	2¹	2²	1²	2hd	Valdivia J Jr	6.60
6May06 6Hol⁶	Putmeinyourwill	LB b	3	116	3	4	4³	3hd	3¹	2½	3¾	Gryder A T	6.40
26Mar06 9SA⁴	Victory Sign	LB	3	119	6	10	10¹	102½	9²	5hd	4¾	Valenzuela P A	2.80
	Sofocles-Brz	LB	4	124	1	8	92½	7¹	6¹	3hd	5¾	Flores D R	28.10
8Apr06 5SA⁵	City Swagger	LB b	3	117	11	7	6¹	6hd	5½	7⁴	62¼	Cohen D	33.00
6May06 6Hol⁴	Paradise Cove	LB b	4	124	5	1	1¹	1⁴	1hd	4¹	71¼	Court J K	5.70
16Apr06 9SA⁸	A Big To'do	LB bf	3	116	2	5	7hd	9½	102½	91½	8¹	Baze T C	39.30
4Sep05 6Dmr⁷	Saporous	LB	3	116	8	6	5½	5¹	8hd	8hd	9⁴	Baze M C	11.90
26Apr06 6Hol⁸	Mritimecommnder	LB b	3	116	7	3	3hd	4³	4hd	102½	102¼	John K	119.90
	Corkonian	LB	3	119	10	11	11	11	11	11	11	Nakatani C S	20.90

OFF AT 2:55 Start Good. Won driving. Course firm.

TIME :22⁴, :45⁴, 1:10¹, 1:22¹, 1:34³ (:22.91, :45.97, 1:10.24, 1:22.37, 1:34.66)

$2 Mutuel Prices:

10 – BRANSFIELD	6.80	3.80	3.00
4 – CAMISADO-FR.		6.20	3.60
3 – PUTMEINYOURWILL			3.80

$1 EXACTA 10–4 PAID $17.00 $2 QUINELLA 4–10 PAID $22.40
$1 TRIFECTA 10–4–3 PAID $69.80 $1 SUPERFECTA 10–4–3–7 PAID $258.10

Dk. b or br. c, (Mar), by Runaway Groom – Butterscotch Sauce , by Clever Trick . Trainer Shirreffs John. Bred by Normandy Farm (Ky).

BRANSFIELD chased three deep then outside a rival, continued outside on the second turn and four wide into the stretch and rallied under urging to get up late. CAMISADO (FR) stalked inside then a bit off the rail, bid outside a foe leaving the second turn, took the lead, kicked clear in the stretch and fought back just off the rail late. PUTMEINYOURWILL saved ground stalking the pace, swung out into the stretch, bid between foes in deep stretch and continued willingly to the wire. VICTORY SIGN bumped and checked at the start,.settled inside then a bit off the rail, continued inside on the second turn, came out for room in midstretch, waited off heels between foes in deep stretch, came out again and finished well. SOFOCLES (BRZ) chased inside then a bit off the rail, angled in again on the second turn, bid inside in the stretch and was outfinished. CITY SWAGGER stalked the pace outside then three deep on the second turn and into the stretch and lacked the needed rally. PARADISE COVE broke outward, had speed outside a rival then angled in and set the pace inside, dueled along the rail leaving the second turn and weakened in the stretch. A BIG TO'DO saved ground off the pace, swung out into the stretch and could not summon the necessary response. SAPOROUS broke a bit awkwardly, chased a bit off the rail then between foes and weakened. MARITIME COMMANDER bumped at the start, was in a good position stalking the pace outside a rival then between horses leaving the second turn and also weakened. CORKONIAN angled in and settled a bit off the rail and was outrun.

Owners– 1, Moss Mr and Mrs Jerome S; 2, Laird P R and Linda; 3, Malibu Farm LLC; 4, Gary and Mary West Stables Inc; 5, Fast Lane Farms Old Friends Inc and TNT Stud; 6, Everest Stables Inc; 7, Maggio Carl S and Way Michael James; 8, Kruger Robert R; 9, Fontana Racing LLC and Pearson Deron; 10, Youkhanna Jr Joel Joel and Joette; 11, Super Horse Inc

Trainers– 1, Shirreffs John; 2, Harty Eoin; 3, Mandella Richard; 4, Frankel Robert; 5, Lobo Paulo H; 6, Canani Julio C; 7, Cardenas Ruben; 8, Van Berg Jack C; 9, Cassidy James; 10, Mayberry Summer; 11, Gallagher Patrick

Scratched– Wildfang (29Apr06 4Hol⁷) , Ebony Light (23Apr06 ¹GG ²) , Bullish Yield (06May06 6Hol⁵)

$2 Daily Double (4–10) Paid $81.80 ; Daily Double Pool $34,559 .
$1 Pick Three (5–4–10) Paid $346.30 ; Pick Three Pool $72,596 .
$1 Pick Four (2–5–4–5/10) Paid $788.40 ; Pick Four Pool $187,871 .
$1 Consolation Pick 3 (5–4–5) Paid $87.00 .
$2 Consolation Daily Double (4–56) Paid $19.40 .

TRAINER STATS FOR TURF

Name	Starts	Wins	Win Percentage	ROI (Based on $2.00 to Win)
Wilson, Lorna S	41	10	0.244	$ 17.60
Waskow, John E	16	5	0.313	$ 15.50
Morales, Nabu	20	6	0.300	$ 14.20
Barbanti, Philip	15	9	0.600	$ 14.20
Houle, William	16	5	0.313	$ 10.20
Miller, Gregory D	13	6	0.462	$ 9.91
Di Marsico, Elaine	34	5	0.147	$ 9.85
Gautreaux, Raymond	17	5	0.294	$ 9.74
Taylor, Robert J	12	6	0.500	$ 9.43
Kasmerski, Len	3	6	0.261	$ 8.81
Pattershall, Mary A	18	5	0.278	$ 8.32
Loney, A. R.	28	9	0.321	$ 7.78
Smith, Tracie L	41	5	0.122	$ 7.63
Reynolds, Ryan	30	8	0.267	$ 7.44
Walsh, Timothy J	54	12	0.222	$ 7.43
Gonzalez, Ramon O	33	6	0.182	$ 7.16
King, James W	34	13	0.382	$ 6.94
Langemeier, John L	24	5	0.208	$ 6.83
Herrington, Paul	25	10	0.400	$ 6.62
Bean, Robert A	47	6	0.128	$ 6.29
Schuh, Tim	33	6	0.182	$ 6.19
Smith, W. B.	26	8	0.308	$ 6.05
Dunn, Stephen D	20	6	0.300	$ 6.01
Whittingham, Michael C	61	7	0.115	$ 5.93
Hofmans, Grant	66	14	0.212	$ 5.80

6

EQUIPMENT CHANGES AND MEDICATION

BLINKERS

TRAINERS USE BLINKERS TO get their horses to focus on running. As you'll see from the lists on pages 107 and 111, the first-blinkers and blinkers-off equipment changes can be valuable and profitable training makeovers. Blinkers come in all varieties—full cup, half-cup, and even an extension blinker for a horse with habitual lugging or drifting running habits. Some conditioners, such as Amy Albright, Tim Schuh, and Kenneth B. Parsley, consistently click with almost three-quarters of their starters when applying the equipment change. Not to mention Rodriguez C. Santiago, who is a perfect 6 for 6 with horses removing blinkers! This is simply an incredible accomplishment. For all our El Commandante racing fans out there, this is one trainer angle for the record books and definitely worth paying close attention to when looking to capitalize on an automatic trainer play.

Typically, the addition or removal of blinkers best assists maidens and horses with limited racing experience. These types of horses are still learning the ropes and may be easily distracted by various external racetrack variables. The key word is *focus*. The addition of blinkers on a horse that characteristically shows some good early gate speed or has a win-early, speed-oriented pedigree is an excellent sign. This type of runner should be able to use its new equipment to stay focused while clearing the field early.

The addition or removal of blinkers is an even more important sign when combined with another trainer maneuver such as a class drop, distance or surface change, or jockey switch. This usually indicates true trainer intent. Fortunately, the DRF Formulator software program allows easy and thorough analyses of these exact scenarios. The good news is that you can even improve upon the general blinker-change Trainer Form stats when combining another factor that may also be intended to enhance a runner's performance.

These types of complete makeovers occur daily and can be found at almost any racetrack in the United States or Canada. Speaking of Canada, let's take a look at a maiden-special-weight route for 3-year-olds and upward on the turf at Woodbine. In this example, trainer Mark Frostad drew the cozy 1 hole for Paradoxical. The Forest Camp gelding was receiving complete alterations in the equipment and medication departments. Frostad is the private trainer for the powerhouse Sam-Son Farms and its talented string of runners. Could Paradoxical fit that description? Frostad's general stats for the current meet (18 2 4 4 .11) and year (31 4 .13) were nothing extraordinary.

Paradoxical
Own: Sam-Son Farms

B. g. 3 (Apr)
Sire: Forest Camp (Deputy Minister) $25,000
Dam: Mimi La Sardine (Tank's Prospect)
Br: Timothy Thornton (Ky)
Tr: Frostad Mark R(18 2 4 4 .11) 2006:(31 4 .13)

Blinkers OFF

L

Life	1 M 0 1	$7,260 47	D.Fst	0 0 0 0	$0 –
2005	1 M 0 0	$357 47	Wet(358)	0 0 0 0	$0 –
2004	1 M 0 1	$6,199 –	Turf(264*)	0 0 1	$7,260 47
WO ⑦	0 0 0 0	$0 47	Dst⑦(341)	0 0 0 0	$7,260 47

24Sep05– 8WO fm 1 ⑦ :23¹ :47¹ 1:13¹1:38¹   Md Sp Wt 68k   47 4 64¾ 53¾ 2hd 1hd 33¼ Wilson E⁵   115 b 27.50 64– 23 Pfifficus120² Arabian Star120¹¼ Paradoxical115ⁿᵏ   Yielded final 1/16th 12
WORKS: Jun16 WO tr.t⑦ 7f fm 1:29 B(d) 3/4   Jun7 WO tr.t⑦ 7f fm 1:31² H(d) 1/2   May24 WO tr.t⑦ 7f gd 1:32 H(d) 2/3   May18 WO 5f gd 1:01³ Hg 18/58   May9 WO 5f fst 1:03 H 28/49   Apr30 WO 4f fst :50¹ B 28/29
TRAINER: +180Days (29 .03 $0.15)   2ndStart(19 .32 $3.02)   1stLasix(6 .50 $3.02)   BlinkOff(2 .50 $3.70)   Turf(134 .12 $0.89)   Routes(124 .12 $0.92)   J/T 2005–06 WO (134 .21 $1.52) J/T 2005–06 (36 .19 $1.44)

Paradoxical was making his second career start off an extended layoff, adding Lasix, and removing blinkers. The Formulator Default Query appeared as the following, which did not take into consideration the addition of Lasix and the removal of blinkers.

Trainer: M. Frostad
Time Frame: Past Five Years
Days/Starts: Second Career Start

Horses	Starts	Wins	ITM	Win%	ITM%	$2ROI	Median Payoff
92	92	24	53	26%	58%	$2.18	$7.15

Without even adding the equipment and medication filters, Frostad was already showing a positive ROI with any horse making its second career start. We could have stopped right there with the Formulator filtering process and considered him a definite threat based on other handicapping factors. Paradoxical had shown good positional speed in his debut on the green at long odds (27–1). He battled gamely for the front before fading to third. What went amiss after that promising start is hard to say, but he had a steady string of six works since the second week of April, including one seven-furlong stamina drill on the grass itself a week earlier. It was another encouraging sign. By adding the First Time Lasix angle, Frostad's percentage started a steady climb. However, his ROI showed a small decline.

Trainer:	M. Frostad
Time Frame:	Past Five Years
Days/Starts:	Second Career Start
Lasix:	**First Time Lasix**

Horses	Starts	Wins	ITM	Win%	ITM%	$2ROI	Median Payoff
18	18	5	12	28%	67%	$2.09	$7.40

As discussed in earlier chapters, one of the downfalls when there are multiple trainer angles and patterns at work simultaneously is that your Formulator sample becomes too small and less meaningful. If we were to link up all the equipment, layoff, and medication factors in play, we'd be left with the following limited sample.

Trainer:	M. Frostad
Time Frame:	Past Five Years
Blinkers:	Blinkers Off
Days/Starts:	Second Career Start
Lasix:	First Time Lasix
Surface:	Turf

Horses	Starts	Wins	ITM	Win%	ITM%	$2ROI	Median Payoff
6	6	1	5	17%	83%	$1.23	$7.40

With only six races to evaluate, we have little concrete data to assess. However, the 5-of-6 in-the-money percentage is probably a good enough reason to conclude that Paradoxical is a live mount this afternoon. A more realistic sample is to keep the filters at a more wide-ranging search. By adding just the Blinkers Off filter, Frostad's win percentage climbs to a favorable 29 percent with a positive ROI, which is far greater than his 13 percent mark for the year.

BLINKS AND BIANCONE

TRAINER PATRICK BIANCONE LEARNED his trade from his father while growing up in Chantilly, France. He is a true master of his craft. As a former rider and now an established trainer for several decades, there are not too many horsemen in the world matching his extreme talent. He first came to attention in the United States by winning the 1983 Horse of the Year title with the French filly All Along, and has since trained some gifted runners on both grass and dirt, including Whywhywhy, Zavata, Lion Heart, Gorella, and Mayakovsky.

Mayakovsky happened to be one of my personal favorite sprinters. I was fortunate enough to be doing some book-publishing business with Mayakovsky's exercise rider a few months before his debut at Saratoga back in 2001. When the rider assertively proclaimed, "He's the fastest horse I've ever worked in the morning," I was immediately sold on his ability and anxiously awaited his arrival in the entry box. As touted, Mayakovsky not only went on to win his 5½-furlong debut, but broke a long-standing track record at the Spa while doing so.

The only negative factor with backing runners from the Biancone barn is that they are usually heavily bet at the windows. Therefore, finding value can be tricky. When Biancone makes an equipment change, it's usually in the handicapper's best interest to take notice.

When Patrick Biancone's highly regarded 3-year-old-colt Kilimanjaro, by Boundary, turned up in the entries on February 3, 2006, at Santa Anita, I was expecting a big performance.

1 Kilimanjaro
Own: Michael B. Tabor, Derrick Smith and Mrs.
2–1 Royal blue, orange ball, orange stripes
Leparoux J R (25 5 5 4 .20) 2006:(554 172 .31)

Dk. b or br c. 3 (Feb) FTFFEB05 $400,000
Sire: Boundary (Danzig) $10,000
Dam: Wayage (Mr. Prospector)
Br: Lucy G. Bassett(Ky)
Tr: Biancone Patrick L (11 2 2 3 .18) 2006:(80 21 .26)

Blinkers ON
Ⓛ 118^{5}

Life	4	1	0	0	$32,370	87	D.Fst	3	0	0	0	$5,370	87
2006	2	0	0	0	$3,120	87	Wet (407)	1	1	0	0	$27,000	73
2005	2	1	0	0	$29,250	73	Turf (302)	0	0	0	0	$0	-
Kee	0	0	0	0	$0	-	Dist (404)	1	0	0	0	$2,250	62

4Mar06-10TP fst 1$\frac{1}{16}$◈ :23^{3} :47^{3} 1:12^{2} 1:46^{4} JBttgliaMm100k 74 10 7$4\frac{1}{4}$ 7$4\frac{1}{4}$ 7$3\frac{1}{4}$ 8$4\frac{1}{4}$ 7$3\frac{3}{4}$ Leparoux J R 115 *2.20 84-19 Lity121½ PirofKings115½ NwAwkning115^{nk} 3 wide, lacked bid 12
3Feb06-7SA fst 1 :22^{3} :46 1:10^{2} 1:36 Alw 53600N1X 87 4 9^{14} 8^{12} 6$6\frac{1}{2}$ 4$4\frac{1}{2}$ 4$5\frac{1}{4}$ Solis A B118 12.00 83-20 OnUnn118$2\frac{1}{4}$ *PntDtrmnd* 120^{3} *Rfnr* 118^{hd} Bumped strt,missed 3rd 9
20Aug05-5Sar my^{S}7f :22 :45^{1} 1:12^{1} 1:26^{1} Md Sp Wt 45k 73 10 3 8$5\frac{3}{4}$ 6$5\frac{1}{2}$ 2^{hd} 1$\frac{3}{4}$ Stevens G L 118 *1.60 73-22 Kilimnjro118$\frac{3}{4}$ Pulpitr118^{4} FlshyBull118$2\frac{1}{4}$ Split rivals, gamely 12
30Jly05-5Sar fst 6f :22^{3} :46 :58^{1} 1:11^{2} Md Sp Wt 45k 62 3 10 10^{11} 9$8\frac{1}{4}$ 6^{11} 4$9\frac{1}{4}$ Stevens G L 118 4.50 74-17 *PrvtVow* 118$2\frac{1}{4}$ FlshyBull118$4\frac{1}{2}$ ThoWrror118$2\frac{1}{2}$ Checked stretch 12

WORKS: ●Apr12 TP 4f fst :49 B *1/18* Apr5 TP 6f fst 1:14^{1} Bg *1/3* Mar24 TP 4f fst :48 B *2/34* ●Mar1 TP 4f fst :47^{1} B *1/10* ●Feb23 TP 5f fst 1:00^{2} B *1/22* ●Feb17 TP 4f fst :48^{1} B *1/26*

TRAINER: 1stBlink (16 .06 $0.25) BlinkOn (20 .10 $0.32) Route/Sprint (18 .28 $2.26) 31-60Days (50 .24 $1.91) Dirt (163 .22 $1.51) Sprint (82 .30J/T 2005-06 KEE (11 .18 $1.91) J/T 2005-06 (63 .29 $1.86)

The $400,000 colt had won a maiden race at Saratoga as a 2-year-old on a muddy track, and his potential looked promising heading into his 3-year-old season. After a troubled beginning, Kilimanjaro made an eye-catching middle move against eventual winner One Union and the Bob Baffert-trained Derby hopeful Point Determined. Kilimanjaro was a soundly beaten fourth, by 5¼ lengths, but it was a decent performance considering the almost six-month layoff. His next start came on March 4 over Turfway Park's new Polytrack, in a minor stakes at 1$\frac{1}{16}$ miles. After looking at the Biancone colt's incredibly sharp morning drills over the new surface, I was confident that he would gobble up the competition despite the outside post draw. To my surprise, as the 2–1 favorite with leading rider Julien Leparoux aboard, Kilimanjaro ran a disappointing seventh.

Five weeks later, when Kilimanjaro was entered in a nonwinners-of-two allowance sprint at Keeneland, I was willing to give him one more shot starting from the golden inside post position. Biancone was also giving his colt a complete makeover, adding both Lasix and blinkers to the mix. At first glance, the First Time Blinkers (1stBlink 16 .06 $0.25) and Blinkers On (Blink On 20 .10 $0.32) angles looked like a losing proposition for the stable. However, after running the following queries through the Formulator program, we did expose an improved win ratio that was clearly better than what was available in the past-performance lines.

Trainer:	Patrick L. Biancone
Time Frame:	Past Five Years
Blinkers:	**Blinkers On**
Lasix:	**First Time Lasix**

Horses	Starts	Wins	ITM	Win%	ITM%	$2ROI	Median Payoff
23	23	6	10	26%	43%	$1.41	$4.50

In this scenario I was able to combine some valuable trip notes with a favorable Formulator pattern for a $9 payoff, which seemed generous for a colt that was listed as the 2–1 second choice in the morning line.

FOURTH RACE
Keeneland
APRIL 15, 2006

6 FURLONGS. (1.07³) ALLOWANCE . Purse $54,000 (includes $8,100 KTDF – KY TB Devt Fund) FOR THREE YEAR OLDS WHICH HAVE NEVER WON TWO RACES. Weight, 123 lbs. Non–winners Of $19,200 Allowed 3 lbs. Non–winners Of A Race Other Than Claiming Allowed 5 lbs.

Value of Race: $52,380 Winner $33,723; second $9,180; third $5,400; fourth $2,700; fifth $1,377. Mutuel Pool $463,508.00 Exacta Pool $311,836.00 Trifecta Pool $198,738.00 Superfecta Pool $59,598.00 Quinella Pool $12,701.00

Last Raced	Horse	M/Eqt.	A.	Wt	PP	St	¼	½	Str	Fin	Jockey	Odds $1
4Mar06 10TP7	Kilimanjaro	L	3	118	1	3	3¹	3⁴	2²	1¹	Leparoux J R⁵	3.50
18Mar06 7GP1	In Certain Circles	L	3	123	2	1	2½	1½	1hd	2¹¹¾	Douglas R R	4.40
10Jly05 10CD9	Fifty Seven Flat	L	3	123	6	2	1hd	2¹	3³½	3¹½	Bejarano R	10.20
25Mar06 7TP6	Miner's Lamp	L b	3	123	3	5	6	6	4hd	4³½	Guidry M	15.60
5Nov05 2CD2	He's a Dixie Boy	L	3	120	4	4	5⁴	5⁴	5⁵	5¹³½	Castanon J L	22.30
8Mar06 3GP1	Prize Cat	L	3	123	5	6	4²½	4¹½	6	6	Velazquez J R	0.60

OFF AT 2:48 Start Good. Won driving. Track fast.
TIME :22, :45³, :57⁴, 1:10¹ (:22.05, :45.71, :57.90, 1:10.34)

$2 Mutuel Prices:

1 – KILIMANJARO.....................	9.00	4.40	3.20
2 – IN CERTAIN CIRCLES..............		4.40	3.40
6 – FIFTY SEVEN FLAT................			4.20

$2 EXACTA 1–2 PAID $30.60 $2 TRIFECTA 1–2–6 PAID $178.40
$2 SUPERFECTA 1–2–6–3 PAID $839.80 $2 QUINELLA 1–2 PAID $19.40

Dk. b or br. c, (Feb), by Boundary – Wayage , by Mr. Prospector . Trainer Biancone Patrick L. Bred by Lucy G Bassett (Ky).

KILIMANJARO, nicely positioned in behind the dueling leaders from early on, eased out four wide leaving the turn, collared front-running IN CERTAIN CIRCLES a furlong out and bested that one under pressure. IN CERTAIN CIRCLES went up inside to vie for the lead early, battled with FIFTY SEVEN FLAT, gained the edge on the turn, held on well until deep stretch but couldn't contain KILIMANJARO while superior to the others. FIFTY SEVEN FLAT drifted out while bobbling at the start, went up soon after to gain a slim lead, battled with IN CERTAIN CIRCLES to the stretch and couldn't keep pace. MINER'S LAMP, three or four wide, was outrun to the lane, made a mild run into the upper stretch but failed to continue the effort. HE'S A DIXIE BOY, four wide most of the way, wasn't a serious factor. PRIZE CAT bobbled when breaking awkwardly, quickly recovered, tracked the pace four wide for a half and tired.

Owners– 1, Tabor Michael B Magnier Mrs John and Smith Derrick; 2, WinStar Farm LLC; 3, Van Meter II Thomas and Hendrickson Doug; 4, Overbrook Farm; 5, McClinton Donald G; 6, Jones Aaron U and Marie D

Trainers– 1, Biancone Patrick L; 2, Asmussen Steven M; 3, Nicks Ralph E; 4, Stewart Dallas; 5, Bindner Walter M Jr; 6, Pletcher Todd A

$2 Pick Three (6–4–1) Paid $99.60 ; Pick Three Pool $65,111 .

MONDAY AT THE MEADOWLANDS

ON A MONDAY AFTERNOON in June 2006, the Meadowlands Racetrack in East Rutherford, New Jersey, was holding an all-grass card. It was the first of a few all-grass Monday events that were actualy part of the Monmouth Park racing meet. The first scheduled event a week earlier had been washed off by heavy rains. Monmouth Park had yet to open its newly remodeled turf course, which was being handled delicately in preparation for the 2007 Breeders' Cup. For those looking to take an extended lunch or perhaps suffering from the Monday doldrums, there was no better remedy than live Thoroughbred racing in East Rutherford. The Meadowlands offered just that with full, competitive fields on a brilliantly sunny early-summer work afternoon.

In the fifth race, Biancone entered his 3-year-old filly Kitty Hawk in the small $60,000 Trenton Stakes. It was to be contested at 1 1/16 miles. Kitty Hawk was lightly raced, with only five lifetime starts, and two of those starts took place in Ireland and France. It was no surprise that Biancone was adding blinkers this afternoon. His filly had broken awkwardly and slowly in her last start at Churchill Downs, and in the race before that she was rank and forced to steady in a small stakes at Santa Anita. Blinkers seemed like the perfect remedy for her today while breaking from the advantageous 1 post. In addition, Kitty Hawk had the sizzling up-and-coming rider Julien Leparoux aboard. A recent June 6 workout at Saratoga, presumably with the new gear on, produced a solid five-furlong drill— 1:00⅕B on the good turf. All systems looked like a go. The only possible roadblock was finding a fair betting price.

The Formulator Default Query for Kitty Hawk appeared as follows:

Trainer: Patrick L. Biancone
Time Frame: Past Five Years
Blinkers: First Time Blinkers

Horses	Starts	Wins	ITM	Win%	ITM%	$2ROI	Median Payoff
58	58	12	25	21%	43%	$1.67	$4.85

The trainer stat of 21 percent wins with blinkers on was nothing to get overly excited about, considering that the Biancone barn was already clicking at a superb 26 percent on all starters for the year (129 34 .26). However, anyone who had been watching Biancone closely for the last several weeks would have recognized that Leparoux had become his go-to guy at Churchill Downs, and that this dynamic duo had even started to win races at a strong clip nationwide. To further prove this theory, we had the Formulator statistics to back up our general assumption.

Time Frame: Past Five Years
Blinkers: First Time Blinkers
Today's Jockey: **Leparoux J R**

Horses	Starts	Wins	ITM	Win%	ITM%	$2ROI	Median Payoff
8	8	4	5	50%	63%	$2.95	$4.50

Unfortunately, Kitty Hawk ran into a greatly improving filly from the Bill Mott barn named Quite a Bride, who took advantage of the speed-favoring turf course and refused to be reeled in by the late-closing Kitty Hawk. Despite the loss, her good effort still substantiated the fact that the Biancone barn is live with the addition of blinkers and that all his entrants adding the equipment for the first time must be respected.

FIFTH RACE

Meadowlands

JUNE 12, 2006

$1\frac{1}{16}$ MILES. (Turf) (1.39²) TRENTON S. Purse $60,000 FOR FILLIES, THREE YEARS OLD. No fee to nominate, $600 to pass the entry box with starters to receive a $400 refund. Weight: 123 lbs. Non-winners of a sweepstakes in 2006 allowed 2 lbs.; $28,000 in 2006, 4 lbs.; $18,000 since March 1, 2006, 6 lbs. (Maiden, claiminig and starter races not considered.) The winning owner to receive a trophy. Closed Sunday, May 28, 2006 with 35 nominations. $400 supplemental nominations were made at time of entry, Saturday, June 10, 2006.

Value of Race: $60,000 Winner $36,000; second $12,000; third $6,600; fourth $3,000; fifth $600; sixth $600; seventh $600; eighth $600. Mutuel Pool $111,597.00 Exacta Pool $116,965.00 Trifecta Pool $87,032.00

Last Raced	Horse	M/Eqt. A. Wt	PP	St	¼	½	¾	Str	Fin	Jockey	Odds $1
14Apr06 9GP1	Quite a Bride	L 3 119	2	1	1hd	2½	2½	12	12¾	Castro E	1.70
5May06 5CD4	Kitty Hawk-GB	L b 3 121	1	5	6½	72	72	31	2¾	Leparoux J R	1.90
5May06 5CD5	Southern Protocol	L 3 117	6	3	4hd	4½	4½	2½	32	Castellano J J	4.00
14Apr06 9GP6	Robyns Anthem	L b 3 117	8	8	8	8	8	74	4½	Lopez C C	96.30
8Apr06 10GP1	Meribel	L 3 117	7	7	7½	6½	51	6hd	51½	Bravo J	5.80
30Apr06 1Aqu4	Celestial Woods	L 3 117	4	2	3½	3hd	3hd	51½	6no	Migliore R	16.80
25Mar06 8TP5	Capozzene	L 3 117	3	4	2½	1hd	1hd	4hd	74	Decarlo C P	12.10
8Apr06 4Tam1	Karla's Number	3 117	5	6	51	51	6½	8	8	Velez J A Jr	89.00

OFF AT 3:33 Start Good. Won driving. Course good.

TIME :24², :48¹, 1:11³, 1:35⁴, 1:41⁴ (:24.59, :48.36, 1:11.71, 1:35.82, 1:41.87)

$2 Mutuel Prices:

2 – QUITE A BRIDE	5.40	3.00	2.40
1 – KITTY HAWK–GB		2.80	2.20
7 – SOUTHERN PROTOCOL			2.40

$2 EXACTA 2–1 PAID $14.80 $1 TRIFECTA 2–1–7 PAID $19.30

Ch. f, (Mar), by Stormy Atlantic – Wise Bride , by Blushing Groom–Fr . Trainer Mott William I. Bred by Haras Santa Maria de Araras SA (Fla).

QUITE A BRIDE moved off the inside and under a rating hold early, vied for command outside a rival, held the advantage turning for home then responded to pressure while drawing clear. KITTY HAWK (GB) saved ground into the far turn, moved out for the drive and finished steadily while earning the place. SOUTHERN PROTOCOL close up early outside, raced four wide turning for home and advanced into midstretch then lacked the needed late response. ROBYNS ANTHEM saved ground to the lane, eased out and offered a mild gain. MERIBEL raced just off the inside into the lane and was checked between rivals when lacking room nearing the furlong marker dropping back. CELESTIAL WOODS close up early inside, lodged a three wide bid on the final turn, drifted in some nearing the eighth pole and tired. CAPOZZENE moved up inside approaching the clubhouse turn and vied for the lead, continued to save ground to the lane, came out slightly nearing the furlong marker and weakened. KARLA'S NUMBER stumbled at the start, raced forwardly placed from the outside to the far turn and tired.

Owners– 1, Haras Santa Maria de Araras; 2, Lakin Lewis G; 3, Humphrey G Watts Jr; 4, Petro Michael P; 5, Hancock III Arthur B and Clay Catesby W; 6, Evans Robert S; 7, My Purple Haze Stables; 8, Lambholm Stable

Trainers– 1, Mott William I; 2, Biancone Patrick L; 3, Arnold George R II; 4, Petro Michael P; 5, Clement Christophe; 6, Kimmel John C; 7, Pletcher Todd A; 8, Lerman Roy S

Scratched– Lady Raj (11Jun06 7Bel6)

$1 Pick Three (2–10–2) Paid $252.70 ; Pick Three Pool $15,841 .

TRAINER STATS FOR 1st Blink

Name	Starts	Wins	Win Percentage	ROI (Based on $2.00 to Win)
Albright, Amy	8	6	0.750	$ 11.40
Anderson, Robert J	8	5	0.625	$ 9.91
King, Gary M	10	6	0.600	$ 9.72
Hall, Dru S	14	8	0.571	$ 8.34
Simon, Stuart C	19	5	0.263	$ 7.25
Schuh, Tim	7	6	0.857	$ 7.03
Kenney, Daniel	17	5	0.294	$ 6.86

DeLima, Clifford	20	7	0.350	$ 6.68
Shockey, Dale E	12	5	0.417	$ 6.68
Gilbert, Bryon J	12	6	0.500	$ 6.03
Montano, Sr., Angel	28	5	0.179	$ 5.62
Kamps, Richard	18	11	0.611	$ 5.30
Fout, Paul D	17	5	0.294	$ 5.29
Hassenpflug, Chad	10	7	0.700	$ 5.18
Scott, Joan	17	8	0.471	$ 5.11
Marquez, Alfredo	13	5	0.385	$ 5.00
Hurtak, Daniel C	33	8	0.242	$ 4.91
Synnefias, Dimitrios	30	7	0.233	$ 4.90
Campbell, D. M.	19	5	0.263	$ 4.85
Connelly, William R	35	5	0.143	$ 4.79
Bettis, Charles L	15	5	0.333	$ 4.79
Petro, Michael	26	7	0.269	$ 4.77
Lopez, Daniel J	21	10	0.476	$ 4.75
Retteld, Richard R	25	10	0.400	$ 4.69
Cartwright, Ronals C	18	6	0.333	$ 4.67

Trainer George Weaver has been conditioning his own string and stable since November 2002. He was the barn foreman for Hall of Fame trainer D. Wayne Lukas, and also spent six years with Todd Pletcher, yet another extraordinary Lukas disciple. There's no doubt Weaver has learned his trade from the industry's best, and he was fortunate enough to have his first Triple Crown entrant, Greeley's Legacy, in 2006.

One of the profitable trainer angles for this stable is the Blinkers Off maneuver. In fact, despite his mediocre 14 percent win clip, Weaver did make our Top 25 trainer list for this particular equipment change because of his attractive ROI. He frequently sends out live longshots when removing the blinkers.

At Belmont Park on June 21, 2006, Weaver entered his 3-year-old gelding Indian Hawke in the sixth race, a one-mile optional-claiming event for nonwinners of two. Weaver was looking to end his 0-for-15 skid at the Belmont meet. Indian Hawke had last run in an off-the-turf route at Belmont on May 12, and was the favorite that afternoon. He battled for the early lead before tiring late while beaten nearly six lengths. It was a solid effort. Since that attempt six weeks ago, Indian Hawke had had four solid works over the main track, including a six-furlong stamina drill in 1:15⅗. Three races back, on the Aqueduct inner track, he had earned an impressive Beyer Speed Figure of 86, drawing off to win by four at today's scheduled distance.

6 Indian Hawke	Gr/ro g. 3 (Feb) SARAUG04 $140,000	Blinkers OFF	Life 7 2 0 0 $55,814 86 D.Fst 5 2 0 0 $53,514 86

6 Indian Hawke
Own: Flanagan, Donald. F.
8–1 Royal Blue and Peach Diamonds, Blue
Santos J A (95 12 8 10 .12) 2006:(362 57 .16)

Sire: Indian Charlie (In Excess*Ire) $25,000
Dam: Georgialina (Affirmed)
Br: Joseph Mangine & Theresa Mangine(NY)
Tr: Weaver George (15 0 2 4 .00) 2006:(130 15 .12)

Blinkers OFF   L 117

Life 7 2 0 0 $55,814 86   D.Fst 5 2 0 0 $53,514 86
2006 4 1 0 0 $29,130 86   Wet (380) 1 0 0 0 $2,300 64
2005 3 1 0 0 $26,684 66   Turf (315) 1 0 0 0 $0 51
Bel 1 0 0 0 $2,300 64   Dist (382) 1 1 0 0 $26,400 86

12May06–4Bel gd 1⅛ ⊗:46¹¹:104¹:371¹:511 3+ ⑤Alw 46000N2X   64 5 2½ 2ʰᵈ 2½ 22½ 45¾ Santos J A   L116 fb *1.55 69–21 MKndTn122²½ SccssflAffr122³ SrFrdd122½   Vied inside, tired 6
7Apr06–8Keefm 1 ⑦:221 :46 1:114¹:374   Trnsylvn-G3   51 9 64½ 65¾ 94½ 9⁸ 9 11½Bejarano R   L117b 14.50 67–16 ChnHgh117¹ LPlx117¾ Whrthstbgns117¹½   Weakened,far turn 10
4Mar06–2Aqu fst 1 ☒:232:474¹:14 1:393   ⑤Alw 44000N1X   86 8 32½ 32½ 2½ 15¼ 1⁴ Santos J A   L118 fb 5.20 85–19 IndnHk118⁴ WhWhtWn120³½ PrncRff118½   3 wide move, clear 8
20Jan06–1Aqu fst 6f ☒:221 :451 :58 1:111   ⑤Alw 43000N1X   38 6 3 51½ 5⁵ 6¹² 6 14½Santos J A   L122 fb 6.20 69–12 Remorse118ʰᵈ PhillipX.1224½ PrincofPc122¹   3 wide trip, tired 7
31Dec05–1Aqu fst 170 ☒:231 :474¹:123 1:424   ⑤Alw 44000N1X   66 6 3² 2½ 2ʰᵈ 2¹ 55½ Santos J A   L122 fb 12.90 79–10 Eprtc118½ PschtcRctn 120⁴ PhilFrn118ⁿᵏ   Lost whip midstretch 9
15Dec05–4Aqu fst 170 ☒:24 :491 1:152 1:454   ⑤Md Sp Wt 42k   59 7 1ʰᵈ 11½ 1¹ 12½ 12½ Santos J A   L120 fb 8.00 69–22 IndnHk120²½ LthlMssl120¹½ IWn'tDnc120ⁿᵒ   Set pace, driving 10
23Nov05–6Aqu fst 5½f :22² :46² :583 1:051   ⑤Md Sp Wt 41k   26 9 7 85¾ 8⁸ 8¹³ 8 15½Castellano J J   L120f 3.80 — — PhllpX1155½ OthnPh120ʰᵈ PrcfPc 1151½   Wide throughout, tired 10

WORKS: Jun15 Bel 6f fst 1:15³ B 1/2   Jun9 Bel 5f sly 1:01³ H 1/3   Jun1 Bel 5f fst 1:00⁴ B 13/28   May25 Bel 4f fst :50⁴ B 29/36   ● May9 Sar tr.t 4f fst :49 B 1/12   Apr29 Kee 4f fst :48⁴ B 7/34

TRAINER: BlinkOff (21 .19 $2.72)   31–60Days (107 .19 $2.08)   Dirt (198 .19 $1.95)   Routes (258 .17 $2.12)   Alw (120 .17 $1.82)   J/T 2005–06 BEL (9 .00 $0.00) J/T 2005–06(45 .18 $1.75)

Unfortunately, an unusual amount of scratches in this race left us with only a field of five. In all likelihood, the short field would ultimately destroy the price on what would have been a lucrative longshot. Despite the diminished field, Indian Hawke was still hovering around 4–1—certainly decent odds considering the circumstances. The Formulator Default Query for his trainer appeared as the following:

Trainer:	George Weaver
Time Frame:	Past Five Years
Blinkers:	Blinkers Off
Days:	31–60 Days

Horses	Starts	Wins	ITM	Win%	ITM%	$2ROI	Median Payoff
79	184	27	75	15%	41%	$2.48	$8.00

The 15 percent win ratio was average, but some general Formulator massaging on the Weaver gelding produced even more lucrative results. The addition of filters for Routes and Surface (Dirt) not only improved his win percentage, but inflated the ROI as well. Indian Hawke determinedly held off the game Pay Attention and paid a modest $9.80 for his backers.

Trainer:	George Weaver
Time Frame:	Past Five Years
Blinkers:	Blinkers Off
Distance:	**Routes (>= 1 Mile)**
Surface:	**Dirt**

Horses	Starts	Wins	ITM	Win%	ITM%	$2ROI	Median Payoff
54	139	30	67	22%	48%	$3.45	$6.40

SIXTH RACE

Belmont

JUNE 21, 2006

1 MILE. (1.32¹) ALLOWANCE OPTIONAL CLAIMING . Purse $46,000 FOR THREE YEAR OLDS AND UPWARD FOALED IN NEW YORK STATE AND APPROVED BY THE NEW YORK STATE–BRED REGISTRY WHICH HAVE NEVER WON TWO RACES OTHER THAN MAIDEN, CLAIMING, OR STARTER OR WHICH HAVE NEVER WON THREE RACES OR OPTIONAL CLAIMING PRICE OF $25,000. Three Year Olds, 119 lbs.; Older, 123 lbs. Non–winners of $26,000 at a mile or over since April 21 Allowed 2 lbs. (Races where entered for $20,000 or less not considered in allowances).

Value of Race: $45,080 Winner $27,600; second $9,200; third $4,600; fourth $2,300; fifth $1,380. Mutuel Pool $225,734.00 Exacta Pool $187,960.00 Trifecta Pool $98,793.00

Last Raced	Horse	M/Eqt.	A.	Wt	PP	St	¼	½	¾	Str	Fin	Jockey	Cl'g Pr	Odds $1
12May06 4Bel4	Indian Hawke	L	3	117	3	2	2½	2½	1hd	11½	1½	Santos J A		3.90
29May06 1Bel1	Pay Attention	L	5	123	5	1	41½	41½	31	2hd	21½	Castellano J J	25000	6.10
13May06 9Bel1	Shuffling Maddnes	L b	3	119	4	4	5	5	4hd	3hd	32½	Migliore R		3.10
27May06 7Bel2	Trading Pro	L b	3	117	2	3	11½	1½	2hd	48	416¾	Gomez G K		0.80
28Apr06 7Aqu8	Jumping Jack Louie	L b	4	121	1	5	3½	3hd	5	5	5	Luzzi M J		21.50

OFF AT 3:36 Start Good. Won driving. Track fast.

TIME :23³, :47, 1:11³, 1:37² (:23.75, :47.08, 1:11.66, 1:37.55)

$2 Mutuel Prices:

6 – INDIAN HAWKE	9.80	4.70	3.90
9 – PAY ATTENTION		5.90	3.70
7 – SHUFFLING MADDNES			2.90

$2 EXACTA 6–9 PAID $50.00 $2 TRIFECTA 6–9–7 PAID $130.00

Gr/ro. g, (Feb), by Indian Charlie – Georgialina , by Affirmed . Trainer Weaver George. Bred by Joseph Mangine & Theresa Mangine (NY).

INDIAN HAWKE raced with the pace from the outside, drew clear when roused then dug in determinedly and prevailed after a long drive. PAY ATTENTION raced close up while three wide and finished gamely outside. SHUFFLING MADDNES was rated along early, raced between rivals and finished well while in tight quarters in deep stretch. TRADING PRO set the pace along the inside and weakened in the stretch. JUMPING JACK LOUIE raced inside and tired.

Owners– 1, Flanagan Donald F; 2, Schwartz Herbert T and Carol A; 3, Trinacria Usa Stable; 4, Klaravich Stables Inc; 5, Anstu Stables Inc

Trainers– 1, Weaver George; 2, Schwartz Scott M; 3, Carroll Del W II; 4, Violette Richard A Jr; 5, Barbara Robert

Pay Attention was claimed by Winning Move Stable; trainer, Contessa Gary C.

Scratched– Step It Up (03Jun06 7Bel3) , Lethimthinkhesboss (25May06 7Bel5) , Who What Win (29May06 1Bel2) , Crop Buster (28Apr06 7Aqu7)

$2 Pick Three (1–10–6) Paid $927.00 ; Pick Three Pool $56,775 .

TRAINER STATS FOR BlinkOff

Name	Starts	Wins	Win Percentage	ROI (Based on $2.00 to Win)
Santiago, Rodriguez C	6	6	1.000	$ 36.80
Brown, James I	8	6	0.750	$ 26.60
Garcea, Eric	12	5	0.417	$ 24.90
Reinstedler, Anthony L	29	8	0.276	$ 13.70
Parsley, Kenneth B	8	6	0.750	$ 12.80
Story, Chad	11	5	0.455	$ 11.60
Glennon, Darren C	11	6	0.545	$ 11.30
Polsinelli, Dominic J	20	6	0.300	$ 11.00
Hall, Darrel V	20	6	0.300	$ 9.92
Huarte, Frank	9	5	0.556	$ 9.78
Johnson, Gary L	15	7	0.467	$ 9.33
Musgrave, Shawn	12	6	0.500	$ 8.93
Wilson, John R	18	6	0.333	$ 8.67
Fahey, III, John	12	7	0.583	$ 8.07
Northrop, Jr., George	9	6	0.667	$ 7.73
Segura, Kearney	20	7	0.350	$ 7.45
Guerrero, J. G.	9	5	0.556	$ 7.33
Specht, Steven	9	6	0.667	$ 7.20
Root, Ben	16	8	0.500	$ 7.05
Barrera, Jr., Oscar S	13	5	0.385	$ 6.97
Weaver, George	85	12	0.141	$ 6.91
Pogue, William R	13	6	0.462	$ 6.80
Farro, Patricia	22	5	0.227	$ 6.58
Miceli, Michael	18	9	0.500	$ 6.36
Dollase, Wallace A	19	8	0.421	$ 6.34

MEDICATION

THE ADMINISTRATION OF proscribed medication is a lot less common on the racetrack than you might think. In fact, intentional medication abuse in the racing industry is extremely rare. To help distinguish between performance-affecting agents and substances with no effect on a race, the industry has classified more than 500 medications with regard to their impact on a horse's race performance. The Association of Racing Commissioners International (ARCI), which is followed by most racing states across the country, divides medications into various categories. Testing has become increasingly accurate and precise. In fact, prerace testing in most states can easily detect minute amounts of substances over a long period of time. Racing chemists are able to measure substances on a parts-per-billion (ppb) basis, thus exposing performance-altering substances as well as legal, therapeutic medications.

Despite adequate pre- and postrace testing within the industry, we've still all heard of trainers that are "juicing" or using illegal drugs and medications. In most of these cases there is no substantial evidence to prove that these individuals are utilizing illegal means to enhance a runner's performance. Fortunately, for our purposes in this text, we're only interested in Lasix and how the addition of the medication from trainer to trainer enhances a runner's performance. Lasix, a diuretic with the generic name furosemide, is used to treat bleeding in a horse's respiratory system after strenuous activity. It is believed that Lasix lowers blood pressure and reduces strain on the capillaries in the lungs.

The issue of whether or not treating a bleeder with Lasix can actually enhance that horse's performance remains debatable. However, a study conducted by Ohio State University some 10 years ago, which included more than 16,000 racehorses treated with Lasix, did provide some very interesting results. According to the published results in *Journal of the American Veterinary Medical Association*, horses that were treated with Lasix earned more money and hit the board more frequently than those who were not.

Medical implications and rumors of cheating trainers aside, what we do know is that the addition of first-time Lasix results in a profitable ROI trainer angle for hundreds of conditioners. Therefore, it merits the handicapper's respect when the little black circle with the white L symbol shows up in a horse's past performances.

TOO GOOD TO BE TRUE

ON ONE EARLY-SUMMER Monday afternoon at the low-profile upstate New York track Finger Lakes, there was an interesting maiden-special-weight sprint race for 3-year-old fillies. Two horses from this field of nine had what appeared to be outstanding first-time Lasix statistics. They were number 2, Xciting Kitty (1stLasix 8 .63 $7.51), trained by meet leader Chris Englehart, and number 4, Bronzesgirl (1stLasix 9 .56 $3.40), conditioned by sixth-ranked Michael Ferraro. Both Englehart and Ferraro have simply owned the Finger Lakes meet, with one or the other holding the title of leading trainer for the last nine years. The pair had such a strangle-hold on the upstate circuit that whatever they brought onto the Finger Lakes strip merited respect.

2 **Xciting Kitty**
Own: Joseph S. Parisi
6–1 White and Blue Triangular Thirds, White
Nicol P A Jr (204 42 32 26 .20) 2006:(279 51 .18)

B. f. 3 (Mar) EASSEP04 $32,000
Sire: Tomorrows Cat (Storm Cat) $7,500
Dam: Last Boat East (Eastern Echo)
Br: Barry R. Ostrager & Mary Kay Vyskocil(NY) ❶ 120
Tr: Englehart Chris (134 38 26 18 .28) 2006:(256 60 .23)

	Life	0 M 0 0	$0	–	D.Fst	0 0 0 0	$0	–
	2006	0 M 0 0	$0	–	Wet (334)	0 0 0 0	$0	–
	2005	0 M 0 0	$0	–	Turf (273)	0 0 0 0	$0	–
	FL	0 0 0 0	$0	–	Dist (320)	0 0 0 0	$0	–

WORKS: Jun12 FL 5f fst 1:02 Bg 3/7   May29 FL 3f fst :37¹ Bg 8/17   May5 Bel 4f fst :49³ B 17/32   May3 Bel 3f fst :49 B 17/41   Apr30 Bel 4f fst :50 B 36/44   Apr27 Bel 3f fst :37² Bg 4/12
Apr18 Bel 4f fst :49 B 24/33   Apr11 Bel 4f fst :49 B 8/24   Apr6 Bel 4f gd :49² B 2/7   Mar30 Bel tr.t 4f fst :51 B 40/43

TRAINER: 1stStart (15 .13 $1.16) 1stLasix (8 .63 $7.51) Dirt (952 .23 $1.80) Sprint (693 .22 $1.67) MdnSpWt (66 .26 $1.59)   J/T 2005-06 FL (14 .00 $0.00) J/T 2005-06 (87 .18 $1.71)

4 **Bronzesgirl**
Own: Frank J. Corigliano
10–1 Red, White Triangular Panel, Green
Buckley P R (64 13 10 5 .20) 2006:(131 20 .15)

B. f. 3 (Jun)
Sire: Taberg Spirit (Galaxy Guide)
Dam: Bronze Vale (Image of Greatness)
Br: Joseph Belscher & Barbara J. Perkins(NY) ❶ 120
Tr: Ferraro Michael S (32 5 6 7 .15) 2006:(33 5 .15)

	Life	1 M 0 0	$270	–	D.Fst	1 0 0 0	$270	–
	2006	1 M 0 0	$270	–	Wet (324*)	0 0 0 0	$0	–
	2005	0 M 0 0	$0	–	Turf (237*)	0 0 0 0	$0	–
	FL	1 0 0 0	$270	–	Dist (255*)	0 0 0 0	$0	–

22May06–6FL fst 5½f :22² :47²1:004 1:08   ⒻⓈMd Sp Wt 18k   — 7 7 7¹³ 7¹⁴ 7¹² 7¹¹½Buckley P R   120   12.50 64–16 Ryn'sGlory120¹ DItnNwMssy120² Wtrlrgngdncr120ⁿᵏ   Outrun 7
WORKS: Jun13 FL 6f fst 1:20¹ Bg 6/6   May15 FL 6f fst 1:18³ Bg 6/6   May7 FL 4f fst :51³ Bg 9/13   Apr28 FL 3f fst :36² Bg 6/29   Apr15 FL 3f fst :39⁴ B 43/49

TRAINER: 2ndStart (11 .27 $1.68) 1stLasix (9 .56 $3.40) Dirt (350 .19 $1.47) Sprint (201 .18 $1.35) MdnSpWt (39 .21 $1.31)   J/T 2005-06 FL (3 .00 $0.00) J/T 2005-06 (3 .00 $0.00)

A careful evaluation of these statistics using the Formulator software, however, proved that when the general first-time Lasix stat is critiqued alone, without taking into account other race specifics such as class, race conditions, last racing date, etc., the number can be deceptive. The Lasix angle for both of these fillies was not as strong as what appeared in print, thus proving that using first-time Lasix as a stand-alone handicapping factor is never a judicious decision. The two fillies finished eighth and ninth, beaten nearly 30 lengths over the sloppy and sealed track.

FOURTH RACE 6 FURLONGS. (1.081) MAIDEN SPECIAL WEIGHT . Purse $15,000 FOR MAIDENS, FILLIES
THREE YEARS OLD. Weight, 120 lbs.

Finger Lakes

JUNE 19, 2006

Value of Race: $15,000 Winner $9,000; second $3,000; third $1,500; fourth $750; fifth $300; sixth $150; seventh $150; eighth $150. Mutuel
Pool $33,750.00 Exacta Pool $38,697.00 Trifecta Pool $35,551.00

Last Raced	Horse	M/Eqt. A. Wt	PP	St	¼	½	Str	Fin	Jockey	Odds $1
22May06 6FL6	Little Broadway	L 3 122	9	1	1³	1⁶	1⁴	1nk	Gutierrez J A	15.80
29May06 5FL5	Then Again	L 3 120	4	4	4²½	3²	2¹	2nk	Grabowski J A	4.90
29May06 5FL8	By the Hour	L 3 120	5	8	8¹⁵	6²	3hd	3²½	Davila M A Jr	2.45
22May06 6FL4	Cyn's Dixieglitter	L 3 120	7	2	3hd	4½	5¹½	4⅘	Camejo O	8.40
6Jun06 5FL3	B J's Rodeo	L 3 120	8	5	5hd	7¹	7½	5²½	Suarez G	5.80
27May06 3FL2	Foxy Madison	L b 3 120	6	3	6¹	5¹	6hd	6no	Ignacio R	5.70
5Nov05 1FL6	Tara Drive	L b 3 120	2	6	2²	2¹	4¹	7²½	Osorio J D	16.40
	Xciting Kitty	L 3 120	1	7	7½	8¹⁵	8¹⁸	8²⁷½	Nicol P A Jr	3.65
22May06 6FL7	Bronzesgirl	L 3 120	3	9	9	9	9	9	Buckley P R	31.00

OFF AT 2:32 Start Good. Won driving. Track sloppy (Sealed).

TIME :221, :461, :592, 1:141 (:22.25, :46.20, :59.58, 1:14.22)

$2 Mutuel Prices:

9 – LITTLE BROADWAY	33.60	10.60	11.40
5 – THEN AGAIN		6.10	4.50
6 – BY THE HOUR			3.60

$2 EXACTA 9–5 PAID $336.00 $2 TRIFECTA 9–5–6 PAID $1,214.00

Ch. f, (Apr), by City Zip – Little Peak , by Hagley . Trainer Perdue Edward C. Bred by E & D Enterprises (NY).

LITTLE BROADWAY broke sharply, sprinted clear, showed the way along the three path, widened into the lane and then was all out for the win. THEN AGAIN was never far back along the rail on the turn, eased out in the stretch, asked and finished with good energy. BY THE HOUR lagged back, gained on the turn, angled out and rallied. CYN'S DIXIEGLITTER was well placed along the three path, four path on the turn and then lacked the late needed response. B J'S RODEO was unhurried along the four path and then improved her position. FOXY MADISON three path, angled out five wide midway on the turn, gained some and then flattened out. TARA DRIVE tracked the winner along the rail to the lane and tired. XCITING KITTY saved ground, was outrun. BRONZESGIRL fractious in the gate and then showed nothing.

Owners– 1, Zeppetelli Mary J and Perdue Agnes J; 2, Gatsas Thoroughbreds LLC; 3, Flying Zee Stable; 4, West Shore Stable; 5, Lathrop David; 6, Aquino Mario; 7, Tedeschi Dominic; 8, Parisi Joseph S; 9, Corigliano Frank J

Trainers– 1, Perdue Edward C; 2, Ferraro M Anthony; 3, Barrera Oscar S Jr; 4, Anderson Bruce D; 5, Lathrop David; 6, Aquino Mario; 7, Raposa Joseph J; 8, Englehart Chris; 9, Ferraro Michael S

Scratched– Peace Princess (27May06 3FL 3)

Another example of how certain Lasix trainer data can lead to wagering miscues occurred on a Monday afternoon at Delaware Park exactly one week later. Three consecutive days of heavy rains and scattered thunderstorms left most of the East Coast tracks a sea of slop. This particular afternoon at Delaware Park was no exception. The fifth race was a 5½- furlong maiden-special-weight sprint for 2-year-olds. Trainer Graham Motion, better known for his expertise on the turf and for handling some of the country's most competitive grass runners, such as Film Maker and Better Talk Now, was sending out a first-time starter named Dangerfield on the main track. Dangerfield was a $100,000 purchase sired by leading stallion Distorted Humor, who quickly gained a solid reputation as a superior sire over the last few years with the Grade 1 successes of Funny Cide, Flower Alley, Commentator, and Awesome Humor.

5	**Dangerfield**			

5 Dangerfield
Own: Dogwood Stable
Green Green, Yellow Dots, Yellow Bands On
CARABALLO J C (143 26 22 26 .18) 2006: (302 59 .20)

Ch. c. 2 (Mar) OBSFEB06 $100,000
Sire: Distorted Humor (Forty Niner) $150,000
Dam: Tassa (Tasso)
Br: ClassicStar (Ky)
Tr: Motion H Graham(45 6 9 4 .13) 2006:(218 39 .18)

118

	Life	0	M	0	0	$0	–	D.Fst	0	0	0	0	$0	–
	2006	0	M	0	0	$0	–	Wet(413)	0	0	0	0	$0	–
	2005	0	M	0	0	$0	–	Turf(282)	0	0	0	0	$0	–
	Del	0	0	0	0	$0	–	Dst(404)	0	0	0	0	$0	–

WORKS: Jun22 Fai 5f fst 1:04 B 1/2   Jun10 Fai 4f fst :46³ B 2/14   Jun3 Fai 4f fst (W) :51 B 3/4   May27 Fai 4f fst :49² Bg 2/11   May20 Fai 4f fst :50¹ Bg 2/5   May13 Fai 4f fst :52 B 7/11
         May5 Fai 3f fst :37¹ B 1/2   Apr14 Fai 4f fst :51³ B 4/6   ● Apr7 Fai 3f fst :37³ B(d) 1/4
TRAINER: 1stStart(87 .13 $1.43) 1stLasix(20 .40 $3.36) 2YO(129 .17 $1.21) Dirt(417 .19 $1.54) Sprint(230 .17 $1.36) MdnSpWt(222 .18 $1.80)

J/T 2005-06 DEL (31 .10 $1.01) J/T 2005-06 (62 .16 $1.31)

The first-time Lasix Trainer Form data for Dangerfield and trainer Graham Motion looked extremely promising (1stLasix 20 .40 $3.36). The colt had a nice series of well-spaced three-, four-, and five-furlong workouts dating back to April 7, and a tremendous off-track Tomlinson Rating of 413 for today's wet going. Although there were some encouraging handicapping angles that might have landed you on this 10–1 first-time starter, the first-time Lasix angle should *not* have been one of them. The Formulator Default Query for this well-bred colt produced the following results:

Trainer:	Graham H. Motion
Time Frame:	Past Five Years
Days/Start:	**First Time Starters**
Lasix:	First Time Lasix

Horses	Starts	Wins	ITM	Win%	ITM%	$2ROI	Median Payoff
175	175	21	53	12%	30%	$1.55	$8.60

Motion's actual 12 percent win ratio was a far cry from the general 40 percent first-time Lasix data listed from the limited medication information in Dangerfield's past performances. Although Graham Motion had shown success when first applying Lasix, this was not the case with his first-time starters. A further filtering process using just 2-year-old first-time-starters produced similar weak results with a dwindling ROI of $0.77.

Trainer:	Graham H. Motion
Time Frame:	Past Five Years
Age:	**2 YOs Only**
Days/Start:	First Time Starters
Lasix:	First Time Lasix

Horses	Starts	Wins	ITM	Win%	ITM%	$2ROI	Median Payoff
82	82	9	26	11%	32%	$0.77	$5.80

FIFTH RACE

Delaware

JUNE 26, 2006

5½ FURLONGS. (1.02³) MAIDEN SPECIAL WEIGHT . Purse $36,000 (plus $600 Starters Bonus) FOR MAIDENS, TWO YEAR OLDS. Weight, 118 lbs.

Value of Race: $36,600 Winner $21,600; second $7,200; third $3,960; fourth $2,160; fifth $1,080; sixth $300; seventh $300. Mutuel Pool $69,749.00 Exacta Pool $73,737.00 Trifecta Pool $60,238.00

Last Raced	Horse	M/Eqt. A. Wt	PP	St	¼	⅜	Str	Fin	Jockey	Odds $1
23Apr06 ²Kee²	Daytona	L	2 118	3	3	4⁴	3¹½	3⁴	1²	Dominguez R A	0.70
	True Wink	L	2 118	5	2	2⁵	2⁵	1½	2³¾	Elliott S	4.30
4Jun06 ⁵Pha²	Musical Step	L	2 118	7	1	1ʰᵈ	1ʰᵈ	2²	3¾	Carmouche K	4.50
	Wicked Retort	L	2 118	1	4	3ʰᵈ	4⁶	4⁶	4²	Castillo O O	6.90
	Bosun's Mate	L	2 113	2	6	7	6³	6⁷	5¹¾	Napravnik A R⁵	24.10
	Dangerfield	L	2 118	4	5	5¹½	5¹½	5²	6²³	Caraballo J C	10.30
	Dance to Glory		2 118	6	7	6¹½	7	7	7	Martin C W	62.00

OFF AT 2:34 Start Good. Won driving. Track sloppy (Sealed).

TIME :22, :46, :59³, 1:06² (:22.04, :46.10, :59.69, 1:06.55)

$2 Mutuel Prices:

3 – DAYTONA	3.40	2.60	2.10
6 – TRUE WINK		3.60	2.60
8 – MUSICAL STEP			2.60

$2 EXACTA 3–6 PAID $12.00 $2 TRIFECTA 3–6–8 PAID $32.00

B. c, (Jan), by Johannesburg – Kirby's Babe , by Sultry Song . Trainer Pletcher Todd A. Bred by Don Graham & Ocala Oaks (Ky).

DAYTONA was slow to settle, rallied three wide through the furlong grounds and ran past the leader in the late stages under strong handling. TRUE WINK dueled inside into the stretch, shook clear leaving the furlong marker but couldn't turn back the winner while second best. MUSICAL STEP dueled two wide to mid stretch then weakened in the final furlong. WICKED RETORT was fractious in the gate then flashed brief speed. BOSUN'S MATE failed to threaten. DANGERFIELD was no factor. DANCE TO GLORY showed little.

Owners– 1, Magnier Mrs John Tabor Michael and Smith Derrick; 2, Wienkowitz Walter; 3, Maple Leaf Farm; 4, Bloom William; 5, Meyerhoff Harry C and Thomas O; 6, Dogwood Stable; 7, Dependable Stables

Trainers– 1, Pletcher Todd A; 2, Ritchey Tim F; 3, Houghton T Bernard; 4, Donk David; 5, Delp Grover G; 6, Motion H Graham; 7, Hamer William E

Scratched– Houston Ridge , Cash Rich

$2 Daily Double (6–3) Paid $16.40 ; Daily Double Pool $10,926 .
$2 Pick Three (6–6–3/4/9) Paid $77.20 ; Pick Three Pool $7,499 .

TRAINER STATS FOR 1stLasix

Name	Starts	Wins	Win Percentage	ROI (Based on $2.00 to Win)
Klesaris, Peter	6	5	0.833	$ 36.20
Irion, Sue	11	6	0.545	$ 18.20
Betancourt, Eli	13	5	0.385	$ 17.00
Bolen, Bradley C	10	6	0.600	$ 16.00
Reinacher, Robert	21	5	0.238	$ 11.80
Procino, Gerald	22	6	0.273	$ 11.10
Thornton, Nancy	9	5	0.556	$ 9.56
Grimm, Margaret E	9	5	0.556	$ 9.38
Lawrence, Robert L	12	5	0.417	$ 8.67
Simon, Lynn M	28	5	0.179	$ 8.62
Murphy, Tom G	7	5	0.714	$ 8.34
Axmaker, Peter M	22	5	0.227	$ 8.15
Danger, Kevin	19	5	0.263	$ 7.51
Kopycinski, Larry	7	5	0.714	$ 6.91
Balding, Andrew	10	5	0.500	$ 6.87
Uelmen, Larry R	24	9	0.375	$ 6.84
Randolph, Amy	15	5	0.333	$ 6.56
Forster, Grant T	28	12	0.429	$ 6.44
Hendricks, Dan L	18	5	0.278	$ 6.24
King, Yolonda Y	16	5	0.313	$ 6.11
Rutland, Jeffrey T	14	5	0.357	$ 5.96
Gerace, Janis L	24	6	0.250	$ 5.84
Lucas, Joe	34	7	0.206	$ 5.82
Eoff, Terry	14	6	0.429	$ 5.74
Yetsook, George G	24	8	0.333	$ 5.73

7

FIRST-TIME STARTERS, 2-YEAR-OLDS, AND MAIDENS

CONTRARY TO POPULAR BELIEF, lightly raced and inexperienced horses offer some of the most lucrative betting opportunities available. The old adage that it's best to pass maiden races because they're impossible to handicap is just not true in today's modern betting era. For those nonbelievers or anyone interested in mastering the maiden and 2-year-old game, I strongly recommend picking up a copy of Dan Illman's *Betting Maidens & 2-Year-Olds: Analytical Approach to Future Winners* (DRF Press 2005). His chapter on the dam factor alone is worth the entire price of the book. Maiden races offer some of the best betting opportunities, and comprehensive trainer data is a big part of uncovering potential juvenile winners.

There are many trainers that have a knack for scoring with first-time starters or runners with limited racing experience. One interesting piece of information you will find in the trainer data collected for this chapter is that the compiled lists of profitable-ROI first-time-starter and debut trainers do not include many of the big-name training outfits you may be accustomed to seeing and betting. Trainers such as Todd Pletcher, Bob Baffert, Steve Asmussen, and Eoin Harty have an incredible assemblage of well-bred, expensive juvenile runners from the most affluent owners in the business. However, although their win percentage with these types of runners is exceptional, the ROI for these outfits is far below what should be most handicappers' betting expectations and profit requirements. Although these trainers win a multitude of races for their well-off owners, the mutuel payoffs are nominal at best for their loyal, chalk-eating fans.

Our overall goal is to use the Formulator-program trainer data to uncover a group of lesser-known trainers that consistently pop with lightly raced longshots. A horseman with a lucrative ROI and a fair-to-average win percentage is much more advantageous for our purposes than a trainer who clicks with 35 percent of his debut or second-time runners but only shows an ROI of $2.20. Despite the expansive debut trainer statistics sold commercially and on the Internet, there are still a handful of trainers that have managed to stay under the watchful and insightful radar of the general betting public. Most of the conditioners listed in this chapter fall under this unique category.

We can also use the reputation of some of the more renowned trainers to our advantage when attempting to rifle out bad favorites. There's no better handicapping scenario than to be able to confidently throw out a 6–5 or even-money favorite from a pick-three or pick-four sequence as a result of a horrendous first-time-starter trainer stat, and the Formulator software is the key to uncovering this kind of information. One such example includes the talented New Jersey native Ben Perkins Jr. and his success with first-time starters.

PERKINS POWER

A SECOND-GENERATION HORSEMAN, Ben Perkins Jr. is the son of Ben Perkins Sr., who trained in the Mid-Atlantic region for nearly 50 years before retiring in 1999. A college graduate who opted to forsake the world of business in favor of training Thoroughbreds, Perkins junior campaigns stables in Maryland, New Jersey, Pennsylvania, and occasionally ships some of his better horses to New York. His roster of stakes winners includes Storm Tower, Stormy Pick, Mass Market, Max's Pal, Richly Blended, and two Breeders' Cup Sprint entrants—Delaware Township in 2000 and Wildcat Heir in 2005. The 2003 Breeders' Cup Sprint winner, Cajun Beat, who was trained by Steve Margolis, was also under Perkins's supervision in 2002 before moving into the Margolis barn as a 3-year-old.

The Perkinses have long been recognized as experts in the preparation of 2-year-olds and have a solid reputation for sending out live first-time starters. Their success can be attributed to acquiring babies with win-early pedigrees, and patiently working their juveniles in the privacy of their own training establishment. When a Perkins 2-year-old hits the racetrack, it's almost a guarantee that he or she is well-accustomed to the ins and outs of the starting gate. In addition, these babies are already used to the unavoidable racetrack racket and various other distractions. These types of diversions frequently unglue inexperienced runners, but will rarely distract a Perkins entrant from running its "A" race.

Trainer Kelly Breen, who worked for Ben Perkins Sr. from 1994–2000, has also had tremendous success with juvenile runners. Breen obviously learned a trick or two from the Perkins family regarding the proper preparation of a 2-year-old. As of the end of June 2006, Breen was the leading trainer at Monmouth Park with 18 wins, of which 13, or 72 percent, came from horses making their first start.

Despite the obvious success of Ben Perkins Jr.'s juvenile runners, there is one interesting and valuable piece of information regarding his overall first-time-starter record. Let's take a look at this little piece of trainer data that could be considered a small diamond in the rough.

On February 5, 2006, Perkins had his 3-year-old filly Sister Silver entered in a six-furlong maiden-special-weight sprint. Sister Silver was a $215,000 purchase by the talented sire Saint Ballado, and the filly had some snappy drills on her work tab and was debuting with Lasix. One eye-catching move was a four-furlong bullet drill on January 20 at the Belmont training track in 47, handily. The work was the best of 93 for that morning.

---

9 Sister Silver

4–1 Own: New Farm
Purple, Black Diamond, Black Diamonds
Coa E M (224 54 37 26 .24) 2005:(1351 206 .15)

Gr/ro f. 3 (Jan) EASMAY05 $215,000
Sire: Saint Ballado (Halo) $125,000
Dam: Marvellous Silver (Silver Deputy)
Br: Double R Stables, LLC, Pollock Farms & Taylor M: **L 120**
Tr: Perkins Ben W Jr (9 3 2 2 .33) 2005:(179 33 .18)

Life	0 M 0 0	$0	–	D.Fst	0 0 0 0	$0	–
2006	0 M 0 0	$0	–	Wet (385)	0 0 0 0	$0	–
2005	0 M 0 0	$0	–	Turf (279)	0 0 0 0	$0	–
Aqu⊡	0 0 0 0	$0	–	Dist (379)	0 0 0 0	$0	–

WORKS: Feb2 Bel tr.t 3f fst :38⁴ B 20/21   Jan27 Bel tr.t 4f fst :48 Bg 3/54   ●Jan20 Bel tr.t 4f fst :47 H 1/93   Dec31 Bel tr.t 4f fst :48⁴ B 31/153   Dec23 Bel tr.t 4f fst :48¹ B 10/74

TRAINER: 1stStart (15 .20 $2.80)   Dirt (171 .20 $1.48)   Sprint (118 .17 $1.33)   MdnSpWt (38 .21 $1.69)

The first Trainer Form data stat for the filly was representative of Perkins's training reputation for getting horses to run at first asking. It read: 1stStart (15 .20 $2.80). Although the printed Trainer Form stat was correct, it was misleading in that it did not take into account the age differences between all of the Perkins first-time starters. Only those handicappers keeping their own trainer-stat records, or those using the Formulator program, would discover the massive disparity between a Perkins 2-year-old and 3-year-old first-time starter. A five-year query of 3-year-old first-time starters taken during the month of February 2006 from the Perkins stable revealed a dismal record of 3 for 50, or 6 percent wins. There was a tremendous discrepancy between that number and the 20 percent first-time-starter data listed in the past performances. It was obvious from these results that Ben Perkins Jr.'s expertise was with juvenile horses making their debuts, and not older runners. This was a valuable

FOURTH RACE	6 FURLONGS. (1.074) MAIDEN SPECIAL WEIGHT . Purse $43,000 INNER DIRT (UP TO $8,170 NYSBFOA) FOR MAIDENS, FILLIES THREE YEARS OLD. Weight, 120 lbs.

Aqueduct

FEBRUARY 5, 2006

Value of Race: $43,000 Winner $25,800; second $8,600; third $4,300; fourth $2,150; fifth $1,290; sixth $215; seventh $215; eighth $215; ninth $215. Mutuel Pool $393,829.00 Exacta Pool $346,304.00 Quinella Pool $31,920.00 Trifecta Pool $270,057.00

Last Raced	Horse	M/Eqt. A. Wt	PP	St	¼	½	Str	Fin	Jockey	Odds $1
8Jan06 2Aqu3	Fiery Pursuit	L b 3 120	4	4	4½	41½	22½	14¾	Mojica O	4.60
8Jan06 2Aqu2	Bella Lago	L 3 115	2	3	1hd	12	1½	21½	Morales P5	3.20
31Dec05 2Aqu3	Alittlemoreaction	L 3 120	6	6	3½	3hd	31	31½	Dominguez R A	6.20
	Risky Agenda	f 3 120	5	5	7½	78	710	4nk	Samyn J L	55.25
16Sep05 6Bel4	S. S. Belle	L bf 3 120	3	9	62½	63	4hd	51½	Arroyo N Jr	15.60
	Exorcise the Demon	L 3 120	7	1	2½	21	52	62	Garcia Alan	9.70
	Sister Silver	L 3 120	9	7	5½	5½	6hd	75¾	Coa E M	1.55
	Kit Kat Club	L 3 120	1	8	8hd	9	9	81	Jara F	26.00
8Jan06 2Aqu5	Tenure Track	L b 3 120	8	2	9	81½	8½	9	Hill C	69.00

OFF AT 1:56 Start Good. Won driving. Track good.

TIME :224, :453, :58, 1:102 (:22.82, :45.75, :58.06, 1:10.40)

$2 Mutuel Prices:	5 - FIERY PURSUIT	11.20	4.70	3.30
	3 - BELLA LAGO		4.20	3.00
	1 - ALITTLEMOREACTION			4.20

$2 EXACTA 5–3 PAID $31.40 $2 QUINELLA 3–5 PAID $16.40
$2 TRIFECTA 5–3–1 PAID $120.00

Ch. f, (Jan), by Carson City – Engaging , by Private Account . Trainer Lukas D Wayne. Bred by Overbrook Farm (Ky).

FIERY PURSUIT raced close up along the inside, advanced inside nearing the stretch, angled out for the drive and drew away late, driving. BELLA LAGO set the pace along the inside, was no match for the winner in the stretch and continued on to hold the place. ALITTLEMOREACTION stumbled at the start, chased the pace while three wide and lacked a rally. RISKY AGENDA was outrun early, raced inside and offered a mild rally inside. S. S. BELLE raced inside and lacked a rally. EXORCISE THE DEMON chased the pace from the outside and tired in the stretch. SISTER SILVER raced wide and tired. KIT KAT CLUB had no response when roused. TENURE TRACK raced greenily and tired.

Owners– 1, Overbrook Farm; 2, West Point Stable; 3, Lejeune Carey Grubard Marc and Medico Stable; 4, Fox Ridge Farm Inc; 5, Schifrin Hyman; 6, Sleeper Stables; 7, New Farm; 8, Our Canterbury Stables; 9, T Street Associates Stable

Trainers– 1, Lukas D Wayne; 2, McLaughlin Kiaran P; 3, Contessa Gary C; 4, Kelly Patrick J; 5, Miceli Michael; 6, Terranova John P II; 7, Perkins Ben W Jr; 8, Hertler John O; 9, Hills Timothy A

Scratched– Royal Good

$2 Pick Three (5–1–5) Paid $148.00 ; Pick Three Pool $60,925 .

piece of trainer-data information, and one that could have easily persuaded you from backing Sister Silver as the lukewarm 1.55–1 favorite in this field of nine.

Exactly 13 days later, Perkins showed up at Aqueduct with another 3-year-old, a colt named Old Time Tale, under almost identical racing circumstances.

It was another maiden-special-weight sprint for 3-year-olds, and Old Time Tale was by the hot sire Tale of the Cat. He had a steady string of 12 printed works dating back to October, and was also debuting with Lasix. Once again the printed Trainer Form data looked very promising: 1stStart (16 .19 $2.62). However, as in the case of Sister Silver, the figures were deceptive. Even the last line of the handicapper's "Closer Look" printed in that edition of *Daily Racing Form* led bettors down a path of unintentional falsehood. It read:

> **Old Time Tale:** Sire wins with approx. 20% of his first-time starters and this is the first foal from dam who won 2 of 18 starts for 31K; dam is a 1/2 to G2 winner Dice Dancer (5–34, 404 K); this barn is very good with 1st-time starters, so must respect.

Old Time Tale was not as popular as Sister Silver at the betting windows and was dismissed at nearly 12–1. He ran to his odds with a sixth-place finish, beaten over 13 lengths, and proved yet another case of the unreliability of older Ben Perkins Jr. horses making their initial start. On the other hand, it proved the advantage of using the Formulator trainer-data program.

FOURTH RACE
Aqueduct
FEBRUARY 18, 2006

6 FURLONGS. (1.07⁴) MAIDEN SPECIAL WEIGHT . Purse $43,000 INNER DIRT (UP TO $8,170 NYSBFOA) FOR MAIDENS, THREE YEAR OLDS. Weight, 120 lbs.

Value of Race: $43,000 Winner $25,800; second $8,600; third $4,300; fourth $2,150; fifth $1,290; sixth $287; seventh $287; eighth $286. Mutuel Pool $457,667.00 Exacta Pool $414,956.00 Quinella Pool $33,701.00 Trifecta Pool $260,740.00 Superfecta Pool $56,924.00

Last Raced	Horse	M/Eqt.	A. Wt	PP	St	¼	½	Str	Fin	Jockey	Odds $1
	Dontfearthereaper		3 120	8	1	43½	21½	12½	1¹	Santos J A	8.00
27Jan06 4Aqu²	Mass Charles	L b	3 120	6	3	3ʰᵈ	3ʰᵈ	3⁶	26¼	Messina R	5.40
21Jan06 6Aqu²	Johnny Spreadsheet	L bf	3 115	4	2	21½	1½	2ʰᵈ	31¼	Kaenel K⁵	1.95
	Nelson St. Swing	L b	3 120	7	6	6³	5½	4ʰᵈ	42¼	Coa E M	2.50
21Jan06 6Aqu³	Little Cherokee	L	3 120	2	4	1ʰᵈ	42½	52½	52½	Castillo H Jr	8.00
	Old Time Tale	L f	3 120	5	5	7¹⁰	7¹²	7¹⁵	62½	Bermudez J E	11.60
	The Rio Kid		3 120	3	8	5½	62½	6¹	713¼	Espinoza J L	14.90
	Angel City	L	3 120	1	7	8	8	8	8	Jara F	38.50

OFF AT 1:57 Start Good. Won driving. Track fast.

TIME :22³, :46³, :59¹, 1:12¹ (:22.77, :46.69, :59.35, 1:12.26)

$2 Mutuel Prices:

9 – DONTFEARTHEREAPER	18.00	8.30	4.50
7 – MASS CHARLES		5.60	3.60
5 – JOHNNY SPREADSHEET			2.60

$2 EXACTA 9–7 PAID $101.50 $2 QUINELLA 7–9 PAID $44.80
$2 TRIFECTA 9–7–5 PAID $276.50 $2 SUPERFECTA 9–7–5–8 PAID $674.00

Dk. b or br. g, (May), by Stormin Fever – Pleasant Scholar , by Pleasant Tap . Trainer Dutrow Richard E Jr. Bred by Lonnie R Owens & Rick Nord (Ky).

DONTFEARTHEREAPER raced with the pace from the outside, took over after a half mile, drew clear and was kept busy to the wire. MASS CHARLES raced with the pace along the inside, angled out in the stretch and finished gamely. JOHNNY SPREADSHEET contested the pace from the outside and tired in the final furlong. NELSON ST. SWING raced outside and posed no real threat. LITTLE CHEROKEE contested the pace along the inside and tired in the stretch. OLD TIME TALE had no response when roused. THE RIO KID was finished early. ANGEL CITY trailed throughout.

Owners– 1, Winged Foot Stables; 2, Baker Charlton; 3, Walsh Elizabeth; 4, Evans Ralph M; 5, Buckley James J and Cabin Creek Stable; 6, New Farm; 7, Our Canterbury Stables; 8, Trade Winds Farm

Trainers– 1, Dutrow Richard E Jr; 2, Baker Charlton; 3, Cedano Heriberto; 4, Violette Richard A Jr; 5, Duggan David P; 6, Perkins Ben W Jr; 7, Laudati Kim; 8, O'Brien Keith

Scratched– Santa's Special (04Feb06 2Aqu²) , Herecomeshollywood

$2 Pick Three (1–3–9) Paid $506.00 ; Pick Three Pool $71,048 .

As with many other Trainer Form stats and angles we've already reviewed in this text, it's imperative to keep in mind that first-time-starter stats are not always as lucrative as the records appear in print. For example, let's take a look at the first race at Colonial Downs on July 15, 2006, which was Virginia Derby Day. (For those racing fans who have never had the opportunity to visit Colonial Downs, I'd highly recommend taking a road trip with some of your favorite racetrack buddies. The facility is gorgeous, the fans and staff are friendly, and the expertly manicured turf course ensures full fields and competitive racing. More importantly, there are some shrewd training outfits that specifically point to the meet, thus offering giant overlays for those that have the time and patience to do their trainer research.)

On this extremely hot and humid afternoon, the first race was a maiden-special-weight event for 2-year-olds sprinting five furlongs on the turf. The number 4 horse was a first-time starter named Sporting Print, trained by Hamilton Smith. Smith, a top-five trainer at Colonial Downs each of the last several years, always has his stable stacked and ready to run in Virginia, and he had what appeared to be good numbers with debut runners. The printed stats for Smith appeared as follows: 1stStart (45 .24 $2.59). His stats for 2-year-olds also looked very promising (2YO 48 .25 $2.35). The Formulator Default Query, however, painted a much different picture. Although Smith hit the board with 50 percent of his debut runners *on the turf,* he was a horrible 3 for 42 in wins.

4	Sporting Print						
	Own: William M Backer	B. c. 2 (Mar)			Life 0 M 0 0	$0 –	D.Fst 0 0 0 0 $0 –
Yellow	Royal Blue, White Palm Tree, White	Sire: Lear Fan (Roberto) $15,000			2006 0 M 0 0	$0 –	Wet(330) 0 0 0 0 $0 –
	KOBISKIE D (82 18 16 11 .22) 2006: (482 83 .17)	Dam: Knock Off (Fit to Fight)		118	2005 0 M 0 0	$0 –	Turf(292) 0 0 0 0 $0 –
		Br: William Backer (Ky)			Cnl ① 0 0 0 0	$0 –	Dst①(294) 0 0 0 0 $0 –
		Tr: Smith Hamilton A(56 7 8 13 .12) 2006:(187 31 .17)					

WORKS: Jun21 Cnl 5f fst 1:02¹ B 3/5 ● Jun15 Cnl 4f fst :48³ Bg 1/8

TRAINER: 1stStart(45 .24 $2.59) 1stTurf(38 .08 $0.61) 1stLasix(6 .17 $2.40) 2YO(48 .25 $2.35) Turf(226 .17 $2.26) Sprint(193 .16 $1.51)

J/T 2005-06 CNL (2 .00 $0.00) J/T 2005-06 (5 .00 $0.00)

Trainer:	Hamilton Smith
Time Frame:	Past Five Years
Days/Starts:	First Time Starters
Surface:	First Time Turf

Horses	Starts	Wins	ITM	Win%	ITM%	$2ROI	Median Payoff
42	42	3	21	7%	50%	$0.51	$6.20

As the 2–1 second choice, Sporting Print rallied for second place in deep stretch, beaten a solid 5¼ lengths by the race favorite and gate-to-wire winner, Hot Guy, who was making his second career start and adding blinkers for trainer Bruce Jackson. Although it was another rock-solid effort from a Hamilton Smith first-time starter on the turf, once again he failed to hit the winner's circle, taking his mark to 3 for 43.

FIRST RACE

Colonial

JULY 15, 2006

5 FURLONGS. (Inner Turf) (.56) MAIDEN SPECIAL WEIGHT . Purse $24,000 (plus $12,000 VBF – Virginia Breeders Fund) INNER TURF FOR MAIDENS, TWO YEAR OLDS. Weight, 118 lbs. (Hazy. 92.)

Value of Race: $24,720 Winner $13,680; second $5,040; third $2,640; fourth $2,160; fifth $720; sixth $480. Mutuel Pool $36,462.00 Exacta Pool $33,180.00 Superfecta Pool $8,203.00 Trifecta Pool $24,771.00

Last Raced	Horse	M/Eqt. A. Wt	PP	St	$\frac{3}{16}$	$\frac{3}{8}$	Str	Fin	Jockey	Odds $1
18Jun06 5Cnl2	Hot Guy	L b 2 118	3	1	1²	1³	13½	15¼	Karamanos H A	1.10
	Sporting Print	L 2 118	2	4	4²	4²	3⁴	2nk	Kobiskie D	2.40
8Jly06 2Cnl3	Inside Joke	f 2 118	1	3	3³	2²	22½	39	Faine C	7.80
	Cryptogram	b 2 118	6	5	6⁶	5²	5⁴	44¾	Franklin M	46.30
	He's Our Hero	L 2 113	8	7	5¹	6⁵	6⁴	5¹	Bryan K⁵	28.90
	Carefree Hero	2 108	5	6	7½	7¹	7¹	61½	Merson L¹⁰	15.60
	Don't Be Alarmed	L b 2 118	7	8	8	8	8	72½	Kaenel K	20.80
	Talldarkhandsome	L b 2 118	4	2	2hd	3³	41½	8	Camacho E	4.00

OFF AT 1:02 Start Good. Won driving. Course firm.

TIME :21³, :44², :56² (:21.76, :44.43, :56.46)

$2 Mutuel Prices:

5 – HOT GUY	4.20	2.60	2.60
4 – SPORTING PRINT		2.80	3.40
3 – INSIDE JOKE			4.00

$2 EXACTA 5–4 PAID $13.00 $1 SUPERFECTA 5–4–3–7 PAID $260.60
$2 TRIFECTA 5–4–3 PAID $50.60

Dk. b or br. g, (Apr), by Scatmandu – Golden Glimmer–Fr , by Kendor–Fr . Trainer Jackson Bruce C. Bred by Hopewell Investments LLC (Ky).

HOT GUY set the pace and pulled away under a brisk drive. SPORTING PRINT circled horses and gained the place. INSIDE JOKE raced near the rail, chased the pace and faded. CRYPTOGRAM raced along the rail and was no factor. HE'S OUR HERO circled the turn and was outrun. CAREFREE HERO was outrun. DON'T BE ALARMED , steadied when pinched back leaving the starting gate, was outrun. TALLDARKHANDSOME , two wide, chased the pace and gave way.

Owners– 1, Trontz Richard S and KelJer Farm; 2, Backer William M; 3, Emerald Pastures Corp Inc; 4, Lady Olivia Northcliff LLC; 5, Arterburn Lonnie and Walters Dave; 6, Rains Robert E; 7, Gold Rush Stable LLC; 8, Hickory Ridge Farm LLC

Trainers– 1, Jackson Bruce C; 2, Smith Hamilton A; 3, Cronin Daniel; 4, Morgan Carla; 5, Arterburn Lonnie; 6, Parrish George W; 7, Baker Bryan R; 8, Allen A Ferris III

Scratched– Wing Walker , High Noon Boy , Stormin Desire

TRAINER STATS FOR 1stStart

Name	Starts	Wins	Win Percentage	ROI (Based on $2.00 to Win)
Morales, Mario	23	6	0.261	$ 14.80
Simoff, Andrew L	15	5	0.333	$ 14.70
Snyder, Floyd W	19	6	0.316	$ 13.90
Pruitt, Peggy E	31	5	0.161	$ 12.40
Bell, II, Thomas R	61	5	0.082	$ 10.80
Gallo, Louis P	23	6	0.261	$ 10.20
Tracy, Jim	13	5	0.385	$ 9.91
Colee, Frank	8	5	0.625	$ 9.73
Shade, Dale W	11	7	0.636	$ 9.69
Conrad, Paul	7	5	0.714	$ 9.03
Buckridge, Gloria	26	5	0.192	$ 9.02
Hunt, J. S.	10	5	0.500	$ 8.28

Magana, Hector	35	7	0.200	$ 7.99
Buck, Beverly	23	7	0.304	$ 7.86
Drummond, Robert	5	5	1.000	$ 7.40
Livesay, Charles	50	7	0.140	$ 7.09
Morreale, Jake V	51	8	0.157	$ 6.82
Charalambous, John	42	7	0.167	$ 6.81
Nemett, George S	52	17	0.327	$ 6.80
Ruhsam, Joey	19	6	0.316	$ 6.59
Weissman, Michael F	21	5	0.238	$ 6.41
Zahl, Robert	27	7	0.259	$ 6.25
Schultz, Harold F	85	12	0.141	$ 6.17
Thompson, C. E.	36	5	0.139	$ 6.16
Crowder, Mike	46	6	0.130	$ 6.14

TRAINER STATS FOR 2YO

Name	Starts	Wins	Win Percentage	ROI (Based on $2.00 to Win)
Powell, Ron	19	5	0.263	$ 24.50
Gallo, Louis P	20	10	0.500	$ 22.40
Snyder, Floyd W	20	6	0.300	$ 13.80
Kruger, Wendy J	30	5	0.167	$ 13.70
Mourier, Franck	32	9	0.281	$ 10.70
Ashby, Lynnett	15	7	0.467	$ 10.50
Betancourt, Eli	20	5	0.250	$ 10.40
Decker, Kenneth	14	5	0.357	$ 9.93
Richards, Lorne	9	5	0.556	$ 9.18
Bowman, Carl	27	10	0.370	$ 8.98
Webb, Stan	7	5	0.714	$ 8.67
Werneth, Roger	37	6	0.162	$ 8.51
Ruhsam, Joey	15	9	0.600	$ 8.28
Rini, Anthony F	24	7	0.292	$ 7.81
Herrick, Joe	31	5	0.161	$ 7.71
Siravo, Florence G	19	6	0.316	$ 7.06
House, Brian S	40	11	0.275	$ 6.97
Ontiveros, Lalita	11	7	0.636	$ 6.89
Weeks, Michael L	6	5	0.833	$ 6.80
Bagnell, Dale	10	5	0.500	$ 6.48
Morales, Mario	47	9	0.191	$ 6.46
Sparks, Brad	21	5	0.238	$ 6.33

Hurt, Clayton C	44	7	0.159	$ 6.26
Mosco, Robert	14	6	0.429	$ 6.14
Lawrence, Robert D	22	5	0.227	$ 6.07

THE MAIDEN DROPPER

ANY HORSE THAT DROPS down from maiden special weight into a maiden-claiming field for the first time must be respected as a potential win threat, regardless of how many lengths he was beaten in his last start. A lot of things have changed in handicapping over the last three decades, but the reliability and effectiveness of this maneuver has stood the test of time. This type of class drop was considered to be the biggest in racing 30 years ago, and I'm happy to report it's still considered to be the largest class drop today. The angle is even more advantageous when a horse has shown some early zip against maiden-special-weight runners in one of his last two races. Any horse that was on the lead or within two lengths of the lead at the first two running calls (regardless of the distance) in the past performances is a huge threat at a lowered class level. In fact, it makes no difference if the class dropper showed a quick burst of speed, then tired badly, and was soundly beaten 15 to 20 lengths.

A horse that consistently shows some speed against maiden-special-weight competitors will have a tremendous pace advantage when dropping in against claimers. It's as simple as that. These types of horses will frequently score gate to wire and occasionally pay respectable prices, especially if they were badly beaten in their last race. The one exception to this golden rule occurs in high-level maiden-claiming events. A horse moving from maiden special weight to a $100,000 maiden-claiming event is not making that drastic a class drop. Fortunately, these class-drop situations only occur at some of the A-level racing circuits such as New York, Kentucky, and Southern California.

Astute handicappers can frequently uncover horses dropping from maiden special weight to maiden claimers, on both dirt and turf, as they move from minor tracks to the major circuits. This maneuver is even more powerful when the trainer has had past success with that particular class move.

Here are some examples of horses making the maiden-special-weight to maiden-claimer class drop. On July 20, 2006, during clos-

ing week at Belmont Park, trainer Richard Violette Jr. entered his
3-year-old filly Derivative Trader in a one-mile, $45,000 maiden-
claiming event on the turf.

1 Derivative Trader	Ch. f. 3 (Apr) OBSAPR05 $60,000		Life	1 M 0 1	$4,300 62	D.Fst	1 0 0 1	$4,300 62
Own: Klaravich Stables	Sire: Sword Dance*Ire (Nijinsky II) $7,500		2006	1 M 0 1	$4,300 62	Wet (319)	0 0 0 0	$0 –
3–1 White, Red Braces and 'KS,' White and	Dam: Virtuous Lass (Hennessy)	$45,000	2005	0 M 0 0	$0 –	Turf (303)	0 0 0 0	$0 –
Castellano J J (174 33 27 27 .19) 2006:(598 104 .17)	Br: Tony Bowling & Bobby Dodd, & William P. Boone(L 118		Bel ⑦	0 0 0 0	$0 –	Dist (349)	0 0 0 0	$0 –
	Tr: Violette Richard A Jr (59 14 9 5 .23) 2006:(184 35 .19)							

21May06–1Bel fst 6f :22¹ :45² :57⁴1:10⁴ 3↑⑩Md Sp Wt 43k   62 7 4 66¾ 5⁸ 59½ 3⁹¼ Morales P⁵   L113   18.30 75–18 *AnyLimit*118⁹¼ Btids118ⁿᵒ DrivtivTrdr113² Going well outside 8

WORKS: Jly8 Aqu 4f fst :49¹ B 11/17   Jun19 Aqu 4f fst :49¹ B 2/7   May10 Aqu 4f fst :48³ Hg 2/12   May3 Aqu 4f fst :48³ Hg 2/6

TRAINER: 2ndStart (58 .22 $1.71)   MSWtoMCL (19 .32 $3.86)   1stTurf (37 .05 $1.14)   Dirt/Turf (38 .08 $1.38)   Sprint/Route (71 .18 $3.13)   31–60DJ/T 2005–06 BEL (8 .25 $2.96) J/T 2005–06 (18 .22 $2.97)

Rick Violette handles many talented runners for West Point
Thoroughbreds on the New York circuit, and has nearly 25 years
of training experience. He is no stranger to success within the Belmont Park maiden ranks and to conditioning lightly raced runners. In 2005 he won 11 races during the Belmont spring meet,
with five of those victories coming in maiden-special-weight
events. Among those winners were some juicy prices, including
Moon's Halo (10–1). He also had two seconds with longshots
Crunch the Numbers (16–1) and Popular Delusions (15–1). In
2004 at Belmont, he accumulated eight wins, with 50 percent of
those victories coming from the maiden ranks. Overall, Violette
consistently clicks with approximately 20 percent of all his runners, and the 2006 Belmont Park spring meet was no exception
(59 14 9 5 .23). It was another productive session for the stable,
which appeared to be moving full speed ahead to the premier
Saratoga meet upstate.

According to Violette's Trainer Form stats, Derivative Trader had
all the signs of a horse likely to move forward off of her May 21
dirt debut. In that six-furlong sprint, the Violette filly was making
a belated move racing wide in the stretch, and today's mile looked
even more favorable for her running style. Violette's numbers for
second-time starters (2ndStart 58 .22 $1.71) and for drop-downs
from maiden special weight to maiden claiming (MSWtoMCL 19
.32 $3.86) were very encouraging. His turf numbers, however, were
not as lucrative. His first-time turf (1stTurf 37 .05 $1.14) and dirt-
to-turf stats (Dirt/Turf 38 .08 1.38) appeared to be one of the few
Violette weaknesses.

For a clearer representation of what was at play we turned
to Formulator. The Default Query produced similar results to
the stats listed below, but for a better indication of his dirt and
turf comparisons we added the Surface option. Violette was
hovering around the 20 percent win mark with horses making

their second career start and moving from maiden special weight to maiden claimers on the main track.

Trainer:	Richard Violette Jr.
Time Frame:	Past Five Years
Class Moves:	MdnSpWt to MdnClm
Days/Starts:	Second Career Start
Surface:	**Dirt**

Horses	Starts	Wins	ITM	Win%	ITM%	$2ROI	Median Payoff
40	43	9	23	21%	53%	$2.30	$9.90

Although the sample for turf races was not as large as we would have preferred, it was clear that Violette was not as successful on the grass with his maiden-special-weight to maiden-claimer droppers as he was on the main track. As the 2–1 second choice, Violette's filly Derivative Trader was uncovered via Formulator as an excellent bet-against. In this case our stats proved correct.

Trainer:	Richard Violette Jr.
Time Frame:	Past Five Years
Class Moves:	MdnSpWt to MdnClm
Days/Starts:	Second Career Start
Surface:	**Turf**

Horses	Starts	Wins	ITM	Win%	ITM%	$2ROI	Median Payoff
11	11	1	3	9%	27%	$1.25	$13.80

FIFTH RACE
Belmont
JULY 20, 2006

1 MILE. (Turf) (1.31³) MAIDEN CLAIMING . Purse $20,000 (UP TO $3,800 NYSBFOA) FOR MAIDENS, FILLIES AND MARES THREE YEARS OLD AND UPWARD. Three Year Olds, 118 lbs.; Older, 123 lbs. Claiming Price $45,000, if for $40,000, allowed 2 lbs. (If the Stewards consider it inadvisable to run this race on the turf course, this race will be run at One Mile on the main track.).

Value of Race: $20,000 Winner $12,000; second $4,000; third $1,500; third $1,500; fifth $600; sixth $58; seventh $58; eighth $58; ninth $58; tenth $58; eleventh $57; twelfth $53. Mutuel Pool $397,278.00 Exacta Pool $315,207.00 Trifecta Pool $228,887.00

Last Raced	Horse	M/Eqt.	A.	Wt	PP	St	¼	½	¾	Str	Fin	Jockey	Cl'g Pr	Odds $1
15Jun06 9Bel6	Verona Dale	L f	4	121	9	1	2½	21½	12	12	1no	Espinoza J L	40000	9.80
28Jun06 4Bel4	Litethenight	L b	4	123	10	2	41	3½	2½	23½	24¼	Prado E S	45000	9.90
21May06 1Bel3	DH Derivative Trader	L	3	118	7	6	3½	41	41½	33½	3	Castellano J J	45000	2.55
7Jly06 2Bel2	DH Bianca's Jewel		4	121	8	7	10hd	111	101½	7hd	31¾	Hill C	40000	11.80
1Jun06 1Bel8	Tuscan Star	L b	3	118	4	8	9hd	8hd	84½	61½	5½	Velasquez C	45000	6.70
15Jun06 9Bel4	A Stroke a Hole	L	4	123	5	3	8hd	71½	61½	4hd	61¾	Jara F	45000	1.75
4Mar06 12Tam11	Last Chance Gulch		3	116	12	9	5hd	5hd	5½	5hd	7no	Fragoso P	40000	111.75
	Spartan Legacy	L b	3	118	3	11	12	12	116	10hd	82½	Samyn J L	45000	45.00
23Jun06 5Bel4	Kissin Damsel	L f	3	118	1	4	6½	101	9½	1112	91	Gomez G K	45000	32.75
4Jun06 9Bel8	Au Currant	L f	3	118	11	10	7½	6½	7hd	81½	103½	Luzzi M J	45000	21.40
25May06 9Bel8	Libby's Moment	L	3	116	6	5	1½	1hd	3½	9hd	1110½	Sutherland C	40000	57.50
27Nov05 4Aqu11	Princess Corrigan	L	3	118	2	12	111	9hd	12	12	12	Santos J A	45000	48.50

DH–Dead Heat.

OFF AT 3:05 Start Good. Won driving. Course good.
TIME :23⁴, :47², 1:11³, 1:36³ (:23.93, :47.52, 1:11.69, 1:36.77)

$2 Mutuel Prices:

9 – VERONA DALE	21.60	8.60	6.40
10 – LITETHENIGHT		11.40	7.10
1 – DH DERIVATIVE TRADER			2.80
8 – DH BIANCA'S JEWEL			3.80

$2 EXACTA 9–10 PAID $162.50 $2 TRIFECTA 9–10–1 PAID $457.00
$2 TRIFECTA 9–10–8 PAID $611.00

Ch. f, (Mar), by Siphon-Brz – Madam C E O , by Corporate Report . Trainer Morrison John. Bred by Brereton C Jones (Ky).

VERONA DALE raced with the pace from the outside, drew clear into the stretch, dug in inside in the drive and held on. LITETHENIGHT raced close up outside, rallied three wide, finished gamely outside and just missed. DERIVATIVE TRADER raced close up along the inside and had no response when roused. BIANCA'S JEWEL was outrun early, came wide into the stretch and offered a mild rally outside. TUSCAN STAR was outrun early, raced wide throughout and lacked a rally. A STROKE A HOLE raced inside and had no response when roused. LAST CHANCE GULCH raced four wide and tired in the stretch. SPARTAN LEGACY had no rally. KISSIN DAMSEL raced inside and tired. AU CURRANT raced between rivals and tired. LIBBY'S MOMENT contested the pace along the inside and tired in the stretch. PRINCESS CORRIGAN raced wide and tired.

Owners– 1, Tucker Jeffrey; 2, Triple Diamond Stables and White Owl Stable; 3, Klaravich Stables Inc; 4, Jablow Darren; 5, Robinson J Mack; 6, Flying Zee Stable; 7, Lerman Roy S; 8, Froehlich Randolph; 9, Cedar Bridge Stable; 10, A Breed Apart LLC; 11, Imperio Michael and Loftus Elizabeth; 12, Sorin Stables

Trainers– 1, Morrison John; 2, Campo John P Jr; 3, Violette Richard A Jr; 4, Jablow Michael; 5, Alexander Frank A; 6, Martin Carlos F; 7, Lerman Roy S; 8, Hauswald Philip M; 9, Gyarmati Leah; 10, Toner James J; 11, Schettino Dominick A; 12, Walsh Thomas M

A Stroke a Hole was claimed by Ross David A; trainer, Russo Frank J.

Scratched– My Own Story (18Jun06 5Bel5), Hollywood Tale (18Jun06 5Bel8), Bear and Grin It (02Jul06 10Mth8), Gilded Thread (29Jun06 6Mth2)

$2 Pick Three (4–4–9) Paid $510.00 ; Pick Three Pool $51,655 .
$2 Pick Four (8–4–4–9) Paid $396.50 ; Pick Four Pool $123,529 .

GOING BACK TO CALY

ALTHOUGH I GREW UP playing the NYRA circuit, I've recently decided to move my main handicapping tack to Southern California. A successful betting trip to beautiful Del Mar last July with DRF handicapper Dan Illman, a recent pick-six score back in April at Santa Anita, and several other pick-four scores at Santa Anita and Hollywood over the past six months pretty much sealed the deal for me.

I don't have any statistical analysis to prove my theory, but it's become rather obvious to me that there are more generous payoffs in the exotic pools of California than in New York. Whether your preferred play is the daily double, pick three, pick four, or pick six, the exotic pools are simply bigger and better. Generally, you'll get more bang for your buck playing day-to-day on the Southern

California circuit than chasing potential $12 doubles or $35 pick threes in New York. In addition, California is always offering guaranteed $400,000 or $500,000 pick fours and pick sixes, which give the casual bettor an opportunity to win large sums of money with a small-to-medium bankroll.

The first race at Del Mar on July 24, 2006, offered another unique glimpse into the familiar drop-down from maiden special weight to maiden claiming. Trainer Doug O'Neill usually brings a tremendous amount of horseflesh to the Del Mar meet, and even averages close to three entrants per racing day. Although O'Neill is traditionally a huge training success at Santa Anita and Hollywood Park, his Del Mar performance has surprisingly not produced his best numbers. At Del Mar, "Where the Surf Meets the Turf," quantity does not equal quality for O'Neill. His numbers are mediocre at best.

On July 24, his 3-year-old filly Feel the Rush, by Wild Rush, was making a conventionally winning trainer maneuver, dropping from maiden special weight to maiden claimers in a six-furlong dirt sprint.

Although the claiming price was a stiff $62,500, the class drop-down was still significant. Feel the Rush had shown decent speed against classier horses in almost all six of her career starts, and managed to hit the board in four, or one-third, of those races. Today, she was also adding blinkers, which many handicappers could easily argue would carry her speed even farther. O'Neill appeared to have fair-to-good Trainer Form stats based on win percentage in both the class drop-down (MSWtoMCL 45 .20 $0.85) and equipment-change (BlinkOn 90 .16 $1.10) categories.

The general Default Query for Formulator produced the following results for Feel the Rush:

Trainer:	Doug O'Neill
Time Frame:	Past Five Years
Blinkers:	**Blinkers On**
Class Moves:	**MdSpWt to MdnClm**

Horses	Starts	Wins	ITM	Win%	ITM%	$2ROI	Median Payoff
71	74	11	35	15%	47%	$0.66	$3.80

These mediocre ROI stats for O'Neill may have been reason enough to play against the heavy maiden favorite. The play-against option became even more appealing when we added the Formulator track-list option to the query menu. O'Neill's performance at Del Mar, Hollywood Park, and Santa Anita for the maiden-special-weight class dropper and entrant adding blinkers made it appear as if we were possibly investigating two or three different trainers. As the statistics indicate below, Hollywood Park was clearly his best meet for these types of maiden class droppers. Santa Anita was second, and O'Neill was still shooting blanks at Del Mar with an uninviting 0-for-10 record.

Hollywood Park

Trainer:	Doug O'Neill
Time Frame:	Past Five Years
Blinkers:	Blinkers On
Class Moves:	MdnSpWt to MdnClm

Horses	Starts	Wins	ITM	Win%	ITM%	$2ROI	Median Payoff
27	27	6	13	22%	48%	$1.15	$4.70

Santa Anita

Trainer:	Doug O'Neill
Time Frame:	Past Five Years
Blinkers:	Blinkers On
Class Moves:	MdnSpWt to MdnClm

Horses	Starts	Wins	ITM	Win%	ITM%	$2ROI	Median Payoff
29	30	3	14	10%	47%	$0.39	$3.80

Del Mar

Trainer:	Doug O'Neill
Time Frame:	Past Five Years
Blinkers:	Blinkers On
Class Moves:	MdnSpWt to MdnClm

Horses	Starts	Wins	ITM	Win%	ITM%	$2ROI	Median Payoff
10	10	0	4	0%	N/A	N/A	N/A

FIRST RACE
Del Mar
JULY 24, 2006

6 FURLONGS. (1.07³) MAIDEN CLAIMING . Purse $34,000 (plus $1,200 Other Sources) FOR MAIDENS, FILLIES AND MARES THREE YEARS OLD AND UPWARD. Three Year Olds, 120 lbs.; Older, 124 lbs. Claiming Price $62,500, For Each $2,500 To $55,000 1 lb. (Hazy. 87.)

Value of Race: $35,200 Winner $20,400; second $6,800; third $4,080; fourth $2,040; fifth $680; sixth $400; seventh $400; eighth $400. Mutuel Pool $240,415.00 Exacta Pool $139,798.00 Quinella Pool $12,956.00 Trifecta Pool $130,468.00 Superfecta Pool $68,643.00

Last Raced	Horse	M/Eqt. A. Wt	PP	St	¼	½	Str	Fin	Jockey	Cl'g Pr	Odds $1
18Jun06 7Hol³	Feel the Rush	LB b 3 115	6	2	4hd	5²	1½	1¾	Garcia M5	62500	1.30
	Key Lime Pie	LB 3 120	2	8	7⁴	6³	4½	21¾	Baze M C	62500	5.60
8Jun06 6Hol²	Mighty Clever	LB b 4 119	5	5	5⁴	4hd	5³	32½	Arias S5	62500	11.90
	Miss Silver Image	LB 4 124	7	3	2hd	1hd	2hd	4¾	Figueroa O	62500	29.60
	Laura'sinspiration	LB 3 120	1	6	1hd	2hd	3¹	5hd	Pedroza M A	62500	3.10
	Bad Ad	LB 3 120	8	1	6hd	72½	71½	61¾	Baze T C	62500	25.80
12May06 2Hol⁴	Get the Money	LB f 3 117	3	7	8	8	8	7²	Sorenson D	55000	7.50
8Jun06 6Hol⁵	Red Neck Gal	LB 3 115	4	4	31½	3¹	6hd	8	Ochoa J5	62500	9.60

OFF AT 2:01 Start Good. Won driving. Track fast.

TIME :22, :45¹, :58, 1:11 (:22.04, :45.26, :58.09, 1:11.15)

$2 Mutuel Prices:

6 – FEEL THE RUSH	4.60	2.80	2.20
2 – KEY LIME PIE		5.60	3.00
5 – MIGHTY CLEVER			3.00

$1 EXACTA 6–2 PAID $11.30 $2 QUINELLA 2–6 PAID $14.60
$1 TRIFECTA 6–2–5 PAID $60.90 $1 SUPERFECTA 6–2–5–7 PAID $561.30

B. f, (Feb), by Wild Rush – Incommunicado , by Wolf Power–SAf . Trainer O'Neill Doug. Bred by Tomoka Farms Inc (Ky).

FEEL THE RUSH stalked the pace outside, went three deep into the stretch, gained the advantage outside rivals in midstretch and held gamely under some urging. KEY LIME PIE broke a bit slowly, saved ground off the pace, came out on the turn and into the stretch and finished well. MIGHTY CLEVER stalked the pace off the rail on the backstretch and turn, entered the stretch outside a rival and gained the show. MISS SILVER IMAGE dueled three deep on the backstretch and turn, continued outside a foe into the stretch and between rivals in midstretch and weakened. LAURA'SINSPIRATION went up inside to duel for the lead, fought back on the turn and to midstretch and also weakened in the final furlong. BAD AD allowed to settle off the rail then outside a rival on the backstretch, angled in on the turn, came out in upper stretch and did not rally. GET THE MONEY saved ground off the pace, remained inside in the stretch and failed to menace. RED NECK GAL vied for command between horses, dropped back into the stretch and had little left.

Owners– 1, Owners Stable Policzer Milt and Suarez Racing Inc; 2, R G M Stables; 3, Gifford Patrick and Pierce; 4, Blahut Donald and Giammarino Robert; 5, Double Kee LLC; 6, G Five Stable LLC; 7, Lemalu Stable and Flores Richard; 8, Brown Darrell Firestone Brooks and Pananides Alex

Trainers– 1, O'Neill Doug; 2, Matlow Richard P; 3, Wicker Lloyd C; 4, Machowsky Michael; 5, McFarlane Dan L; 6, Puhich Michael; 7, Avila A C; 8, Spawr Bill

Key Lime Pie was claimed by Jawl Michael; trainer, Peery Chuck,
Laura'sinspiration was claimed by Southern Equine Stable LLC; trainer, Guillot Eric.

Doug O'Neill managed to break his five-year skid as Feel the Rush narrowly held off first-time starter Key Lime Pie to score as the 7–5 betting favorite. In retrospect, was she still a favorite worth betting against? Absolutely. Did our Formulator trainer data lead us down a path of doom? Absolutely not. These are the types of favorites we should be trying to beat day in and day out, and the types of situations that will ultimately reward those who consistently play against trainers that do not excel in certain situations.

Anyone who thinks individual race meetings don't affect the performance of a trainer is sadly mistaken. For a variety of reasons, a trainer has different levels of success on different racetracks, despite the fact they are operating on the same circuit. Many of these tracks are frequently within 100 miles of one another, but it makes no difference. Jim Mazur of Progressive Handicapping is a good friend of mine, and has produced meet-specific trainer-stat books for his customers for well over a decade. A unique advantage of Mazur's trainer books (up until the recent development of Formulator) was the fact that they were meet-specific. A successful trainer maneuver at one track does not always result in triumph at another meeting. It's impossible for training outfits to operate at full throttle continuously, and it's natural for trainers to excel at different times of the year and at different tracks. It's our job as handicappers to know when that occurs.

I've already provided several examples throughout the book where the interpretation of some of the general Trainer Form data can be misleading without using a little common sense and some of the useful Formulator tools. In other situations the data is as clear as day and does not require any aggressive or exploratory handicapping techniques to uncover live horses.

This was exactly the case with another maiden-claiming event on July 26, 2006, which was the first day of week two of the 2006 Del Mar meet. The race was a 1 1/16-mile route for 3-year-old California-breds running for a $40,000 price tag. Number 8, Freedom Event, was trained by the talented and ultraconsistent Martin F. Jones. Jones is not listed on our Top 25 ROI list, but he was hovering around 30th place at the time of this writing and certainly should be commended as one of the masters with this maiden class drop. It didn't take a rocket scientist to recognize that Jones was a specialist of the maiden-special-weight to maiden-claimer drop-down maneuver.

8 **Freedom Event**	Dk. b or br g. 3 (Mar)		Life	3 M 0 0		$800	65	D.Fst	1 0 0 0		$0 65
	Sire: Event of the Year (Seattle Slew) $4,000										
Own: Golden Eagle Farm	Dam: Flag of Freedom (Fappiano)	$40,000	2006	3 M 0 0		$800	65	Wet (376)	0 0 0 0		$0 –
6–1 Burgundy, gold eagle on back, gold	Br: Betty L. Mabee(Cal)		L 115 5	2005	0 M 0 0		$0	–	Turf (296)	2 0 0 0	$800 65
Garcia M (32 7 4 4 .21) 2006:(837 205 .24)	Tr: Jones Martin F (–) 2006:(135 22 .16)		Dmr	0 0 0 0		$0	–	Dist (371)	0 0 0 0		$0 –

23Jun06–3Hol fm 1 1/16 ①:23 :47 1:10⁴ 1:41³ 3↑ Ⓢ Md Sp Wt 48k		47 6 11¹¹ 11¹⁶ 11¹⁶ 10¹⁵ 9¹⁵ Garcia M⁵	LB112	6.60 69–13 *CousinJoe* 124³ HighEen 1171⁄4³ WrGel 119⁴	Off bit slow,no threat 12
31May06–8Hol fm 1 1/16 ①:23 :46³ 1:10² 1:41 3↑ Ⓢ Md Sp Wt 48k		65 4 76 10¹⁰ 108³⁄4 88 76³⁄4 Ochoa J⁵	LB112	8.30 81–10 Opa117³ *Cousin Joe* 1243³⁄4 Snoden 124⁰ᵒ	Pulled early,no rally 10
30Apr06–4Hol fst 6 1/2f :21¹ :43⁴ 1:09⁴ 1:16¹ 3↑ Ⓢ PepOakFrm60k		65 12 8 119¹⁄4 11¹⁰ 99³⁄4 79³⁄4 Valdivia J Jr	LB117	60.60 81–08 Bcfss124⁰ᵒ OnDx1175³⁄4 KtKIdKImz124¹⁄2	3wd into lane,no bid 14

WORKS: Jly14 Hol 6f fst 1:13⁴ H 4/6 Jly7 Hol 4f fst :51¹ H 30/38 Jun14 Hol 4f fst :50⁴ H 27/29 May25 Hol 5f fst 1:00³ H 13/44 May19 Hol 6f fst 1:15⁴ H 17/22 May12 Hol 4f fst :50¹ H 24/30

TRAINER: MSWtoMCL (15 .53 $5.08) Turf/Dirt (33 .15 $1.94) 31–60Days (116 .16 $1.92) Dirt (268 .15 $1.82) Routes (128 .16 $1.62) MdnClm (91 .18 $2.36)   J/T 2005–06 (12 .33 $3.60)

The first category of the Trainer Form stats on Freedom Event was a thing of beauty. It read: MSWtoMCL (15 .53 $5.08). Once you are accustomed to reading these stats in the *Daily Racing Form* past performances, it's information like this that just seems to bounce off the page. Only a few years back, when all the comprehensive trainer data was not as easily accessible to the public, you might have expected to get 8–1 or 9–1 on this horse. Today, we don't get as many overlays as we once did; however, good value on specific trainer angles still exists with handicapping patience and perseverance.

The Default Query for Freedom Event strengthened the validity and effectiveness of the Jones maiden-special-weight to maiden-claimer drop-down. It appeared as follows:

Trainer:	Martin F. Jones
Time Frame:	Past Five Years
Class Moves:	**MdnSpWt to MdnClm**
Surface:	Turf to Dirt

Horses	Starts	Wins	ITM	Win%	ITM%	$2ROI	Median Payoff
15	16	7	11	44%	69%	$4.85	$6.80

These favorable stats alone justified a wager on Freedom Event, but a little Formulator track-specific massaging glorified his chances even further. Jones had attempted this same class drop at Del Mar only four times over the past five years, but was victorious in 75 percent of those attempts.

Trainer:	Martin F. Jones
Time Frame:	Past Five Years
Class Moves:	MdnSptWt to MdnClm
Track/Circuit:	**Today's Track**

Horses	Starts	Wins	ITM	Win%	ITM%	$2ROI	Median Payoff
4	4	3	3	75%	75%	$5.90	$8.20

FIRST-TIME STARTERS, 2-YEAR-OLDS, AND MAIDENS

TRAINER STATS FOR MSWtoMCL

Name	Starts	Wins	Win Percentage	ROI (Based on $2.00 to Win)
Baldwin, James	6	5	0.833	$ 10.00
Springer, Frank R	12	6	0.500	$ 9.12
Gothard, Akiko M	19	5	0.263	$ 7.84
Pierce, Jr., Joseph H	19	5	0.263	$ 7.74
Oliver, Vicki	17	6	0.353	$ 7.74
Hartlage, Gary G	25	7	0.280	$ 7.56
Currin, William L	11	6	0.545	$ 7.56
Poliziani, Daniel J	8	6	0.750	$ 7.43
Arceneaux, Victor	16	10	0.625	$ 7.24
Adamo, Anthony	11	6	0.545	$ 6.87
De Gannes, Gregory	11	6	0.545	$ 6.69
Leatherbury, King T	25	9	0.360	$ 6.48
Bernis, Glynn	34	8	0.235	$ 6.13
Hedge, Rick	10	6	0.600	$ 6.07
Maker, Rebecca	29	9	0.310	$ 6.07
Marr, Joel H	17	10	0.588	$ 5.92
Spawr, William	9	5	0.556	$ 5.80
Janks, Christine K	25	11	0.440	$ 5.78
Van Berg, Jack C	21	5	0.238	$ 5.74
Gulick, James M	11	5	0.455	$ 5.67
Bonilla, Candelario	8	8	1.000	$ 5.65
Walters, David	25	9	0.360	$ 5.53
Mandella, Richard E	10	5	0.500	$ 5.46
McKellar, Joseph P	12	5	0.417	$ 5.38
Patrick, R. G.	38	16	0.421	$ 5.28

TRAINER STATS FOR 2ndMdn

Name	Starts	Wins	Win Percentage	ROI (Based on $2.00 to Win)
Spurlock, Lee	9	5	0.556	$ 25.80
Scolamieri, Sam J	15	5	0.333	$ 16.30
Paasch, Christopher S	38	5	0.263	$ 15.00
Inabinett, Johnny	14	7	0.500	$ 12.90
Nunnally, James E	14	5	0.357	$ 12.80
Vaders, Jayne	28	9	0.321	$ 12.30
Ordonez, Aggie	20	7	0.350	$ 12.00
Anderson, Jann P	13	5	0.385	$ 11.80
Meals, Lois	18	5	0.278	$ 11.40
Barney, Edward H	11	5	0.455	$ 10.10
Retamoza, Sr., Ernest P	18	5	0.278	$ 10.10
Speckert, Christopher	17	6	0.353	$ 10.00
Skiffington, Thomas J	38	6	0.158	$ 9.23
Reinacher, Jr., Robert J	26	5	0.192	$ 9.05
Lay, Larry	28	6	0.214	$ 9.04
Schmidt, Denise	42	5	0.119	$ 8.56
Hendrickson, David L	35	14	0.400	$ 8.11
Armata, Vito	22	7	0.318	$ 7.88
Schlich, Joseph P	8	5	0.625	$ 6.83
Furr, Daniel R	46	7	0.152	$ 6.82
Kees, Barbara M	19	5	0.263	$ 6.59
Cart, Jerry D	50	5	0.100	$ 6.45
Novak, Marshall L	9	6	0.667	$ 6.44
Hill, Jimmie E	9	5	0.556	$ 6.42
Taylor, Brant L	35	5	0.143	$ 6.34

TRAINER STATS FOR DebutMCL

Name	Starts	Wins	Win Percentage	ROI (Based on $2.00 to Win)
Cronk, Samuel F	18	5	0.278	$7.63
Brashears, Bill	16	5	0.313	$4.90
Simon, Stuart C	20	5	0.250	$4.85
Sherman, Art	81	23	0.284	$4.48
Harwood, Doris	33	8	0.242	$4.47
Teel, Mike R	15	5	0.333	$4.05
DiMauro, Stephen L	52	8	0.154	$3.94
Hills, Timothy A	41	9	0.220	$3.74
Ziadie, Kirk	22	7	0.318	$3.58
Duncan, Leonard M	35	5	0.143	$3.52
Stall, Jr., Albert M	32	5	0.156	$3.41
Baffert, Bob	21	7	0.333	$3.30
Casse, Mark E	26	6	0.231	$3.30
Fawkes, David	35	7	0.200	$3.08
Pearson, Molly J	19	6	0.316	$3.04
O'Connell, Kathleen	44	10	0.227	$2.95
Zimmerman, John C	16	6	0.375	$2.95
Gilchrist, Greg	19	7	0.368	$2.92
Catalano, Wayne M	17	6	0.353	$2.91
Nicks, Morris G	33	6	0.182	$2.85
Romans, Dale L	30	6	0.200	$2.83
Martin, John F	27	7	0.259	$2.77
Rigattieri, John	14	5	0.357	$2.69
Musgrave, Shawn	31	5	0.161	$2.69
Patrick, R. G.	25	6	0.240	$2.48

8

THE GO-TO GUY OR GAL

IT'S WIDELY ACCEPTED IN today's handicapping realm that the right combination of jockey and trainer has supplementary effects on the outcome of races. Jim Quinn nailed the importance of the class drop, jockey switch, and trainer intention in his book *The Best of Thoroughbred Handicapping.* He stated, "When a horse is primed to win, its chances improve against easier competition and with superior jockeys. Regardless of whether the race is actually easier or the jockey better, trainers perceive these differences and believe the switches favor their horses."

Favorable jockey and trainer stats don't lie, and it's easy to distinguish what combinations are successfully lighting up the tote board at the racetrack or circuit where you are wagering. These successful combos change from meet to meet and year to year due to retirement, injuries, agent changes, etc. Therefore, as a handicapper, it's imperative that you keep an updated and thorough list of what jockeys and trainers are clicking at the circuits you're playing, and also familiarize yourself with the up-and-coming apprentices that are likely to get the live mounts because of their weight allowance.

Daily Racing Form lists the records of jockeys and trainers for the current meet, the current year, and shows the win percentage for specific jockeys and trainers when they team up. They may appear as the following in the printed DRF edition:

Molina V H (259 36 34 .14) 2006: (286 38 .13); Tr: Servis John C (77 10 17 8 .13) 2006: (113 13 .12); J/T 2005–06 PHA (3 .00 $0.00) J/T 2005–06 (3 .00 $0.00).

This information is useful, but the Formulator program allows the bettor to dig even deeper into a specific jockey's strengths and weaknesses. Not only can the handicapper get the data provided above, but you can also get the jockey's success rate for dirt, turf, sprints, routes, and his or her win clip for maiden and nonmaiden races. In addition, you'll get 10- and 30-day win-streak percentages, and the average win payoff for the trainer/jockey combination. Does jockey Edgar Prado typically perform better in turf routes than dirt routes? With the Formulator program, you'll have that indispensable data right at your fingertips.

Following is an extensive listing of the top five DRF jockey/trainer combo stats, which were taken from the beginning of 2004 to the end of July 2006. The list includes most American and Canadian racetracks. They are ranked by ROI with a five-race win minimum. As with any statistical study, the results are constantly changing. Therefore, it's essential that your analysis is continuously updated and maintained for accuracy. The beauty of using the Formulator program is that the jockey and trainer combo statistics are automatically updated daily. This is a huge advantage over those individuals who still rely on accumulating their own data through the tiresome chore of reviewing old racing charts. Whatever your handicapping style may be, I'm confident that you'll find this list helpful in some capacity—hopefully while uncovering the jockeys and trainers that team up at your local circuit to produce juicy overlays year after year. Keep the list handy and in a safe place!

*Please note that some jockeys and trainers that appear on this list are no longer actively riding or training.

AQUEDUCT

Trainer	Jockey	Starts	Wins	Win Pct	ROI
Pederson, Jennifer	Kaenel, Kyle	14	5	0.357	8.07
Carroll, II, Del	Castellano, Javier	13	6	0.462	7.44
Mettinis, Louis N.	Fragoso, Pablo	20	5	0.250	5.72
Barbara, Robert	Dominguez, Ramon A.	10	5	0.500	5.71
McLaughlin, Kiaran P.	Jara, Fernando	71	17	0.239	5.52

ARLINGTON PARK

Trainer	Jockey	Starts	Wins	Win Pct	ROI
Razo, Alejandro	Perez, Eduardo E.	13	5	0.385	9.31
Dini, Michael	Ferrer, Jose C	19	9	0.474	7.65
Gabriel, Bettye A.	La Sala, Jerry	26	7	0.269	6.10
Beam, Ed	Fires, Earlie	23	5	0.217	4.83
Livesay, Charles	Razo, Jr., Eusebio	28	5	0.179	4.49

ATLANTIC CITY

Trainer	Jockey	Starts	Wins	Win Pct	ROI
Voss, Thomas H.	Murphy, Cyril	14	5	0.357	8.07

BAY MEADOWS

Trainer	Jockey	Starts	Wins	Win Pct	ROI
Diaz, Antonio L.	Garcia, Martin	7	5	0.714	7.83
Specht, Steven	Perez, Miguel A.	12	5	0.417	7.30
Jackson, Ellen L.	Harvey, Barrington	34	5	0.147	4.42
Belvoir, Howard	Duran, Francisco	32	5	0.156	3.99
Franko, Daniel	Garcia, Martin	14	5	0.357	3.84

BELMONT PARK

Trainer	Jockey	Starts	Wins	Win Pct	ROI
Albertrani, Thomas	Castellano, Javier	18	5	0.278	5.67
Carroll, II, Del	Migliore, Richard	13	5	0.385	5.62
Aquilino, Joseph	Chavez, Jorge F.	24	8	0.333	5.56
Schettino, Dominick A.	Chavez, Jorge F.	9	5	0.556	5.32
Hough, Stanley M.	Coa, Eibar	25	8	0.320	5.11

BEULAH PARK

Trainer	Jockey	Starts	Wins	Win Pct	ROI
Grace, John R.	Stokes, Joe	14	5	0.357	9.41
Allen, Sr., Ronald D.	Yuranga, Yuri	10	5	0.500	5.86
Rawlins, Jerry	Sanchez, Joseph	28	9	0.321	5.74
Faulkner, Rickey	Melancon, Paul	42	12	0.286	5.46
Gross, Reid	Rojas, Christian	31	12	0.387	5.19

CALDER RACE COURSE

Trainer	Jockey	Starts	Wins	Win Pct	ROI
Mendez, Jose A.	Lezcano, Jose	20	5	0.250	7.39
Chaparro, Dubis	Sanchez, Jeffrey	9	6	0.667	6.93
Morales, Mario	Penalba, Cecilio	15	5	0.333	6.28
Paul, Cecil	Cruz, Manoel R.	11	5	0.455	5.25
Morales, Mario	Cruz, Manoel R.	9	5	0.556	5.26

CANTERBURY PARK

Trainer	Jockey	Starts	Wins	Win Pct	ROI
Donlin, Larry D.	Stevens, Scott A.	17	5	0.294	7.59
McShane, David D.	Essman, David Wilder	13	5	0.385	6.51
Van Winkle, David	Campbell, Joel	16	8	0.500	4.54
Artz, Deborrah J.	Bell, Derek C.	13	5	0.385	3.72
Bango, George A.	Eikleberry, Ry	17	6	0.353	3.49

CHARLES TOWN

Trainer	Jockey	Starts	Wins	Win Pct	ROI
Barr, Donald H.	Russell, Chris	9	5	0.556	8.00
Martinez, Frankie W.	Grafton, Dwayne A.	21	7	0.333	7.48
Cartagena, Keisy	Gustavo, Larrosa	18	6	0.333	7.06
Wells, David J.	Whitacre, Brandon	18	12	0.667	6.66
Merryman, Edwin W.	Cora, David	24	7	0.292	6.18

CHURCHILL DOWNS

Trainer	Jockey	Starts	Wins	Win Pct	ROI
Foley, Vickie L.	Perret, Craig	12	5	0.417	9.23
Flint, Bernard S.	Martinez, Willie	20	6	0.300	6.72
Reinstedler, Anthony	Day, Pat	7	5	0.714	6.00
Maker, Rebecca	Castanon, Jesus Lopez	23	5	0.217	5.69
Margolis, Stephen R.	Martinez, Willie	24	7	0.292	5.61

COLONIAL DOWNS

Trainer	Jockey	Starts	Wins	Win Pct	ROI
Baker, Bryan R.	Sosa, Jr., Peter	25	5	0.200	8.94
Sweeney, Ronald M.	Delgado, Alberto	9	5	0.556	6.42
Garcia, Carlos A.	Garcia, Luis	20	7	0.350	4.76
Feliciano, Jr., Benjamin M.	Fogelsonger, Ryan	8	5	0.625	4.30
Robinson, Catherine H.	Garcia, Luis	28	6	0.214	4.26

DELAWARE PARK

Trainer	Jockey	Starts	Wins	Win Pct	ROI
Sheppard, Jonathan E.	Rose, Jeremy	9	6	0.667	7.24
Canet, Julian	Saez, Gabriel	16	6	0.375	5.30
Pecoraro, Anthony	Pino, Mario G.	9	5	0.556	4.42
Simoff, Andrew L.	Hansby, Antonio E.	34	5	0.147	4.28
Guiterrez, Angel	Umana, Juan	49	5	0.102	4.07

DEL MAR

Trainer	Jockey	Starts	Wins	Win Pct	ROI
Dollase, Craig	Nakatani, Corey S.	14	6	0.429	5.33
Mullins, Jeff	Kerwin, John	12	6	0.500	5.03
Gaines, Carla	Espinoza, Victor	17	7	0.412	4.11
Canani, Julio C.	Flores, David Romero	24	6	0.250	3.88
Canani, Julio C.	Nakatani, Corey S.	13	6	0.462	3.40

DELTA DOWNS

Trainer	Jockey	Starts	Wins	Win Pct	ROI
Huval, Brian A.	Nichols, Jerri Elizabeth	22	8	0.364	9.98
Enis Mouton, Alicea	Maldonado, Edwin	18	5	0.278	4.39
Sam, Thomas W.	Eads, Jason R.	22	5	0.227	4.04
Sam, Thomas W.	Smith, Guy	20	9	0.450	3.99
Segura, Kearney	Woodley, Carl James	25	6	0.240	3.85

EMERALD DOWNS

Trainer	Jockey	Starts	Wins	Win Pct	ROI
Navarro, Jose	Zunino, Jose Luis	18	6	0.333	9.06
Kenney, Daniel	Russell, Ben	30	12	0.400	6.95
Penney, Jim	Perez, Miguel A.	15	8	0.533	6.16
Knapp, Neil	Hoonan, Deborah	14	5	0.357	5.89
Smith, William J.	Ruis, Mick	15	6	0.400	5.83

EVANGELINE DOWNS

Trainer	Jockey	Starts	Wins	Win Pct	ROI
Hendrickson, Lori	Riquelme, Jose	9	5	0.556	6.53
Rayburn, Greg	Clark, Kerwin D.	12	5	0.417	6.43
Herbert, R. Pete	Langlinais, Elvis	28	6	0.214	6.08
Breaux, Samuel	Carmouche, Jr., Sylvester J.	37	6	0.162	5.30
Meaux, William	Nichols, Jerri Elizabeth	13	6	0.462	5.06

FAIR GROUNDS

Trainer	Jockey	Starts	Wins	Win Pct	ROI
Bindner, Jr., Walter M.	Graham, James	16	5	0.313	8.38
Carroll, Josie	Melancon, Gerard	19	5	0.263	7.18
Keen, Dallas E.	Meche, Lonnie	14	5	0.357	5.96
Amoss, Thomas M.	Melancon, Larry	11	6	0.545	5.87
Broussard, Joseph E.	Martin, Jr., Eddie M.	12	5	0.417	4.37

FAIR MEADOWS

Trainer	Jockey	Starts	Wins	Win Pct	ROI
Marshall, Kenneth W.	Kimes, Curtis	8	5	0.625	3.25
Dyer, Debbie Holland	Kimes, Curtis	16	6	0.375	3.09
Armstrong, Zachary	Matz, Nena	28	7	0.250	2.49
Teel, Mike R.	Kimes, Curtis	57	18	0.316	1.86
Ferrell, Jory	Kimes, Curtis	32	10	0.313	1.48

FAIRMOUNT PARK

Trainer	Jockey	Starts	Wins	Win Pct	ROI
Roberts, Robert W.	Caples, Steve	27	6	0.222	8.30
West, David L.	Hernandez, Rafael Manuel	34	12	0.353	5.26
Manley, Steve	Hernandez, Rafael Manuel	27	6	0.222	4.31
Trione, Jr., Thomas E.	Villafan, Roberto	21	6	0.286	4.10
Rednour, Jr., John	Sukie, Danush	18	5	0.278	4.02

FINGER LAKES

Trainer	Jockey	Starts	Wins	Win Pct	ROI
Nicolo, John	Dominguez, Vincente Carlos	16	6	0.375	7.81
Erb, Jim	Dominguez, Vincente Carlos	15	5	0.333	7.50
Armstrong, Bryan R.	Castillo, Elaine	30	5	0.167	5.28
Wright, T. James.	Suarez, Gabriel	24	5	0.208	4.64
Anderson, Bruce D.	Centeno, Daniel	31	5	0.161	4.22

FONNER PARK

Trainer	Jockey	Starts	Wins	Win Pct	ROI
Gaede, Milton M.	Ranilla, Luis	15	5	0.333	8.49
Moss, Joseph A.	Frazier, Don Lee	25	7	0.280	4.11
Parker, Robert W.	Carkeek, Jerome	24	7	0.292	3.98
Conyers, William F.	Collins, Dennis Michael	14	7	0.500	3.73
Strode, Daniel Lee	Beck, Daniel Lee	17	6	0.353	3.47

GOLDEN GATE

Trainer	Jockey	Starts	Wins	Win Pct	ROI
Marshall, John Terry	Rollins, Chance J.	10	5	0.500	6.70
Specht, Steven	Perez, Miguel A.	39	11	0.282	6.38
Morey, William E.	Schvaneveldt, Chad Phillip	13	7	0.538	5.23
Sherman, Art	Miranda, Alfredo	22	7	0.318	5.16
Mason, Lloyd C.	Carr, Dennis	13	5	0.385	5.15

GREAT LAKES DOWNS

Trainer	Jockey	Starts	Wins	Win Pct	ROI
Johnson, Keith M.	Santos, Felipe J.	15	5	0.333	7.56
Lelito, Timothy L.	Bernal, Octavio	38	5	0.132	5.88
Barron, Douglas R.	Santos, Felipe J.	35	6	0.171	5.57
Glenn, Dwaine A.	Knott, Rick L.	15	5	0.333	5.19
Londono, Jr., Odin J.	Bernal Octavio	34	11	0.324	4.99

GULFSTREAM PARK

Trainer	Jockey	Starts	Wins	Win Pct	ROI
Bracken, James E.	Prado, Edgar S.	13	5	0.385	6.23
Hennig, Mark A.	Bravo, Joe	20	5	0.250	5.22
Wolfson, Martin D.	Castro, Eddie	36	8	0.222	4.89
Garcia, Rodolfo	Lopez, Jose E.	10	5	0.500	4.80
Harvatt, Charles R.	Bravo, Joe	12	5	0.417	4.75

HASTINGS PARK

Trainer	Jockey	Starts	Wins	Win Pct	ROI
Morrison, John D.	Stein, Justin	10	5	0.500	8.17
Anderson, Robert J.	Alvarado, Pedro V.	8	5	0.625	7.81
Barroby, Frank E.	Hamel, Richard Harvey	26	7	0.269	7.60
Giesbrecht, Brian	Ward, Anderson	19	6	0.316	6.59
Anderson, Robert J.	Stein, Justin	9	6	0.667	5.94

TRAINER ANGLES

HAWTHORNE

Trainer	Jockey	Starts	Wins	Win Pct	ROI
Kasperski, Jr., Joseph E.	Laviolette, Shane	24	5	0.208	7.00
Hinsley, David H.	Mena, Miguel	32	8	0.250	5.95
Brueggemann, Roger A.	Contreras, Cruz	16	6	0.375	5.10
Roberts, Stanley W.	Morris, Liz	36	6	0.167	4.93
Turner, Kris	Lopez, Uriel A.	30	5	0.167	4.67

HOLLYWOOD PARK

Trainer	Jockey	Starts	Wins	Win Pct	ROI
Gonzalez, Sal	Cohen, David	25	6	0.240	7.72
Becerra, Rafael	Douglas, Rene R.	11	5	0.455	7.11
Hines, Nicholas J.	Gomez, Garrett K.	22	5	0.227	4.60
Gallagher, Patrick	Valdivia, Jr., Jose	37	10	0.270	4.46
Harrington, Mike	Court, Jon Kenton	35	10	0.286	4.43

HOOSIER PARK

Trainer	Jockey	Starts	Wins	Win Pct	ROI
Essenpreis, Eddie M.	Garcia, David	26	7	0.269	5.40
Nance, Michael W.	LeJeune, Jr., Sidney P.	19	6	0.316	5.21
Bennett, Gerald S.	Delgado, Jose J.	25	6	0.240	4.85
Prescott, Rodney A.	Hoskins, Steve	15	5	0.333	4.44
Pompell, Thomas L.	Essenpreis, Eddie M.	25	7	0.280	4.27

SAM HOUSTON

Trainer	Jockey	Starts	Wins	Win Pct	ROI
Hall, Randall J.	Garner, Cathleen J.	17	8	0.471	6.65
Montgomery, Sandra	Rodriguez, Filemon T.	33	5	0.152	5.82
Bennett, William D.	Shepherd, Justin	15	9	0.600	5.68
Hukill, Charles P.	Cruz, Anthony	55	7	0.127	5.62
House, Brian S.	Collier, Jeremy	14	5	0.357	5.06

INDIANA DOWNS

Trainer	Jockey	Starts	Wins	Win Pct	ROI
Hayes, Michael S.	Diego, Inosencio	7	5	0.714	9.69
Shuster, Patricia C.	Delagado, Jose J.	19	7	0.368	6.57
Martin, Joseph R.	LeJeune, Jr., Sidney P.	12	5	0.417	6.40
Zahl, Robert	Stokes, Joe	30	8	0.267	5.79
Scott, Joan	Zuniga, Eddie	7	5	0.714	4.54

KEENELAND

Trainer	Jockey	Starts	Wins	Win Pct	ROI
Sheppard, Jonathan E.	Stevens, Gary L.	7	5	0.714	5.74
Amoss, Thomas M.	Graham, James	22	8	0.364	5.04
Zito, Nicholas P.	Day, Pat	10	6	0.600	4.50
Foley, Gregory D.	Bejarano, Rafael	22	6	0.273	4.05
Holthus, Robert E.	McKee, John	54	7	0.130	3.67

LAUREL PARK

Trainer	Jockey	Starts	Wins	Win Pct	ROI
Grusmark, Karl M.	Whitacre, Brandon	9	5	0.556	7.44
Smith, Hamilton A.	Karamanos, Horacio	19	6	0.316	6.40
Trombetta, Michael J.	Caraballo, Jose C.	11	5	0.455	5.96
Haughton, Donnovan	Dominguez, Ramon A.	8	6	0.750	5.83
King, Yolonda Y.	Monterrey, Jr., Pedro	28	5	0.179	5.56

LONE STAR PARK

Trainer	Jockey	Starts	Wins	Win Pct	ROI
Pish, Danny	Taylor, Larry	17	5	0.294	6.42
Morgan, Tommie T.	Crandall, Amanda L.	24	5	0.208	5.78
Hudson, James C.	Theriot, Jamie	24	9	0.375	5.66
Whitton, Mark	Taylor, Larry	36	6	0.167	5.19
Petalino, Joseph	Hamilton, Quincy	15	7	0.467	4.40

LOUISIANA DOWNS

Trainer	Jockey	Starts	Wins	Win Pct	ROI
Seagle, Stan	Riquelme, Jose	18	5	0.278	8.27
Mayo, Larry A.	Burningham, Jeffery	36	5	0.139	6.22
Gomez, Jorge	Flores, Rico	31	5	0.161	5.66
Mayo, Larry A.	Jacinto, John	25	8	0.320	5.54
Hebert, Doris	Bourque, Steve J.	25	7	0.280	5.46

MEADOWLANDS

Trainer	Jockey	Starts	Wins	Win Pct	ROI
Allard, Edward T.	Vega, Harry	15	9	0.600	6.88
Servis, Jason	Lopez, Charles C.	19	9	0.474	4.65
Broome, Edwin T.	Pimentel, Julian	25	5	0.200	3.62
Shuman, Mark	Gryder, Aaron T.	30	7	0.233	2.53
Pletcher, Todd A.	DeCarlo, Christopher P.	32	9	0.281	1.81

TRAINER ANGLES

MONMOUTH PARK

Trainer	Jockey	Starts	Wins	Win Pct	ROI
Sacco, Gregory D.	Lezcano, Jose	15	6	0.400	5.37
Costa, Frank	Bravo, Joe	9	6	0.667	5.07
Broome, Edwin T.	Clemente, Alfredo V.	31	7	0.226	4.86
Maker, Michael J.	Garcia, Alan	15	5	0.333	4.36
Broome, Edwin T.	Garcia, Alan	34	7	0.206	4.06

MOUNTAINEER PARK

Trainer	Jockey	Starts	Wins	Win Pct	ROI
Gumbell, Thomas A.	Marcial, Benjamin	44	5	0.114	9.06
Wiseman, Kelly L.	Birzer, Gary A.	33	8	0.242	7.16
Reynolds, Ryan	Pereira, Oswald M.	21	7	0.333	6.82
Knipe, Duane	Rini, Wade P.	14	6	0.429	6.31
Rissi, Luiz	Marcial, Benjamin	27	7	0.259	5.72

OAKLAWN PARK

Trainer	Jockey	Starts	Wins	Win Pct	ROI
Cart, Jerry D.	Berry, M. Clifton	9	5	0.556	8.53
Milligan, Sr., Eddie R.	Berry, M. Clifton	17	5	0.294	6.56
Tomlinson, Michael A.	Shepherd, Justin	22	6	0.273	6.39
Whited, Danny W.	Quinonez, Luis S.	31	8	0.258	5.58
Fires, William H.	Rose, Jeremy	15	5	0.333	4.43

PENN NATIONAL

Trainer	Jockey	Starts	Wins	Win Pct	ROI
West, Benjamin F.	Rodriguez, Edilberto	57	7	0.123	6.98
Hendriks, Richard J.	Lee, Katie	22	6	0.273	6.34
Zimmerman, John Charles	Perez, Christian Yermay	15	5	0.333	5.45
Beattie, Stephanie S.	Perez, Edwin	25	9	0.360	5.00
Rojas, Murray L.	Benavides, Daniel	41	11	0.268	4.72

PHILADELPHIA PARK

Trainer	Jockey	Starts	Wins	Win Pct	ROI
Lehman, Edward	Santagata, Nick	17	8	0.471	5.14
Martin, Ramon F.	Mello, David	25	7	0.280	5.08
Bonaventura, Paul	Vega, Harry	21	9	0.429	5.03
Beattie, Todd M.	Perez, Edwin	16	6	0.375	4.76
Taylor, Robert J.	Anderson, Devon	15	5	0.333	4.73

PIMLICO

Trainer	Jockey	Starts	Wins	Win Pct	ROI
Delozier, III, Joseph W.	Camacho, Eric	20	8	0.400	4.57
Delozier, III, Joseph W.	Garcia, Luis	30	10	0.333	4.42
Albert, Linda L.	Garcia, Luis	32	7	0.219	4.08
Haughton, Donnovan	Monterrey, Richard	16	6	0.375	4.05
Dilodvico, Damon R.	Santana, Jozbin Z.	37	11	0.297	4.05

PORTLAND MEADOWS

Trainer	Jockey	Starts	Wins	Win Pct	ROI
Duke, David L.	Zunino, Jose Luis	12	5	0.417	9.42
Caron, Darrell	Gilbert, Jessica	11	5	0.455	6.60
Hunt, Vannessa	Peery, Melissa	35	8	0.229	4.61
Runyon, David P.	Jones, Clark E.	11	6	0.545	4.60
Elliott, Tim	Peery, Melissa	13	6	0.462	4.52

PRAIRIE MEADOWS

Trainer	Jockey	Starts	Wins	Win Pct	ROI
Ashauer, Norman	Torres, Cesar A.	17	5	0.294	7.15
Barkley, Jeff	Doocy, Timothy T.	20	7	0.350	5.52
Bader, Mark S.	Smith, Stormy	25	6	0.240	5.11
Dunbar, Larry	Shino, Ken A.	27	5	0.185	4.51
Dunbar, Larry	Doocy, Timothy T.	27	7	0.259	4.41

REMINGTON PARK

Trainer	Jockey	Starts	Wins	Win Pct	ROI
Engel, Roger F.	Cogburn, Kevin Leon	16	6	0.375	5.11
Albright, Robert	Cogburn, Kevin Leon	20	6	0.300	4.40
Bass, Fred	Landeros, Benny C.	48	7	0.146	4.04
Osborn, O.J.	Hamilton, Quincy	20	5	0.250	4.03
Charlton, Brent W.	Hamilton, Quincy	33	12	0.364	3.53

RETAMA PARK

Trainer	Jockey	Starts	Wins	Win Pct	ROI
Lovell, Michelle	Byrne, John	15	5	0.333	7.89
Asmussen, Cheryl	McNeil, Tony	18	6	0.333	6.09
Pettit, William A.	Taylor, Larry	35	10	0.286	4.30
Evans, Bart B.	Beasley, Jeremy	13	5	0.385	3.83
Doege, Glenn	Taylor, Larry	16	5	0.313	3.44

TRAINER ANGLES

RIVER DOWNS

Trainer	Jockey	Starts	Wins	Win Pct	ROI
England, David P.	Chavez, Casey R.	25	5	0.200	9.62
White, Vincent	Lebron, Victor	25	6	0.240	8.88
Bartholomew, Jennifer A.	Golibrzuch, Siggy	15	6	0.400	8.67
Nocero, Rinzy	Collazo, Sr., Jorge E.	68	16	0.235	4.38
Caramori, Eduardo C.	Rosario, Jr., Hector L.	7	5	0.714	4.31

SANTA ANITA PARK

Trainer	Jockey	Starts	Wins	Win Pct	ROI
Mandella, Gary	Solis, Alex O.	8	5	0.625	7.80
Duncan, Leonard M.	Gomez, Garrett K.	17	5	0.294	6.22
Gaines, Carla	Bisono, Alex	14	5	0.357	6.11
McAnally, Ronald L.	Stevens, Gary L.	25	9	0.360	5.90
Ellis, Ronald W.	Desormeaux, Kent J.	11	5	0.455	5.73

SARATOGA

Trainer	Jockey	Starts	Wins	Win Pct	ROI
Clement, Christophe	Bailey, Jerry D.	8	5	0.625	4.79
Serpe, Philip M.	Castellano, Javier	20	6	0.300	3.92
Frankel, Robert J.	Prado, Edgar S.	19	6	0.316	3.38
Rice, Linda	Velasquez, Cornelio H.	38	8	0.211	3.35
Zito, Nicholas P.	Castellano, Javier	23	5	0.217	2.57

STAMPEDE PARK

Trainer	Jockey	Starts	Wins	Win Pct	ROI
Simpson, Gerald R.	Winters, Perry A.	17	5	0.294	8.32
Brown, Barry D.	Abrego, Nobel	10	5	0.500	5.72
Mullaney, Deryle	Walcott, Rickey	18	6	0.333	4.91
Nicholson, David	Bryan, Desmond	29	6	0.207	4.90
Anderson, Leonard	Stein, Gary Raymond	19	8	0.421	4.64

SUFFOLK DOWNS

Trainer	Jockey	Starts	Wins	Win Pct	ROI
Poxon, Jr., Ernest	Llagas, Walter Enrique	16	5	0.313	6.55
Thornton, Paul	Judice, Joseph C.	12	5	0.417	5.70
Bubolz-Cantlon, Corleen	Clemente, Alfredo	20	5	0.250	5.42
Meade, Sherryl F.	Hole, Taylor M.	22	7	0.318	4.65
Sargent, Sr., Wayne E.	Hole, Taylor M.	30	5	0.167	4.53

SUNLAND PARK

Trainer	Jockey	Starts	Wins	Win Pct	ROI
McArthur, James F.	Lambert, Casey T.	14	6	0.429	4.90
Hartman, Chris A.	Montoya, Daryl	34	5	0.147	4.04
Bringhurst, J. Owen	Gonsalves, Frank Albert	25	6	0.240	3.94
Claridge, Jimmie D.	Noguez, Tony	39	12	0.308	3.89
Hartman, Chris A.	Tohill, Ken S.	16	6	0.375	3.80

TAMPA BAY DOWNS

Trainer	Jockey	Starts	Wins	Win Pct	ROI
Ziadie, Kirk	Zimmerman, Ramsey	18	9	0.500	8.33
Tomillo, Thomas F.	Houghton, T. D.	13	6	0.462	6.06
Burns, David R.	Bush, Vernon	18	7	0.389	6.06
Knipe, Duane	Umana, Juan	34	9	0.265	5.60
Smock, Lori A.	Flores, Jeremias	13	6	0.462	5.54

THISTLEDOWN

Trainer	Jockey	Starts	Wins	Win Pct	ROI
Madrigal, Sr., Rodrigo	Hannigan, Lyndon	37	11	0.297	5.51
Nance, Michael W.	Johnston, Jeff	6	5	0.833	5.30
Silva, Fernando	Rojas, Christian	26	7	0.269	5.18
Martin, Joseph R.	Cloninger, Jr., Weldon T.	44	9	0.205	4.18
Morden, Lyle	Deveaux, Sean R.	22	6	0.273	3.91

TIMONIUM

Trainer	Jockey	Starts	Wins	Win Pct	ROI
Lake, Scott A.	Dunkelberger, Travis L.	7	5	0.714	3.49
Wolfendale, Howard E.	Camacho, Eric	11	5	0.455	2.00

TURFWAY PARK

Trainer	Jockey	Starts	Wins	Win Pct	ROI
King, Warren L.	Sarvis, Dean A.	12	6	0.500	7.25
Hollendorfer, Jerry	Sarvis, Dean A.	13	6	0.462	6.98
Frederick, Edward	Harrison D'Amico, Anthony J.	3	5	0.385	5.83
Hughes, Sr., Donald E.	Martin, Jr., Eddie M.	12	5	0.417	5.42
Banks, David P.	Bejarano, Rafael	5	5	1.000	5.08

TRAINER ANGLES

TURF PARADISE

Trainer	Jockey	Starts	Wins	Win Pct	ROI
Hansen, Dale A.	Keith, Lori	14	5	0.357	8.83
Zimmerman, Jon Phil	Martinez, Orlando A.	34	6	0.176	5.65
Ferguson, Curt	Mawing, Leslie	15	5	0.333	5.29
Brinsley, Monte	Hernandez, Miguel Luis Gaeta	9	5	0.556	4.96
Mills, Glendon	Corbett, Glenn W.	5	5	1.000	4.88

WILL ROGERS DOWNS

Trainer	Jockey	Starts	Wins	Win Pct	ROI
Listen, Robert L.	Kimes, Curtis	12	5	0.417	5.92
Offolter, Joe S.	Landeros, Benny C.	9	5	0.556	4.24
Engel, Roger F.	Birzer, Alex	15	6	0.400	3.52
Wartchow, John	Matz, Nena	21	7	0.333	3.06
Lozano, Martin	Jimenez, Alex	60	20	0.333	3.03

WOODBINE

Trainer	Jockey	Starts	Wins	Win Pct	ROI
Hammett, Jody	Brimo, Julia	10	5	0.500	8.69
Bedford, Janet	Scharfstein, Jillian	47	6	0.128	7.22
Dwyer, David	Montpellier, Constant	16	8	0.500	5.63
Cappuccitti, Audre	Husbands, Simon P.	38	7	0.184	5.58
Wright, Michael W.	Callaghan, Slade	23	5	0.217	5.14

WYOMING DOWNS

Trainer	Jockey	Starts	Wins	Win Pct	ROI
Simpson, Gary	Colledge, Cameron	11	7	0.636	5.24
Simpson, Gary	Williams, Sean	12	5	0.417	4.25

YAVAPAI DOWNS

Trainer	Jockey	Starts	Wins	Win Pct	ROI
Fergason Rolland R.	Gomez, Angel	7	5	0.714	8.43
Knudsen, Kevin	Vergara, Daniel P.	18	5	0.278	7.14
Kumke, Myron D.	Higuera, Alberto R.	17	6	0.353	5.65
Faulkner, Jeffrey	Gomez, Esteban Angel	10	5	0.500	4.88
Mehok, William L.	Kenney, Kristina	21	9	0.429	4.31

ABOUT THE AUTHOR

DEAN KEPPLER IS THE director of DRF Press for *Daily Racing Form.* He has over 25 years of experience handicapping both Thoroughbred and harness racing. Keppler was the 2005 winner of the Freehold Raceway Thoroughbred handicapping contest, and was the proud owner of a 2006 Easter Sunday $91,000 pick-six ticket at Santa Anita Park. He has authored several books and articles on various subjects. He's also contributed to the DRF *Learn to Play the Races* fan guide, *Winning Techniques*, and was a freelance handicapper for the *Saratoga Special* in 2006. In the last six years, Keppler has been responsible for organizing and orchestrating the publication of more than 30 DRF Press book titles. He resides in Yonkers, New York, five minutes from the historic Yonkers Raceway now known as the new and improved Empire City.